SHIP TO SHORE, INC.

SHIP TO SHORE II

CARIBBEAN CHARTER YACHT RECIPES

Author and Publisher......................................Capt. Jan Robinson
Associate Publisher.......................................Waverly H. Robinson
Assistant...Mildred S. Thompson
Title by...F. Marion Meginnis
Artist...Celia A. Flock
Cover Artist...Raid Ahmad

For additional copies use the order blanks in the back of the book, or write directly to:

SHIP TO SHORE, INC.
10500 Mt. Holly Road
Charlotte, NC 28214-9347
1-800-338-6072

First printing: January, 1986
Second printing: June, 1986
Third printing: October, 1987
Fourth printing: March, 1989
Fifth printing: March, 1991

SHIP TO SHORE II Copyright 1985

ISBN 0-9612686-1-1

ACKNOWLEDGEMENT
Special thanks to Mr. Harry Jackson for his wine expertise.

Printed in the United States of America

FOREWORD

Cruising in the beautiful Caribbean aboard a yacht with captain and crew provides the setting for an exciting experience in sailing, swimming, and snorkeling. Most of all, it provides a peaceful setting for relaxation and unique dining experiences. Sunset over the islands quickens the imagination and blue crystal-clear waters, tropical islands, cool breezes, secluded white sand beaches, and exotic beautiful food provide an experience that can never be forgotten. Despite man's encroachment, the trade winds, sea, and sun preserve the islands' tranquility and timeless pace.

This book and Volume I of **SHIP TO SHORE** have captured the spirit and flavor of yachting cuisine and the Caribbean. They are a compilation of proven recipes used by charter yacht chefs every day.

The overwhelming success of the first volume of the **SHIP TO SHORE** cookbook has motivated Jan Robinson to collect new recipes from additional boats. These recipes, great for a Caribbean cruise, are equally exciting to anyone who wishes to please guests at home. They are simple to prepare, using ingredients found at your local supermarket.

SHIP TO SHORE II has gone all out to provide you with more easy culinary delights. The outstanding characteristics of Volume I are included plus these new features:

- Over 100 entrees with individual menus and recipes
- Preparation and cooking times
- A choice of a French and California wine for each entree
- Appetizers, Accompaniments, Desserts
- Informative Potpourri Section

Leisurely follow the main course of the charter yacht chefs through this unique collection of treasured recipes. *Bon Voyage!*

DEDICATION

This book
is dedicated to the
Caribbean Charter Yacht Chefs
who by donating their most treasured
recipes made this book
a truly unique
collection.

TABLE OF CONTENTS

*These sections feature over 100 entrees with individual menus, recipes, and wine selections.

*French and California wines were selected for these menus because of their availability in the Caribbean. Substitutions of your favorite may be made.

BREAKFAST AND BREADS

NOTES

EGGS ON LOBSTER

Preparation time: 5 minutes
Cooking time: 5 - 8 minutes
Serves: 4

Jan Robinson
Vanity

1 lb. raw lobster meat, cut in
chunks
1 small onion, sliced thin
½ green pepper, diced
½ tsp. paprika

½ tsp. pepper
¼ tsp. garlic salt
4 - 6 eggs, poached
2 - 4 Tblsp. butter
6 toasted muffins in halves

Saute onion, green pepper, and seasonings. Add lobster and saute until white. Serve immediately over muffin halves with an egg on top. Delicious!

EGGS BON VIVANT

Preparation time: 20 minutes
Cooking time: 20 minutes
Serves: 8

Annie Scholl
Bon Vivant

12 hard boiled eggs
½ cup flour
¼ cup butter or margarine
4 cups milk
1 medium onion, chopped

White pepper
Salt
6 - 8 English muffins, toasted
Garnish: parsley, paprika

Over medium heat, saute onions in butter until opaque. Sprinkle with salt and pepper. Stir in flour until thoroughly mixed. Add milk slowly, and cook until bubbly and about the consistency of heavy cream. Slice eggs, and add to the sauce mixture. Heat through, and arrange toasted English muffins in a circle. Spoon the eggs and cream mixture in center of each muffin. Garnish with paprika and parsley. *A "hand's down" breakfast favorite!*

VANITY SCRAMBLED EGGS

Preparation Time: 15 minutes   *Bob Robinson*
Cooking Time: 5 minutes   *Vanity*
Serves: 4

6 eggs, beaten
¼ cup evaporated milk or
    1/8 cup milk
¼ cup green onions, chopped
½ tsp. black pepper
4 oz. butter

salt to taste
1 Tblsp. Parmesan cheese, grated
1 Tblsp. Pica Pepper sauce,
    optional

Combine eggs, milk, onions, pepper, salt, and Pica pepper. Fold together lightly. Melt butter in a frying pan over low heat and add egg mixture. Scramble to personal preference. Sprinkle with Parmesan cheese.

CURRIED CREAMED EGGS

Preparation Time: 20 minutes   *Terrie Thorbjornson*
Cooking Time: 15 minutes   *Western Star*
Serves: 4

6 eggs
White sauce (I use packaged)
Garnish: Paprika, Parsley

Curry powder
4 slices of toast

Hard boil the eggs. Make a white sauce, then add curry to taste. Slice about 1½ eggs on each piece of toast, and cover with the curry sauce. Sprinkle on a little paprika, and top with a snip of parsley. *Serve with sausage, Banana Bread, and fresh fruit.*

KELLY EGGS

Preparation Time: 15 minutes
Cooking Time: 30 minutes
Refrigeration Time: over night

Nancy Wilkinson
New Horizons

6 - 8 eggs
6 - 9 slices white bread

Salt and pepper (to taste)
2 cups cooked bacon or sausage,
    crushed

Must be made the night before it is served. Mix eggs, salt, and pepper. In 2 small loaf pans or a large baking pan, place the bread on the bottom of pan. Pour egg mixture over the bread. This mixture should cover the bread thoroughly. Sprinkle the sausage or bacon on top. Cover and refrigerate over night. Next morning, bake at 350°F. for 30 minutes. Serve with melons and muffins. *This donated recipe was from a charter guest. Serves 4 to 6.*

KEDGEREE

Preparation Time: 20 minutes
Cooking Time: 30 minutes
Serves: 6 - 8

Fiona Baldrey
Promenade

1 lb. smoked Haddock
1 (14 oz.) can evaporated milk
1 cup uncooked rice
3 hard boiled eggs

3 oz. butter
2 oz. flour
2 tsp. curry powder
Freshly ground black pepper

Hard boil eggs (7 minutes). Poach Haddock in milk (5 minutes). Boil rice in unsalted water until just soft. Chop eggs. Meanwhile, make up sauce: melt the butter and curry powder. Cook for 1 to 2 minutes, add flour, and cook further for 1 to 2 minutes. Stir in milk from fish. Add boiled eggs. Skin Haddock using 2 forks. There is no need to flake the fish as this happens naturally. Strain rice and add with Haddock mixture. Serve immediately, garnished with a little cayenne pepper (optional). *This is a traditional breakfast served in England, and makes a pleasant change for American guests. Watch out for the salt because smoked Haddock can be very salty.*

CHEESY EGG CASSEROLE

Preparation Time: 15 minutes   Donna Jaggard
Cooking Time: 45 minutes   Thorobred
Serves: 6

2 cups seasoned croutons   ½ tsp. mustard
1 cup grated Cheddar cheese   1/8 tsp. onion powder
4 eggs, slightly beaten   Dash of pepper
2 cups milk   4 slices cooked bacon, crumbled
½ tsp. salt

Preheat oven to 325° F. Grease a 10" x 6" x 1¾" baking dish. Combine croutons and cheese, and put in the bottom of the dish. Combine eggs, milk, mustard, and spices. Pour over croutons and cheese. Sprinkle with crumbled bacon. Bake at 325° for 45-50 minutes.

EGGS MacDOUGLAS

Preparation Time: 15 minutes   Jean Thayer
Cooking Time: 10 minutes   Finesse 60
Serves: 8

8 English Muffins, split   6 oz. Swiss cheese, grated
8 slices ham   Mayonnaise
8 hard-boiled eggs, shelled, sliced

Lightly toast half of the muffins under broiler. Top toasted halves with ham, sliced eggs, and 1 to 2 Tblsp. of mayonnaise. Sprinkle grated cheese on top of mayonnaise.

Toast remaining muffin halves, spread lightly with butter and keep warm. Place ham and cheese muffins under broiler and broil until cheese is melted and mayonnaise is bubbly. *To serve, top each ham/ cheese muffin with plain muffin.*

GRATIN DAUPHINOIS

Preparation Time: 5 minutes
Cooking Time: 30 minutes
Serves: 6

Sheila Smith
Victorious

2 eggs, beaten
3 baking potatoes, peeled
    and sliced
4 - 6 slices of bacon, chopped

1 onion, chopped
Milk
½ cup grated cheese (not vital)
Seasoning: Bay leaf

Preheat oven to 300° F. Place potatoes, bacon, and onion in a sauce-pan, and cover with milk. Season and bring to a boil; cook for 10 minutes. Drain off liquid into a bowl with the eggs and cheese. Place potato mixture in an oven dish and cover with eggs - cheese mixture. Bake at 300° F. for about 20 minutes - until it sets, but do not let it separate. Serve this as breakfast or supper. It is a Scottish dish, and traditionally would use a tiny piece of belly pork. *The bacon is just for flavor, and too much destroys the delicate flavor this dish should have.*

SWEDISH SMORGASBORD

Preparation Time: 20 minutes
Cooking Time: 10 minutes
Serves: 4

Norma Trease
Caroline

1 soft boiled egg per person
    in egg cups
Wasa bread (Swedish flatbread)
    and assorted other breads
Fresh butter

Assorted good jams or marmalades
Sliced ham
Black and red caviar
Sliced tomatoes
Chunk Havarti cheese

Perfect soft boiled eggs: put cold eggs in cold water to cover in pan. Bring to a boil, remove from heat, cover, and allow to sit 4 minutes. Rinse in cold water. Serve in egg cups, and chop off pointy end. Top with caviar and eat from shell with small spoon. Layer together Wasa bread, butter, jam, cheese, ham, tomato, and eat. *Incredibly good taste, and table display is spectacular.*

OMELETTE SANTO DOMINGO

Preparation Time: 15 minutes
Cooking Time: 20 minutes
Serves: 8

Lisa Hawkins
Ariguani

2 Tblsp. olive oil
1 medium onion, chopped
2 cloves garlic
1 medium tomato, chopped
6 eggs, slightly beaten

3 Tblsp. cilantro, chopped or
1 tsp. coriander powder
½ cup grated Monteray Jack cheese
Salt and pepper to taste

Preheat oven to 450° F. Pour olive oil in ceramic quiche dish, and arrange onion, garlic, and tomato in the bottom. Bake for 5 minutes. Beat eggs, cheese, cilantro, salt, and pepper. Pour over vegetables, and bake approximately 20 minutes or until eggs have puffed at center, and omelette has set. Do not over cook. Serve in wedges. Serve with pineapple wedges and Monkey Bread.

For the pineapple wedges: remove the top and bottom of a large pineapple. Slice in half lengthwise, and remove core. Slice each half in 4 wedges. Run your knife between fruit and skin, then chop into cubes. *Serve one wedge on each plate.*

CHOP SUEY OMELETTE

Preparation Time: 5 minutes
Cooking Time: 5 minutes
Serves: 4 - 6

Jan Robinson
Vanity

2 Tblsp. butter
8 eggs, beaten
¼ tsp. garlic powder
¼ tsp. pepper

1 (16 oz.) can chop suey vegetables, drained
4 oz. sliced Swiss cheese

Melt butter in a covered skillet, add eggs, vegetables, seasonings and top with cheese. Cover and cook over low heat until done. Serve with hot buttered English muffins, chilled orange juice and champagne. *This is a super easy breakfast.*

GOMELET

Preparation Time: 10 minutes
Cooking Time: 20 minutes
Serves: 6

Emily Welch
Wind's End

6 slices bacon
¼ cup minced onion
¼ cup minced green pepper
¼ cup minced red pepper
½ tsp. minced garlic

1 cup sliced mushrooms
¼ tsp. ground pepper
6 well beaten eggs
¼ cup milk
½ cup grated Cheddar cheese

In large high-sided skillet at medium high heat, fry bacon until crisp, crumble, and set aside after draining on paper towels. Saute onion, green pepper, red pepper, garlic, and mushrooms. Drain on paper towels, and set aside. Beat eggs, milk, and pepper in medium-sized bowl. Pour into skillet. Sprinkle bacon, pepper, onion, and garlic mixture over top. Follow with grated cheese. With lid on, steam approximately 10 minutes or until set. *Slice as pie, and serve with warm buttered croissants and choice of jams and jellies.*

RASPBERRY RICOTTA OMELETTES

Preparation Time: 10 minutes
Cooking Time: 15 minutes
Serves: 4

Cherie Hughes
Skopbank of Finland

3 Tblsp. unsalted butter
6 eggs
½ cup milk
Garnish: Parsley and orange segments

2 cups Ricotta cheese
4 Tblsp. raspberry jam
Confectioners sugar

Beat together eggs and milk. Make omelettes, filling them with ½ cup of Ricotta cheese, and a bit of jam. Sift confectioners sugar over the top. Heat a metal skewer over a gas flame until red hot. Sear with hot skewer in a criss-cross pattern. Garnish with parsley and orange segments. *Serve with banana bread and fresh pineapple boats.*

APPLE OMELETS

Preparation Time: 15 minutes
Cooking Time: 20 minutes
Serves: 4

Shannon Webster
Chaparral

FILLING:
¼ cup butter
2 Tblsp. apricot jam
2 baking apples, peeled, cored
    and sliced
2 Tblsp. sugar

OMELETS:
4 eggs, separated
2 Tblsp. sugar
2 Tblsp. cornstarch
½ tsp. vanilla extract
2 Tblsp. sweet butter

TOPPING:
Sugar
Whipped cream

Place butter and jam in a saucepan. Heat gently until butter is melted.
Add the apples, cover and cook gently until just soft then stir in the
sugar. In a separate bowl, whisk egg yolks, sugar, cornstarch, and
vanilla extract until thick and creamy. Melt ½ of the butter. Whisk egg
whites, and fold into the mixture. When the butter sizzles in the skillet,
pour ½ of egg mixture. Cook slowly without stirring until the omelet
is golden underneath, and the sides are beginning to set. Place under
broiler until the top is golden. Make a slit in the centre of the omelet.
Spoon ½ of apple mixture and fold over. Sprinkle with sugar. Cover
and make 2nd omelet. *Serve with cream, sausage patties and
Champagne Mimosas.*

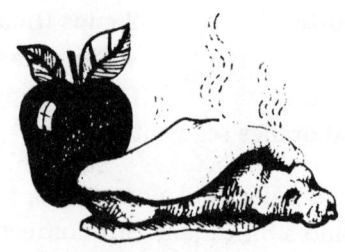

*HINT: Boil sausages 10 minutes. Drain water and brown sausages
lightly in butter and oil. Makes them very tender.*

PINA COLADA FRENCH TOAST

Preparation Time: 15 minutes
Cooking Time: 10 minutes
Serves: 4

Jan Robinson
Vanity

6 eggs
1 tsp. cinnamon
2 Tblsp. rum
1 cup crushed pineapple

4 - 6 slices raisin bread or
Pepperidge Farm toasting
white bread
4 oz. butter

Beat eggs, cinnamon, and rum. Add pineapple and beat again. Put bread in shallow dish and pour over egg mixture. Turn bread a couple times until well soaked. Fry in butter until golden.

Serve with: 1 can Coco Lopez Cream of Coconut
Lime cut in ¼'s

BAVARIAN WAFFLES WITH AMBROSIA

Preparation Time: 10 minutes
Cooking Time: 10 minutes
Serves: 6

Bob and Didgie Belschner
Tequila

AMBROSIA:
½ cup sour cream
½ cup raisins
½ cup yogurt
½ cup nuts
1 cup fruited yogurt
1 apple, cored, sliced
½ cup orange sections
1 banana, peeled, sliced
½ cup pineapple chunks

WAFFLES:
Any batter recipe or Pillsbury's
Ultra-Light Pancake Mix
Shortening
Maple syrup

Garnish:
Kiwi fruit, sliced

Prepare waffles according to the package directions - be sure to brush shortening onto waffle iron. In a large bowl, mix the cut fruit, nuts, raisins, yogurts, and sour cream.

Heat the maple syrup. We like to spoon the ambrosia over the waffle, and then pour the syrup on top. *Garnish with Kiwi fruit.*

TEQUILA GOLD PANCAKES

Preparation Time: 10 minutes   *Bob Robinson*
Cooking Time: 15 minutes   *Vanity*
Serves: 6

2 cups Bisquick
1 cup milk
1 egg
1 Tblsp. vegetable oil

1 banana
1/3 cup Tequila, gold
Syrup: see below

Combine all ingredients in blender. Spoon enough batter for 3 or 4 inch pancakes on hot skillet or electric fry pan. Cook until golden on each side. Remove and place on hot platter in warm oven. Continue process until all batter is used. Garnish with orange twists.

Syrup: Heat apricot preserves with a little butter, add a little gold rum, stir and serve. *A "Good Morning" kick off!*

APPLE STRUDDLE STACK

Preparation Time: 25 minutes   *Sharon Strong*
Cooking Time: 20 minutes   *Promises*
Serves: 6

1 recipe for homemade pancakes
   or premade pancake mix for
   20 pancakes
8 large Granny Smith apples,
   peeled, cored and sliced
1/3 cup brown sugar
1 Tblsp. cinnamon
½ tsp cloves

½ tsp. nutmeg
½ tsp. all-spice
1 Tblsp. butter
¼ cup raisins
¼ cup chopped walnuts
1 Tblsp. lemon juice

Garnish: whipped cream

Get 2 large frying pans sizzling, and make 8-10 large pancakes. Keep in the hot oven or microwave at end. Add extra butter to keep moist between layers. Meanwhile, saute apples with all above ingredients. Put cover on pan, and let steam gently for 10 minutes or until tender. To serve: put pancakes on platter and add ½ apple mixture on top. Dollop with whipped cream if desired (quickly serve before whipped cream slides off). Serve extra apples on the side. Cut into pie wedges. *This is really pretty to serve and so tasty. Try using blueberries or other fruit topping.*

BLINTZES

Preparation Time: 20 minutes
Chilling Time: 30 minutes
Cooking Time: 1 hour
Serves: 8

Jane Glancy
Truant

Crepes:
3 eggs
3 Tblsp. oil
1½ cup milk
1 cup flour
½ tsp. salt
1/3 cup melted butter

Filling:
1 egg yolk
2 Tblsp. sugar
8 oz. softened cream cheese
1 (16 oz.) carton cottage cheese
¼ tsp. vanilla

Topping:
Confectioners sugar
1 cup sour cream
1 cup strawberry or cherry preserves

Crepes: Mix eggs, oil, and milk. Blend well. Add flour and salt, and mix until smooth. Cover and refrigerate for 30 minutes. Cook crepes on one side only.

Filling: Mix egg yolk and sugar until thick and yellow. Add cheeses and vanilla. Stir until well combined.

To fill: Spread 3 Tblsp. of the filling on the browned side of crepe. Fold the two opposite sides over the filling, then overlap ends to cover completely. Melt 1 Tblsp. butter in a skillet. Add half of blintzes seam side down. Saute until golden on both sides. Keep warm and cook remaining blintzes. *Serve hot with sprinkled confectioners sugar, sour cream, and preserves.*

HINT: Hard cooked eggs are easy to peel if you cook them with vinegar (1 - 2 Tblsp.) in the water, and chill immediately after cooking.

APPLE CREAM CHEESE COFFEE CAKE

Preparation Time: 15 minutes
Cooking Time: 15 minutes
Serves: 6

Margo Ann Muckey
Tuff

1 (3 oz.) package cream cheese
¼ cup butter or margarine, firm
2 cups Bisquick
1/3 cup milk
2 Tblsp. sugar
½ tsp. ground cinnamon
1 (20 oz.) can apple pie filling
¼ cup chopped walnuts

Cream Cheese Filling:
8 oz. cream cheese, softened
1/3 cup sugar
2 tsp. lemon juice
1 tsp. grated lemon peel

Preheat oven to 425° F. Cut cream cheese and margarine into Bisquick mix. Stir in milk. Turn dough into surface dusted with Bisquick mix. Knead lightly 8 - 10 times. Roll onto rectangle 12 x 8 inches. Place on a lightly greased cookie sheet. Mix together all ingredients of cream cheese filling and spread down the center of the rectangle. Make cuts 2½ inches long at 1 inch intervals on 12 inch side of rectangle. Fold strips over filling, overlapping. Mix sugar and cinnamon, and sprinkle over the top. Heat oven to 425°, and bake uncovered until golden for about 12 - 15 minutes. Cool for 10 minutes. Spoon apple pie filling down center of coffeecake. Sprinkle with walnuts.

HINT: Make perfect toast on top of your stove by placing bread in teflon or silver stone skillet. Don't use any butter until toast is done on both sides.

OATMEAL COCONUT COFFEE CAKE

Preparation Time: 15 minutes
Cooking Time: 40 minutes
Serves: 15 - 18

D. Stetson
Fantasy

1½ cups boiling water
1 cup rolled oats
¼ cup butter or margarine
1 cup packed brown sugar
1 cup sugar
2 eggs, slightly beaten
1½ cups all purpose flour
1 tsp. baking soda
1 tsp. salt
1 tsp. ground cinnamon
1 tsp. vanilla extract

TOPPING:
1 cup flaked coconut
½ cup chopped pecans or walnuts
½ cup butter or margarine
½ cup packed brown sugar
¼ cup milk
¼ tsp. vanilla extract

Preheat oven to 350° F. Mix the oats and boiling water, and let stand
for 10 minutes. Cream together ¼ cup of butter; gradually add 1 cup
of brown sugar and 1 cup of regular sugar, beating well. Add the other
6 ingredients and mix well. Spoon into a greased 13x9x2 inch baking
pan. Bake at 350° F for 40 minutes, or until a toothpick comes out
clean.
Topping: Combine coconut and pecans. Sprinkle mixture over cake.
Combine remaining ingredients and pour over cake. Return to the oven,
and broil for 1 - 2 minutes until golden brown.

Cut into squares to serve.

ORANGE PUFFS

Preparation Time: 25 minutes   *Jacklyn Johnson Rabinowitz*
Cooking Time: 25 minutes   *Almost Heaven*
Serves: 4 - 6

½ cup plus 2 Tblsp. unsalted   Grated peel and juice (¼ cup)
    butter, softened   of 1 orange
½ cup sugar   ¼ cup milk
1 egg
1-1½ cups all purpose flour   Garnish:
1-1½ tsp. baking powder   1 pineapple
½ tsp. salt   6 peach slices
¼ tsp. grated or ground nutmeg   1 orange

Preheat oven to 350° F. Beat butter and sugar in a bowl; Stir in egg.
In another bowl, mix flour, baking powder, salt, nutmeg, and peel.
Stir dry ingredients into butter mixture, mixing alternately with orange
juice and milk. Half fill greased muffin cups. Bake for 20-25 minutes
until lightly browned. Serve with quartered pineapple (keep the stem
on) topped with 6 peach slices in a spiral pattern. *On the plate, make
an "orange butterfly" of 2 orange wedges back to back with orange peel
sliver as an antennae.*

BREAKFAST GRANOLA OR HAND MUNCHIES

Preparation Time: 30 minutes   *Sylvia Dabney*
Cooking Time: 1 hour   *Native Sun*
Serves: Many

6 cups oatmeal   2 cups chopped almonds or cashews
1 cup wheat germ   1 cup honey
½ cup corn meal   1/3 cup water
½ cup whole wheat flour   2/3 cup vegetable oil
1 cup sunflower seeds   2 cups raisins

Preheat oven to 300° F. Mix dry ingredients together. Mix wet ingredients and blend well. Pour wet over dry and stir until all is coated. Bake
on cookie sheets for one hour or so. After it has cooled, stir in raisins.
Store in airtight containers.

EASY SOUTHERN MADE DOUGHNUTS

Preparation Time: 5 minutes
Cooking Time: 10 minutes
Makes: 10 doughnuts

C. J. Burns
Grace

1 can of buttermilk or
    regular biscuits (10 inside)
Crisco oil

Glaze:
1 cup powdered sugar
3 Tblsp. cold water
1 tsp. vanilla

Heat a 1 or 2 quart, high-sided sauce pan with 2 inches of hot Crisco Oil. (When a small piece of dough floats and fries, the oil is ready). Open the can of biscuits and separate. Put your thumb in the center and pull a hole in the middle of each. Fry 2 at a time. Meanwhile, have the glaze ready to dip hot doughnuts in immediately before draining. You can dip one or both sides. Hide the can! No one will believe you made them! Kids love them. *They melt in your mouth. They are also great for dessert.*

BARB'S BREAKFAST SCONES

Preparation Time: 10 minutes
Cooking Time: 20 minutes
Serves: 4 - 6

Sheila Smith
Victorious

2 cups plain white flour
¼ cup bran flour
Pinch of salt
1 egg in a measuring cup, make up to 6 oz. of liquid with buttermilk
    (or sour milk by adding lemon juice)

¼ cup oil (or less)
1 level Tblsp. baking powder

Preheat oven to 400° F. Place all dry ingredients in a bowl, and rub in oil (will be like "peas"). Add milk and egg mixture; blend thoroughly. Make 6 - 8 scones (just balls in floured hands). Place on a greased baking tray, and cook at 400° for 20 minutes or until golden brown. *Serve with butter and selections of jam for breakfast, or at 4 p.m. with tea - a lovely change from cocktails!*

MEXICAN CORN BREAD

Preparation Time: 15 minutes   *Lisa Hawkins*
Cooking Time: 30 minutes   *Ariguani*
Serves: 8

1½ cups self-rising cornmeal   1 medium bell pepper, chopped
3 eggs   1 can whole kernel corn
½ cup salad oil   (medium-sized)
1 cup sweet milk   2 jalapeno peppers, chopped
1 medium onion, chopped   1 cup sharp Cheddar cheese, grated

Preheat oven to 400° F. Combine the first 4 ingredients. Add remaining ingredients, and pour into greased pan. Bake in oven for 30 minutes or until center is done, and top is golden brown. *Serve piping hot with butter.*

SWEET ONION BREAD

Preparation Time: 30 minutes   *Mardy Array*
Cooking Time: 40 minutes   *Emerald Lady*
Serves: 6

3 onions, thickly sliced   3/4 tsp. salt
4 Tblsp. butter   1½ tsp. sugar
3 Tblsp. brown sugar   1 egg, well beaten
2 cups flour   1 cup milk
4 tsp. baking powder   ¼ cup oil

Preheat oven to 350° F. Saute thick slices of onion separated into rings in skillet with 3 Tblsp. butter. Spread remaining Tblsp. butter in a 9-inch round cake pan. Sprinkle the bottom of pan with brown sugar. Arrange golden sauteed onions on top of brown sugar. For bread: combine flour, baking powder, salt, and sugar. Add egg, milk, and oil. Batter should be thinner than biscuit dough. Spoon over onions spreading evenly. Bake for 35-40 minutes. Let cool for 5 minutes. Serve in pan shaped wedges. *Great with poultry dishes or barbeque feasts!*

ONION CHEESE BREAD

Preparation Time: 10 minutes
Cooking Time: 20 minutes
Serves: 6 - 8

D. Stetson
Fantasy

½ cup chopped onion
1 Tblsp. vegetable oil
½ cup milk
1 egg, beaten

1½ cups Bisquick
1 cup shredded Cheddar cheese,
    divided
2 Tblsp. fresh parsley
2 Tblsp. melted butter

Preheat oven to 400° F. Saute onion in oil in a small skillet until tender. Combine milk, egg, and Bisquick in a medium bowl. Stir just until moistened. Add onion, ½ cup Cheddar cheese, and parsley; stir well. Spread batter in a greased 8 inch round cake pan. Drizzle with the melted butter. Bake for 15 minutes. Sprinkle with remaining ½ cup of cheese. Bake an additional 5 minutes.

TOMATO BREAD

Preparation Time: 30 minutes
Rising Time: 2 hours
Cooking Time: 1 hour
Serves: 8 - 10

Judith Meyers Vegiard
Ruach

1 (10 oz.) can tomato soup
½ cup milk
¼ cup butter, softened
4 cups flour

2 tsp. dry yeast
1 tsp. salt
1 large egg

Preheat oven to 350° F. Dissolve yeast in milk heated to 80° - 90° F. In a large bowl combine tomato soup, egg, softened butter, and salt. Add yeast and milk mixture. Add flour, one cup at a time, to form stiff dough. Knead dough, and then place in a bowl. Cover the bowl with a damp towel. Place the bowl somewhere where air temperature is 80° - 90° F. for one hour in order for the bread to rise. Punch down dough and knead again. Place dough in a buttered bread pan. Let rise again for 1 hour. Bake at 350° 1 hour. *This makes a nice lunch when served with fresh fruit and cheese platter.*

PUMPKIN BREAD

Preparation Time: 20 minutes
Cooking Time: 50 minutes
Serves: 12

Marita M. Tasse
Flower of the Storm

2/3 cup shortening	2 tsp. baking soda
2-2/3 cup sugar	1 tsp. baking powder
4 eggs	1½ tsp. salt
1 (16 oz.) can pumpkin	1 tsp. cinnamon
2/3 cup water (½ wine optional)	1 tsp. cloves
	2/3 cup walnuts
3-1/3 cup flour	2/3 cup raisins

Preheat oven to 350° F. Cream shortening and sugar. Add eggs, beat well, and add pumpkin. Add previously mixed dry ingredients alternately with water (water + wine). Add nuts and raisins. This large recipe makes 2 spring form tube pans or 2 - 9 x 4 inch loaf pans plus 6 muffins. Bake at 350° for about 50 minutes, slightly longer for loaf pans, less for muffins. *Bread keeps well in refrigerator, and stays moist longer.*

PEAR/CHEESE BREAD

Preparation Time: 5 minutes
Cooking Time: 60 minutes
Serves: 6 - 8

Shannon Webster
Chaparral

1 package nut or date quick bread mix	½ cup shredded Cheddar cheese
¾ cup finely diced canned pears	1/8 tsp. cinnamon
½ cup pear liquid	1 egg

Preheat oven to 350° F. Generously grease, and flour bottom only of loaf pan. In a large bowl, combine all ingredients, and stir 50 - 75 strokes until dry particles are moistened. Pour into prepared pan. Bake 55 - 65 minutes.

CHEDDAR CRISSCROSS

Preparation Time: 10 minutes
Cooking Time: 20 minutes
Serves: 6

Barbara Lowe
My Way

1 package crescent dinner rolls
Prepared mustard

¾ cup Cheddar cheese

Preheat oven to 375° F. Spread dough out on ungreased cookie sheet, and squeeze perforations together. Spread mustard down center 1/3 of the dough. Shred cheese and sprinkle over the mustard. Make diagonal cuts down the outer thirds of dough at 1'' intervals. Overlap opposite strips to cover cheese. Bake at 375° for 20 minutes. *An easy and attractive accompaniment to any meal!*

CHEESE BREAD

Preparation Time: 20 minutes
Rising Time: 1½ hours
Cooking Time: 50 minutes
Serves: 10

Sue Griffin
Endless Summer I

2 cups milk
2 cups water
1 tsp. sugar
4 tsp. yeast
6½ cups all purpose flour

Salt
½ cup grated Cheddar cheese
1 beaten egg
½ cup Parmesan cheese, grated
1 tsp. mustard

Preheat oven to 350° F. Warm milk and one cup of water. Mix in sugar and yeast, and allow to rise 10 minutes. Add to flour and salt, and beat until the mixture leaves the sides of the bowl, adding more water if needed. Add Cheddar cheese and mustard. Allow to rise covered with damp towel for 1½ hours. Knock down and knead gently. Cook in desired shape or tin. Egg wash, and sprinkle with Parmesan. Cook for 50 minutes. *Delicious sliced and toasted for breakfast.*

SAUSAGE BREAD

Preparation Time: 30 minutes
Cooking Time: 1 hour
Makes: 1 loaf

Jane Glancy
Truant

1 loaf frozen dough (thawed)
1 lb. (16 oz.) Italian sausage
   (cooked and drained)
2 eggs

½ cup chopped onion
Crushed red pepper
Oregano
½ cup shredded Mozzarella

Preheat oven to 350°F. Let the dough rise in an oiled bowl covered with a wet towel. Roll dough into a rectangle (10" x 20"). Mix the cooked sausage with one egg, and spread evenly over the dough. Spread the onion and cheese over that. Shake lots of crushed red pepper over that (don't be afraid), and oregano to taste. Roll up like a jelly roll, and brush with a beaten egg. Arrange on a pan in a horseshoe shape. Bake for 1 hour. Cool and slice. *This is a great hors d'oeuvre sliced thin. It is also good for lunch with a salad or soup.*

MOM'S SUMMER STRAWBERRY BREAD

Preparation Time: 15 minutes
Cooking Time: 1 hour
Makes: 2 loaves

Cindy Harhen
Impervious Cover

3 eggs
1½ cups sugar
1 cup salad oil
1 Tblsp. vanilla
2 cups flour
1 cup quick oats

1 Tblsp. cinnamon
1 tsp. baking soda
1 tsp. salt
½ tsp. baking powder
2 cups crushed strawberries
   (you can use frozen without sugar)

Preheat oven to 350° F. Beat eggs and sugar. Add oil and vanilla. Mix in flour, oats, cinnamon, soda, salt, and baking powder. Add strawberries and mix well. Pour into 2 greased and floured 4 x 8 inch loaf pans. Bake for 1 hour at 350° F. These loaves freeze well, and are delicious with cream cheese. *Paul's mom always has a few loaves in the freezer as a special treat for guests. Delightful!*

MONKEY BREAD

Preparation Time: 15 minutes   *Lisa Hawkins*
Cooking Time: 40 minutes   *Ariguani*
Serves: 8

½ cup chopped pecans	3 cans biscuits
½ cup sugar	¾ cup brown sugar
1 tsp. cinnamon	½ cup butter

Preheat oven to 350° F. Heat the brown sugar with ½ cup butter. Sprinkle pecans on bottom of bundt pan. Roll biscuits, and cut in quarters. Roll each quarter in sugar and cinnamon. Layer in pan. Pour hot sugar-butter mixture over dough, and bake for 30 - 40 minutes. Let cool 10 minutes before serving. *Invert onto plate, and let the guests devour!*

BANANA-NUT MUFFINS

Preparation Time: 10 minutes   *Bob Belschner*
Cooking Time: 45 minutes   *Tequila*
Makes: 12 muffins

1¾ cups all purpose flour	1/3 cup cooking oil
¼ cup sugar	2 eggs, well beaten
2½ tsp. baking powder	¾ cup chopped bananas
¾ cup milk	½ cup chopped walnuts or pecans
½ tsp. salt	

Preheat oven to 400° F. Measure out flour in a large mixing bowl. Add sugar, baking powder, and salt. In a separate bowl, mix milk, oil, and eggs. Add this mixture to dry ingredients all at once. Stirring until just moistened, fold in bananas and nuts. Fill well greased muffin pans ¾ full. Bake at 400° F for 45 minutes or until brown.

FRENCH BREAD IN A HURRY

Preparation Time: 10 minutes   *Jane Glancy*
Rising Time: 30 minutes   *Truant*
Cooking Time: 20 minutes
Makes: 2 or 3 loaves

1½ cups warm water   1½ Tblsp. dry yeast
1 Tblsp. honey   4 cups unbleached white or all
1 tsp. salt   purpose flour

Heat the oven to 450° F. Combine water, honey, salt, and yeast in a
bowl. Stir to combine, and let stand 5 - 10 minutes until the yeast
starts to bubble. Add the flour in small amounts until the dough no
longer sticks to the sides of the bowl. Some of the flour should be
left over. Turn the dough onto a well floured surface. Coat hands and
dough with flour, and shape the dough into an oval. Cut into 2 or 3
pieces. Shape each piece into a long loaf by gently pulling on it, or
rolling it between your hands. Place loaves in a well greased pan, cover,
and let sit in a warm place for 20 minutes. Make 3 shallow slashes in
each loaf, and spray with salted water. Bake 20 minutes, and cool on a
wire rack. To freeze loaves, bake only 15 minutes, cool completely,
and wrap in plastic. To reheat, spray with salted water, and cook at
450° for 10 minutes.

SUPER MUFFINS

Preparation Time: 10 minutes   *Jacklyn Johnson Rabinowitz*
Cooking Time: 20 minutes   *Almost Heaven*
Serves: 4 - 6

1 pint vanilla ice cream, softened   2 cups sifted self rising flour

Preheat oven to 350° F. Blend ice cream and flour until flour is just
moistened (batter will be lumpy). Fill 10 well greased muffin cups
¾ full. Bake in preheated 350° oven for 20 minutes until toothpick
comes out dry. Serve in a basket with a gaily checked napkin. *Serve
with a glass bowl of cantaloupe melon balls, and a side bowl of vanilla
yogurt garnished with walnuts and kiwi fruit.*

CINNAMON BUNS

Preparation Time: 40 minutes
Cooking Time: 30 minutes
Rising Time: 1 hour
Serves: 8 - 10

Rosalind Rice
Endless Summer II

2 tsp. dried yeast	4 tsp. brown sugar
1 tsp. white sugar	½ cup butter
½ cup tepid water	1 tsp. cinnamon
2 cups all purpose flour	1 cup raisins
4 tsp. white sugar	1 cup confectioners sugar

Preheat oven to 400° F. Dissolve 1 tsp. white sugar in tepid water. Stir in yeast until well mixed. Leave in a warm place to work, about 30 minutes. Rub ¼ cup butter into flour until well combined. Stir in the white sugar. When yeast mixture is frothy pour into flour and knead for 8 - 10 minutes. When it feels spongy, place on a floured board and roll into an oblong pan approximately 6" x 12". Dot remaining butter over dough, and sprinkle brown sugar, raisins, and cinnamon. Roll up like a jelly roll and cut into 12 - 14 pieces. Place in a well greased round 9" cake pan, working from outside in. Leave to rise in a warm place about 30 minutes. When well risen, place in hot oven, 400° F., for about 30 minutes or until nicely browned. Remove from the oven, and allow to cool. Mix confectioners sugar with sufficient cold water to make a fairly stiff mixture, and while the buns are still warm, dribble it over the top.

LOUISE BRENDLINGER on RING-ANDERSEN omits the confectioners sugar mixture, and sprinkles the greased cake tin with 1 Tblsp. brown sugar and 2 Tblsp. Karo Syrup.

HONEYDEW ON "THE PORTSIDE"

Preparation Time: 10 minutes *Betsi Dwyer*
Marinating Time: 12 hours *September Morn*
Serves: 8

1 honeydew melon Garnish: Orange slices
1 cup port wine

Cut a hole 1" in diameter into the side of the melon and remove the "plug." Pour wine into melon and insert plug. Refrigerate for 8 - 12 hours or overnight. Drain wine before serving. Cut into the number of slices needed, remove seeds, and garnish with a twisted orange slice. *This also makes a nice dessert after a heavy meal. Try watermelon with rum, but use 2 - 3 cups of liquid.*

PEACH AMBROSIA

Preparation Time: 10 minutes *D. Stetson*
Chilling Time: 1 hour minimum *Fantasy*
Serves: 10 - 14

1 (15 oz.) can pineapple tidbits **½ cup flaked coconut**
½ cup green grapes **½ cup sour cream**
½ cup orange sections **14 peach halves**
½ cup minature marshmallows **½ cup slivered toasted almonds**

Combine the first five ingredients, tossing gently; chill. Before serving add the sour cream to fruit mixture; mix well. Spoon ¼ cup of fruit into each peach half, and top with almonds.

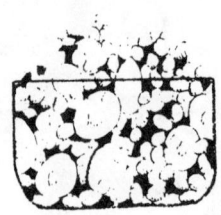

LUNCHEONS

NOTES

FISHERMAN'S SALAD

Preparation Time: 40 minutes
Marinating Time: 20 minutes
Serves: 6

Cindy Harhen
Impervious Cover

Salad ingredients: lettuce
    scallions, red pepper, etc.
2 - 3 cups cooked fish (salmon,
    turbot, dolphin, cod, sole,
    or swordfish)
Salt and pepper
¼ cup lemon juice

¼ cup minced shallots or scallions
¼ cup capers
½ cup chopped parsley
1 cup diced raw vegetables, (celery,
    pepper, cucumber, etc.)
2 Tblsp. olive oil
½ cup good mayonnaise
¼ cup sour cream

Pick through cooked fish to remove any bones and skin. Flake it into a
bowl, and season carefully folding in salt, pepper, lemon juice, minced
shallots, capers, parsley, diced vegetables, and olive oil. Let marinate for
20 minutes, tossing gently twice. Drain, if necessary, and fold in enough
mayonnaise and sour cream mixture to coat fish. *To make a colorful
luncheon salad, use curly endive lettuce. Put a mound of Fisherman's
Salad on top, then dress the plate with black olives, red pepper strips,
boiled shrimp in their shells, and a long, slim scallion. Very elegant!
Serve with Gazpacho in chilled mugs with cucumber swizzle stick, hot
buttered crescent rolls, and warm peach cobbler.*

FLUTE'S KOSHER SALAD

Preparation Time: 25 minutes
Cooking Time: 5 - 8 minutes
Serves: 6

Lee Ann LaCesa
Flute

2 medium heads of Iceberg lettuce
1 medium red onion, sliced
1½ lbs. Nova Salmon in strips
1 lb. cream cheese in small chunks
    (reserve 4 oz. in bowl)
12 bagels

Butter
DRESSING:
½ cup red wine vinegar
½ cup olive oil
1½ Tblsp. pepper

Layer in order, lettuce leaves, onion, salmon, and 12 oz. of cubed
cream cheese. Butter bagels and broil until light brown and bubbly.
Toss salad in dressing and place on plate. Garnish with 2 bagel halves
and serve. Put extra bagels and reserved cream cheese on table. *Serve
with a chilled dry white wine. This is an absolute rave!*

THE CHEF'S SALAD

Preparation Time: 35 minutes
Cooking Time: 5 minutes
Serves: 4

Jacklyn Johnson Rabinowitz
Almost Heaven

2 hard boiled eggs, crumbled
    or sliced
1/3 lb. each of turkey, ham
    and roast beef
½ lb. Provolone cheese
Variety salad greens (Iceberg,
    Romaine, Spinach,
    Watercress)
1 tomato
1 carrot

½ cucumber
½ green pepper
½ red pepper
¼ Bermuda onion
Black pitted olives
¼ cup shredded red cabbage
1 (8 oz.) jar marinated artichoke
    hearts
1 tsp. paprika

Slice meats and cheese into thin strips. Wash and dry greens. Cut tomato into wedges, carrot into diagonal slices, cucumber into half peeled slices, and the onion and pepper into rings. Assemble salads creatively, and top with eggs, pitted olives, artichoke hearts, and sprinkle with paprika. *Serve with your homemade dressing, a crusty loaf of French bread, dry white wine and fresh fruit. A favorite lunch!*

CALYPSO SALAD

Preparation Time: 15 minutes
Chilling Time: overnight
Serves: 4

Margo Ann Muckey
Tuff

1 cup mayonnaise
1 Tblsp. curry powder
1 Tblsp. soy sauce
½ tsp. ground ginger
1 Tblsp. ketchup
1 Tblsp. lemon juice
1 lb. lump crabmeat, tuna,
    lobster, chicken, or turkey

1 cup chopped green pepper
1 cup seedless grapes
1 (8 oz.) can pineapple chunks,
    drained
1 (2 oz.) jar chopped pimento,
    drained
1 cup slivered almonds, toasted
Lettuce
Garnish: avocado, cantaloupe

Combine first 7 ingredients in large bowl. Add next 4 ingredients, and mix well. Cover and chill overnight. When ready to serve, shape lettuce into cups on individual plates. Add ½ almonds to salad and toss lightly. Divide among lettuce cups. Sprinkle with remaining almonds. *Garnish with cantaloupe and avocado, if desired.*

SALADE NICOISE

Jean Thayer
Finesse 60

Preparation Time: 20 minutes
Cooking Time: 20 minutes
Serves: 8

6 new potatoes
1 medium red onion, thinly sliced
2 boxes frozen whole green
    beans, defrosted, patted dry
3 heads Bibb lettuce, washed,
    dried, separated
5 tomatoes, quartered
1 lb. smoked marlin - sliced and
    separated into large flakes
    or: 2 (6½ oz.) cans tuna,
    drained
3 Tblsp. capers, drained
5 hard-boiled eggs, peeled, halved

DRESSING:
1 Tblsp. lemon juice
3 Tblsp. wine vinegar
2 Tblsp. Dijon mustard
1 clove garlic, minced
½ Tblsp. dried basil
1 Tblsp. chopped fresh parsley
2/3 cup olive oil
Salt, freshly ground pepper
    to taste

Garnish: Anchovies (optional)

Combine all ingredients for dressing in a small bowl, whisking in the olive oil. Set aside. Steam potatoes 15 to 20 minutes or until tender. Cool. Peel and slice. Drizzle a bit of white wine over potatoes and set aside. Pat lettuce dry and toss with 2 Tblsp. of dressing. Line a large platter with lettuce. Top with green beans and potatoes. Arrange flaked marlin and onion rings across the center; tomato quarters and egg halves around rim of platter. Sprinkle olives, capers and anchovies over salad. Spoon dressing over salad. *Serve with hot French bread.*

SALMON & AVOCADO SALAD

Preparation Time: 20 minutes
Chilling Time: 30 minutes
Serves: 4

Sylvia Dabney
Native Sun

1 (1 lb.) can Red Salmon,
   picked over
2 Tblsp. finely chopped celery
2 hard boiled eggs, chopped
4 Tblsp. mayonnaise

1 tsp. curry powder
2 avocados
1 large crushed garlic
Juice of 1 lemon
Garnish: Paprika

Flake salmon, add celery, eggs - toss. In another bowl, mix mayonnaise with curry, pour over salmon - refrigerate. When you are ready to eat, halve avocados, brush with lemon juice and fill with salmon mixture. Garnish with a dusting of paprika and serve on a bed of lettuce. *The filling makes a delicious cracker spread and croissant sandwich.*

ARTICHOKE RICE SALAD

Preparation Time: 20 minutes
Cooking Time: 15 - 20 minutes
Serves: 10 - 12

Shannon Webster
Chaparral

2 cups white rice
2 chicken bouillon cubes
2 (6½ oz.) jars marinated
   artichoke hearts
½ - ¾ cup mayonnaise
1 - 1½ tsp. curry powder
Salt and pepper, to taste

4 green scallions, thinly sliced
½ green or red pepper, chopped
15 pimento stuffed olives, sliced
½ cup chicken, or shrimp,
   cooked (optional)
½ cup chopped almonds (optional)
Garnish: lettuce and cherry
    tomatoes

Cook rice in water as directed, but add bouillon to water. Cool in a large bowl. Drain artichoke hearts but save the juice. Cut hearts in half. Combine with mayonnaise, curry powder, salt and pepper. Mix rice with artichoke liquid. Then add onions, pepper (green or red), and olives. Toss artichoke hearts with rice mixture. Add chicken, also shrimp and almonds if desired. Better if allowed time to set. Can be put into a mold. *Serve on a bed of lettuce with cherry tomato flowerettes.*

FISH *NECTARINE SALAD

Preparation Time: 25 minutes
Cooking Time: 10 - 15 minutes
Chilling Time: Several hours
Serves: 4 - 6

Shannon Webster
Chaparral

4 cups fish, grouper, snapper,
    etc. (cooked and flaked)
1½ cups cubed and peeled
    nectarines
1 (8 oz.) can water chestnuts,
    drained and sliced
¼ cup pecans, chopped
2 Tblsp. green pepper, chopped

½ cup mayonnaise
1 Tblsp. lemon juice
1¼ tsp. salt
¼ tsp. pepper
1/8 tsp. thyme
Garnish: lettuce leaves
    and nectarine slices

Combine fish with nectarines, water chestnuts, pecans and green pepper. Then mix mayonnaise, lemon juice and seasonings. Toss with fish mixture. Chill. *Peaches may be substituted for Nectarines. *Serve over lettuce leaves, and garnish with nectarine slices. A refreshing light luncheon entree .*

FIESTA CRAB SALAD

Preparation Time: 30 minutes
Serves: 6

Margo Hall
Winji

1 lb. crab meat or sea legs
1 head lettuce
½ lb. fresh sliced mushrooms
6 small tomatoes, diced
8 oz. Cheddar cheese

8 oz. Monterey Jack cheese with
    green onions
8 oz. sour cream
Guacamole dip
1 bag Tostado chips

Shred lettuce in individual salad bowls. Add mushrooms and tomatoes. Grate equal amounts of cheeses on top. Arrange crab meat or legs on top of cheese. Arrange Tostado chips around the edges of salad bowls, and top with a scoop of sour cream and guacamole. *A very pretty and easy lunch! A best seller on Winji.*

LOBSTER SALAD WITH CREAM DRESSING

Preparation Time: 35 minutes
Cooking Time: 5 minutes
Serves: 6

Sharon Strong
Promises

2½ lbs. cooked lobster meat
   coarsely chopped
½ cup minced celery
Juice of 1 lemon
Salt and pepper
2 Tblsp. parsley, finely chopped
1 medium cucumber, chopped,
   peeled, and seeded
2 Tblsp. scallions, finely chopped
Garnish:
½ head lettuce, Butterleaf or Bibb
4 small firm tomatoes

4 hard boiled eggs and
   1 yolk for garnish
1 can asparagus spears
6 lobster half shells

DRESSING:
3 egg yolks
3 Tblsp. butter, softened
1 tsp. salt, dry mustard, and sweet
   Hungarian paprika
1 cup scalded light cream
3 Tblsp. white wine vinegar

Arrange lettuce leaves inside ½ lobster shells. In a bowl, mix the lobster meat, cucumber, celery, parsley, ½ the dressing and juice of 1 lemon with salt and pepper. Cut the tomatoes with 5 incisions (not cutting all the way to the bottom) width-wise. Use egg slicer to cut eggs, and place one slice into each incision of the tomato. You now have a tomato-egg fan. Place 4 asparagus spears alongside each lobster shell and a tomato fan nearby. Sprinkle each lobster meat shell with the hard boiled yolk sieved through a strainer for color. If you have a little red caviar you can crown each with ½ tsp. Serve remaining dressing on the side.

DRESSING: Combine the egg yolks, butter, and dry ingredients. Pour 1 cup into the egg yolk mixture in a stream, stirring constantly. Transfer the mixture to a saucepan, and cook over low heat, stirring constantly until thickened. Do not let boil. Strain into a bowl, and slowly beat into the vinegar. Let cool. *Serve with Chilled Coconut Soup and Parmesan bread.*

NOTE: Avocado shells may be used for base of salad instead of lobster shells.

CRAB/SHRIMP OR LOBSTER SALAD

Preparation Time: 45 minutes   *Sharon Strong*
Serves: 6   *Promises*

3 large avocados, peeled and
    pitted, coarsely chopped
2½ lbs. lobster meat (or crab
    or shrimp)
½ cup finely chopped celery
½ cup thinly sliced red radishes
¼ cup lemon juice
¼ cup vinegar
3 Tblsp. olive oil

2 Tblsp. finely chopped shallots
¼ tsp. cayenne and salt
Garnish:
Carrot flowers from 1 carrot
Cucumber spears
4 hard boiled eggs
3 lemons, scalloped halves
½ head of lettuce
LOUIE DRESSING:
See recipe below

Mix all ingredients and attractively place on individual plates with cucumber spears, carrot flowers, hard boiled egg slices and lemon scallops. *Serve with Cold Zucchini Soup or Conch Chowder.*

LOUIE DRESSING

1 cup mayonnaise
¼ cup chili sauce
1 Tblsp. horseradish
2 Tblsp. chopped parsley

1 Tblsp. finely chopped onions
1 Tblsp. finely chopped chives
Salt and pepper
¼ cup heavy cream, whipped

Mix all ingredients to pepper. Fold in the whipped cream. Serve in a separate bowl.

This crab/shrimp/or lobster salad can be served in a conch shell. Tortellini can be substituted for avocados. The conch shell presentation is beautiful. The shredded lettuce fills up the holes in the shell. Make sure the conch shell is one that sits up steadily.

A large flour tortilla shell is another nice presentation. Fry one in a wok with oil and use an empty coffee can with pressure from a large stainless spoon to form the cavity. Always collect leaves and use them throughout the charter. With a conch shell and tortilla shell, place grape (seagrape) leaves at base. Use little leaves on top of sorbets and poached pears.

TUNA SHELL SALAD

Preparation Time: 15 minutes
Chilling Time: 30 minutes
Serves: 4

Barbie Haworth
Ann-Marie II

1 (6½ oz.) can white tuna in water, drained
1-1½ cups macaroni shells, cooked
½ cup green pepper, chopped
¾ cup celery, chopped
6 eggs, hard-cooked, chopped

2 Tblsp. Dip-idy Dill (onion, parsley, dill, salt, garlic, spices)
1-2 cups mayonnaise*
2 tsp. Dijon mustard
Romaine lettuce leaves
Italian dressing

Garnish: green pepper strips, tomato wedges, red onion rings, carrots, celery strips, Hearts of Palm or artichoke hearts, black olives, sprouts

Combine all ingredients except tuna. Flake tuna and fold into sauce. Chill. Salad can be served on individual plates or on a platter. Place on Romaine and arrange garnishes on top and around the salad. Pour Italian dressing around the Romaine and garnishes. *Can use ½ cup sour cream or yogurt.

CHICKEN WITH TONNATO SAUCE

Preparation Time: 10 minutes
Cooking Time: 30 minutes
Chilling Time: several hours - overnight
Serves: 8

Jean Thayer
Finesse 60

8 whole boneless chicken breasts, halved and skinned
White wine for poaching

TONNATO SAUCE:
7 oz. can tuna, drained
6 anchovies, rinse, pat dry
1 cup mayonnaise

Garnish: capers and lemon wedges

In large skillet, poach breasts in wine over very low heat, turning once. Poach until no longer pink, do not overcook! Drain breasts and refrigerate several hours or overnight. Immediately before serving make Tonnato sauce, blend tuna, anchovies and mayonnaise in food processor, stopping once to scrape down. Place two halves of chicken on each plate - spoon Tonnato sauce on side, sprinkle with capers and garnish with lemon wedges. *Serve with Potato Pie and Gazpacho Andaluz.*

CURRIED CHICKEN IN PINEAPPLE BOATS

Preparation Time: 20 minutes
Cooking Time: 15 minutes
Serves: 6

Sharon Strong
Promises

3 pineapples
6 - 8 chicken breasts, deboned
    and cut into bite-size pieces
¾ cup onion, chopped
½ cup celery, chopped
Salt and pepper to taste
¾ cup sour cream

½ cup sliced almonds
1 Tblsp. butter
1/3 cup chopped dried apricots
1/3 cup raisins
2 Tblsp. curry powder (or use Hol-
    land House Curry Sauce, mild)
2 cups cooked rice (optional)

Halve pineapples, remove flesh and cut in bite-size pieces. Save pineapple shells. Lightly toast almonds in 1 Tblsp. butter. Use slotted spoon and remove. Save. In a large skillet, lightly saute onions and celery. Add chicken pieces, salt, and pepper. Stir until cooked. Add sour cream and curry, and let simmer a few minutes. Meanwhile, put pineapple chunks, apricots, and raisins in another skillet, and heat through. To serve: spread chicken mixture over a bed of rice (if desired) in each pineapple half shell. Add pineapple mixture, and sprinkle almonds on top. Garnish with a flower on pineapple stem. Serve with nut or coconut bread. Do prep work the night before or morning, and spend only 15 minutes cooking for a hot and easy lunch. *Serve chutney on the side. Guaranteed to get attention!*

CHICKEN GALANTINE

Preparation Time: 20 minutes
Cooking Time: 1 hour
Chilling Time: 1 hour
Serves: 10

Sue Griffin
Endless Summer I

4 - 6 lb. chicken
1 lb. sausage, veal or
    ground beef
4 Tblsp. sour cream

2 mushrooms
1 red pepper
1 green pepper
Seasonings

Preheat oven to 375° F. Bone chicken keeping as whole as possible, but not essential. Mix sausage, sour cream and seasonings. Divide into 4 parts. Lay chicken in a pan skin side down. Alternate sausage mixture and different vegetables for a contrast of color. Keep the vegetables as whole as possible but keep flat. Roll up the chicken, and wrap in foil. Seal and bake for 1 hour. Chill. When cold, slice ¼ inch thick and serve.

CURRIED CHICKEN IN AVOCADO HALVES

Preparation Time: 30 minutes
Cooking Time: 30 minutes
Chilling Time: 2 hours
Serves: 4

Jacklyn Johnson Rabinowitz
Almost Heaven

4 chicken breasts
2 avocados
1 small green pepper, diced
1 small red pepper, diced
1 scallion, chopped
¼ cup slivered almonds
1 tomato, cut in wedges
Lettuce
¼ cup raisins

CURRY DRESSING:
½ cup sour cream
½ cup mayonnaise
1 tsp. Dijon or Pommery mustard
½ tsp. paprika
¼ tsp. pepper
2 Tblsp. curry powder, to taste
Garnish: 2 hard boiled eggs, sliced

Cook, cool and dice chicken. Add vegetables, almonds and dressing to chicken. Stir together and chill 2 hours but overnight is best. Halve avocados, and stuff with mixture when ready to serve. Garnish with raisins and sliced eggs. Surround and anchor avocados with lettuce and tomato. *Serve with crackers and Cucumber Dill Salad.*

ZUCCHINI PITA PIZZAS

Preparation Time: 15 minutes
Cooking Time: 20 minutes
Serves: 6

Barbara Lowe
My Way

2 large onions, sliced
4 - 5 zucchini, cut in half
   and sliced
1 Tblsp. basil
3 pita bread pockets

¼ cup olive oil
¼ cup grated Parmesan
1½ cups grated Mozarella
1 pkg. slice pepperoni

Preheat oven to 400° F. Cook onions and zucchini in oil, add basil. Cut pita pockets in half forming 2 complete rounds of each. Sprinkle bread with Parmesan. Top with cooked zucchini and onions and cover with shredded Mozarella and 6 slices pepperoni. Bake 15 minutes in hot oven till pitas are crisp and cheese is melted. *Accompany with a chilled soup or just with chips or a fruit salad of some sort.*

TRAWLER'S PIE

Preparation Time: 35 minutes
Cooking Time: 1 hour
Serves: 6

Fiona Baldrey
Promenade

20 oz. white tuna in water
26 oz. can whole tomatoes
6 hard boiled eggs, peeled
    and sliced
1 pint Bechamel sauce
    (see recipe p. 91)

6 sliced green onions
3 lbs. potatoes, mashed with 3 oz.
    butter and 3 oz. milk
3 Tblsp. breadcrumbs
2 Tblsp. grated Parmesan cheese

Preheat oven to 350° F. Prepare Bechamel sauce, and set aside. Hard boil the eggs for 6 - 8 minutes. Peel potatoes, and boil until just soft. Meanwhile, drain tuna and tomatoes (reserve 2 oz. tomato liquid). Crush tomatoes, layer with tuna, and then moisten with tomato liquid. Layer peeled and sliced eggs. Spread Bechamel sauce on top. Drain and mash potatoes adding milk and butter. Layer on top of sauce. Flatten and score with a fork. Sprinkle with breadcrumbs and Parmesan cheese. Bake in moderate oven for 1 hour. *Serve with a mixed salad.*

ZUCCHINI PIE

Preparation Time: 20 minutes
Cooking Time: 20 minutes
Serves: 8

Irene McClain
Solskin II

1 can crescent rolls
2 tsp. Dijon mustard, optional
4 cups zucchini, thinly sliced
1 cup coarsely chopped onion
¼-½ cup margarine
1 minced clove garlic
2 eggs

½ lb. shredded Mozzarella cheese
¼ tsp. basil
¼ tsp. oregano
¼ tsp. pepper
½-3/4 tsp. salt
2 Tblsp. parsley

Preheat oven to 350° F. Saute onion, garlic, and zucchini in margarine. Meanwhile, break dough into triangles, and form into a crust in a large pie pan. Spread crust with mustard, if desired. Mix eggs, cheese, and spices together. Add to vegetables. Pour into pie pan, and bake for 18 - 20 minutes. If crust starts to brown too quickly, cover with tin foil. Let rest 10 minutes before serving. *I serve this dish with a green salad, hot rolls, and butter with apple crisp and whipped cream for dessert.*

SPINACH AND FETA PIE

Preparation Time: 30 minutes
Cooking Time: 20 - 30 minutes
Serves: 8

Lisa Hawkins
Ariguani

2 (10 oz.) pkgs. frozen spinach, cooked
1 medium onion, chopped
1 cup mushrooms, sliced

1 large jar Feta cheese, crumbled
2 eggs
12 or more sheets filo dough
1½ cups butter, melted

Preheat oven to 375° F. Squeeze water from cooked spinach and chop. Combine spinach, onion, mushrooms, Feta, and eggs. Add salt and pepper to taste. With a pastry brush, butter the bottom of baking dish. Layer 4 sheets of filo buttering between each sheet. Spread ½ spinach mixture over filo. Layer 4 more sheets of filo buttering between each sheet. Spread remaining spinach mixture over filo. Layer 4 more sheets filo buttering between each layer and top sheet. Bake for 20 - 30 minutes or until bubbling and golden. *Serve with Sauteed Summer Squash and Minted Fruit Salad.*

POTATO PIE

Preparation Time: 1 hour
Cooking Time: 1 hour and 45 minutes
Serves: 6 - 8

Jean Thayer
Finesse 60

3 large baking potatoes
12 oz. container cottage cheese, mashed through a strainer or sieve
¼ cup Half & Half
1 Tblsp. butter
2 eggs

1 cup freshly grated Parmesan cheese
1 tsp. chopped chives
1 Tblsp. chopped parsley
2 Tblsp. fresh bread crumbs
½ Tblsp. butter

Bake potatoes at 450° F. for 1 hour or until tender. While potatoes are warm, cut in half and scoop out flesh. In a medium bowl, mash potatoes with the sieved cottage cheese, Half n' Half, and butter. Beat in eggs, one by one, and add ¾ cup of the Parmesan and the chives and parsley. Butter a 9" pie pan with ½ Tblsp. butter. Sprinkle bread crumbs and remaining ¼ cup of Parmesan over bottom and sides. Spoon potato mixture into pan. At this point the dish may be refrigerated and baked later in the day. To bake - preheat oven to 350° F and bake 35 to 45 minutes until puffy and brown. May be served warm or at room temperature or even quickly re-heated. *Great with: Chicken with Tonnato Sauce and Gazpacho Andaluz.*

VEAL TROPICANA

Preparation Time: 15 minutes
Cooking Time: 15 - 20 minutes
Serves: 6

Nicky Cahi
Once Upon A Time

6 Veal Scallopinis
6 slices Prosciutto
6 bananas
Dijon mustard

1 egg
Bread crumbs
Cocktail sticks/toothpicks (vital)
Garnish: parsley and lemon slices

Beat scallopini to about ¼ inch pieces. Spread with layers of Dijon mustard. Place slice of Prosciutto over mustard, then place bananas in centre and roll veal and Proscuitto around banana. Secure with toothpicks. Roll in egg and bread crumbs. Fry veal in hot oil (about ½ inch in pan) placing seam in oil first to seal. When cooked, allow to cool slightly, then cut into ½ inch rounds. Looks very attractive seeing layers of banana, Proscuitto, and veal. *Garnish with parsley and lemon slices. Serve with tossed green salad.*

GAZPACHO ANDALUZ

Preparation Time: 15 minutes
Chilling Time: 4 hours
Serves: 6

Jean Thayer
Finesse 60

3 large tomatoes, peeled, halved
1 large cucumber, peeled, halved
1 medium onion, peeled, halved
1 medium green pepper,
    quartered, seeded
1 pimento - drained

24 oz. tomato juice
2 drops tabasco
¼ cup olive oil
¼ cup red wine vinegar
Salt, fresh ground pepper to taste
2 cloves garlic - minced
½ cup croutons

In blender combine 2 tomatoes, ½ cucumber, ½ onion, ½ green pepper, pimento, and ½ cup tomato juice. Blend, covered at high speed 15 seconds. In large bowl, mix pureed vegetables with remaining juice, oil, vinegar, tabasco and salt and pepper. Refrigerate, covered, 4 hours. Chop remaining vegetables and refrigerate in separate bowls. Immediately before serving, mince garlic and stir into soup. *To serve, spoon into chilled cups and set out bowls of chopped vegetables and croutons as accompaniments.*

SWEET AND SOUR FISH FILLETS

Preparation Time: 10 minutes
Cooking Time: 10 minutes
Chilling Time: overnight
Serves: 4

Wendy Smith
Stampede

8 Tblsp. olive oil
2 large onions, sliced
1 Tblsp. lemon juice
2 Tblsp. dry white wine
Salt and pepper

2 tsp. sugar or more
2 oz. pine nuts
2 oz. raisins
Flour for dusting
4 fish fillets

Heat oil and gently cook onions for 5 minutes until soft. Add lemon,
wine, salt, pepper, and sugar. Bring to a boil, and simmer for 2 minutes.
Add raisins and pine nuts. Dust fish fillets with flour. Shallow fry for
1 minute on each side. Drain, and arrange in shallow serving dish.
Spoon the mixture over the fish, cover, and chill overnight. This is a very
old Italian recipe. I often make the sauce and serve it hot over almost
any fish. *Serve with rice salad, lettuce, and tomatoes.*

HAM MORNAY

Preparation Time: 5 minutes
Cooking Time: 30 minutes
Serves: 4

Sheila Smith
Victorious

8 slices boiled ham
2 slices pineapple (canned
    is fine)

Cheese sauce made with Cheddar
    cheese
Tomatoes for garnish

Preheat oven to 300° F. Roll ham around ½ slice of pineapple, and
place it in a baking dish. Pour cheese sauce over, and garnish with
tomato slices. Bake for 30 minutes. Serve as a light supper with parsley-
potatoes, and salad, or on its own for lunch. *Everyone loves it, so don't
be put off by how easy it is.*

CHICKEN CREPES

Preparation Time: 15 minutes
Cooking Time: 35 minutes
Serves: 4

Barbie Haworth
Ann-Marie II

2 cups cooked chicken chunks
2 Tblsp. butter
½ green pepper, chunks
¼ cup canned mushrooms, drained
½ cup petit peas, drained
1 cup cheese, grated (any kind - optional)
1 (10¾ oz.) can cream of mushroom, celery, or chicken soup
2 Tblsp. white wine
½ tsp. celery salt
½ tsp. basil

CREPE BATTER: (9 crepes in 10" skillet)
1 cup Bisquick
1 egg, beaten
1 cup milk
Garnish: parsley

In a 2 qt. saucepan, saute green pepper and onions for 2 minutes (so they're still crispy). Add rest of ingredients, mix well. Heat slowly over low flame, stir occasionally (use flame tamer). Crepes may be made ahead. (You do not have to layer each with paper towel). At time of service, heat each crepe in skillet, lay on plate, spoon ¼ cup of chicken mixture in each, roll up. Two crepes per serving. Garnish with parsley on top. *Note: you may substitute 2 (6½ oz.) cans tuna in water, drained, and 1 tsp. curry powder for chicken and have TUNA CURRY CREPES. Serve with coleslaw and Banana Bread.*

SEATTLE STYLE ENCHILADAS

Preparation Time: 20 minutes
Cooking Time: 15 minutes
Makes: 12

Joan Della Dora
Bluewater

12 flour tortillas
2 (10¾ oz.) cans cream of chicken
   soup, undiluted
1 cup green chilies, cut up
2 - 3 chicken breasts, cooked,
   boned, and shredded
1 cup sour cream

1 (8 oz.) brick Monterey Jack
   cheese with jalapenos
2 bunches of green onions, chopped
1 (16 oz.) can Enchilada sauce
   (or homemade)
4 oz. grated Cheddar cheese
Black olives, sliced

Heat the oven to 350° F. While preparing filling, place tortillas in oven, wrapped in foil, to soften, and make more pliable. Heat soup and add chilies, chicken, and sour cream. In tortilla, place several slices of Monterey cheese, then chicken filling. Top with onions, and roll up. Place seam side down into a 9" x 13" casserole dish, which has been lightly greased. Cover with remaining chicken mixture. Add ½ - ¾ can Enchilada sauce over top. Add grated Cheddar cheese evenly over top and sliced black olives. Bake about 15 minutes, just until cheeses melt and blend together. *Serve with Spanish Rice, Mexican Sangria, Fresh Fruit Salad.*

CARIBBEAN CONCH FRITTERS

Preparation Time: 30 minutes
Cooking Time: 15 minutes
Serves: 6 - 8

Kimberly Foote
Oklahoma Crude II

2 cups chopped conch
2 cups Bisquick
2/3 cup milk
2 tsp. baking powder
2 eggs, lightly beaten

4 Tblsp. cocktail sauce, bottled
½ tsp. each of curry powder, celery
   salt, onion powder, garlic
   powder and parsley
Oil for frying

Mix all ingredients in a bowl. Drop by spoonful in large frying pan with hot oil. When golden brown, drain on a paper towel. *Jan Robinson on Vanity adds ¼ cup each of diced celery, onion and green pepper to this recipe. Serve on large party platter on bed of lettuce with bowl of seafood cocktail sauce in center.*

SPICY CEVICHE

Preparation Time: 30 minutes
Chilling Time: 24 hours
Serves: 8

Shannon Webster
Chaparral

2 - 3 lbs. fresh tuna
1 packet dry Italian dressing mix
¼ cup olive oil
¾ cup vegetable oil
¼ cup fresh coriander leaves
½ cup black olives, sliced
½ cup chopped celery
1½ cups minced Spanish onions

2/3 cup fresh lime juice
3 minced cloves garlic
2 bay leaves
Fresh pepper, to taste
1 pinch salt
1 tsp. fresh thyme
3 drops tabasco
½ cup fresh chopped scallions

Place tuna in shallow bowl. Blend oils and Italian dressing mix, coriander, thyme, tabasco, salt, and pepper. Combine oil mixture with olives, celery, onions, lime juice, garlic, and bay leaves. Pour marinade over fish. Cover bowl and chill for 24 hours. Serve cold on a bed of lettuce with some of the marinade. Sprinkle with fresh scallions. Serve with French bread or crackers. *It's worth the 24 hour wait! Serve as a lunch or starter to a meal.*

TAKE IT EASY SPINACH QUICHE

Preparation Time: 20 minutes
Cooking Time: approximately 1 hour
Serves: 6

Lisa Ferry
Tefra

3 (10 oz.) packages frozen
    creamed spinach
2 packages shredded
    Swiss cheese
1 can French fried onion rings,
    crushed

4 eggs
1 tsp. nutmeg
Fresh ground pepper to taste
2 shallow or 1 deep dish frozen
    unbaked pie shell

Preheat oven to 350° F. Cook spinach according to package directions. Empty into bowl, add Swiss cheese and French fried onion rings. Beat in eggs and seasonings with wooden spoon. Empty into pie shell(s), and bake for 50 - 60 minutes. Center should be firm when done. *Serve with a Greek salad.*

S & S TOMATOES

Preparation Time: 15 minutes   *Denise Wright*
Cooking Time: 20 minutes   *Parandah*
Serves: 6

6 large tomatoes, suitable   2 Tblsp. dry sherry
   for stuffing   ½ cup bread crumbs
1 pint scallops   2 Tblsp. chopped parsley
3 - 4 green onions, chopped   ¼ cup Parmesan cheese
2 Tblsp. butter   Garnish: parsley, black olives

Slice scallops. Saute onions in butter. Add scallops. Add few Tblsp. bread crumbs and sherry. Simmer for 10 minutes. Cut a large star shaped hole in the tops of tomatoes. Using a spoon, empty tomatoes. Add parsley to scallop mixture. Spoon into tomato shells. Top with remaining bread crumbs and Parmesan cheese. Broil for about 5 minutes until light brown. Top with a sprig of parsley and 2 black olives. *Serve on a bed of alfalfa sprouts with carrot sticks, purple grapes, and orange slices. Serve with hot French bread.*

STIR-FRY VEGGIES

Preparation Time: 15 minutes   *Candice Carson*
Cooking Time: 3 minutes   *Freight Train*
Serves: 6

1 cup each of thinly sliced: Celery
   Zucchini   ½ cup red or green onions, chopped
   Summer squash   4 large Syrian or pita breads
   Red pepper   8 slices Muenster cheese
   Green pepper   Peanut oil
   Mushrooms

Fry vegetables in hot peanut oil. I use my wok, but a large frying pan would work. Be careful not to overcook them, they should be crispy. Cut bread in half, and put a slice of cheese in each pocket. Spoon in the vegetables. Any vegetables you have on hand are fine: bamboo shoots, water chestnuts, broccoli, sprouts, snow peas, etc. All work great but the ones listed keep well on a sailboat.

CHICKEN QUICHE

Preparation Time: 25 minutes
Cooking Time: 1 hour
Chilling Time: 1 hour
Serves: 6 - 8

Barbie Haworth
Ann-Marie II

8 INCH CRUST:
1 cup flour
½ tsp. salt
2-2/3 Tblsp. shortening
2-2/3 Tblsp. cold water

FILLING:
¾ cup Cheddar or Swiss cheese, grated
1½ cup cooked chicken pieces
½ cup cooked chopped broccoli
½ cup cooked chopped onions
1 cup evaporated milk
2 eggs, beaten
Pepper
½ tsp. salt
1/8 tsp. nutmeg

Preheat oven to 325° F. Make pie crust and chill. Roll out pie crust, and place in an 8 inch deep pie pan, and flute the edge. Layer the ingredients. Combine eggs, milk, salt, pepper, and nutmeg. Blend thoroughly. Pour over pie shell. Bake in oven for 1 hour or until quiche is set (insert knife). Can be cooked on stove top at low temperature for 30 - 35 minutes with flame tamer in skillet or Dutch oven. *Serve with crisp tossed salad, and Banana or Pumpkin bread. Note: Can be made with Muenster cheese, chicken or shrimp and spinach.*

FESTIVE ITALIAN QUICHE

Preparation Time: 20 minutes
Cooking Time: 50 minutes
Serves: 6

Donna Jaggard
Thorobred

1 - 9 inch pie shell
2 Tblsp. oil
2 cups chopped zucchini
½ cup chopped onion
1 minced clove garlic
1¼ cup shredded Mozzarella
3 beaten eggs
1 cup cottage cheese
1/3 cup milk
½ tsp. salt
Dash of pepper
HERBED TOMATO SAUCE:
1 (15 oz.) can tomato sauce
1 Tblsp. parsley flakes
1 tsp. oregano
½ tsp. basil, crushed
1 minced clove of garlic
Salt and pepper, to taste

Preheat oven to 350° F. Bake crust for 10 minutes. Cool. Increase oven to 375°. Heat oil. Add zucchini, onion, garlic, and saute for 10 minutes. Spread in pie shell. Mix 1 cup Mozzerella with eggs, cottage cheese, milk, salt, and pepper. Spoon over vegetables. Sprinkle with remaining ¼ cup Mozzarella. Bake 40 minutes. Serve with the Herbed Tomato Sauce. To make, simmer all sauce ingredients for 15 minutes. *Serve with a tossed salad and chilled white wine.*

CAULIFLOWER QUICHE

Preparation Time: 20 minutes
Cooking Time: 1 hour
Serves: 6

LeeAnn LaCesa
Flute

1 fold-out refrigerator pie crust
1 cup grated Cheddar cheese
½ cup grated Monterey Jack cheese
1 tomato, sliced
1 med. Cauliflower, in flowerettes
1½ cups sour cream
2 eggs
½ cup whipping cream
2½ Tblsp. Italian seasoning
1 Tblsp. sweet basil

Preheat oven to 350° F. In 9-inch pie pan layer fold-out crust (as per instructions), cheeses, tomato slices, and cauliflower flowerettes. Mix remaining five ingredients until smooth and pour over cauliflower. Bake in 350° oven for 1 hour or until it's browned around the edges and puffed up. Let cool 5 minutes. Slice and garnish each with a parsley sprig. *Serve with a Pineapple/Apple Salad and a nice white wine.*

QUICHE AUX EPINARDS
QUICHE AUX CHAMPIGNONS

Preparation Time: 30 minutes   *Laura Greces*
Cooking Time: 30 - 45 minutes   *Mistral*
Serves: 6

2 - 9 inch pastry crusts

4 eggs

2 cups heavy cream

½ cup grated Swiss cheese

2 Tblsp. butter

¼ cup minced shallots or
    green onions

4 Tblsp. butter

1 (8 oz.) can sliced mushrooms

1 tsp. salt

1 tsp. lemon juice

2 Tblsp. port or sherry

1 (10 oz.) package frozen chopped
    spinach, thawed and drained

½ tsp. salt

1/8 tsp. pepper

Pinch of nutmeg

This recipe makes 2 quiches - 1 mushroom and 1 spinach. I offer guests a choice.

Preheat oven to 375° F. Cook shallots in butter for 2 minutes. Place half in another saucepan. In first saucepan, add spinach, and stir over moderate heat for several minutes to evaporate all water. Stir in salt, pepper, and nutmeg. In second saucepan, over moderate heat, stir in mushrooms, salt, lemon juice and port. Boil until most liquid evaporates. Beat eggs and cream together. Stir in equal amount of this mixture into each saucepan. Pour each saucepan into separate pastry crusts (if more liquid is needed, add a little milk into the pastry crust and stir). Sprinkle with cheese. Dot with butter. Bake for 30 minutes or until cooked. *Serve with tossed green salad.*

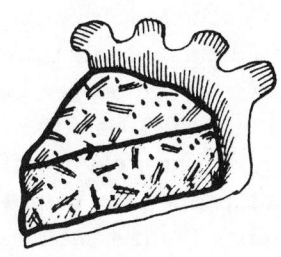

ASPARAGUS QUICHE

Preparation Time: 10 minutes   *Fiona Baldrey*
Cooking Time: 40 minutes   *Promenade*
Serves: 6

1 (7½ oz.) packet frozen   6 oz. whipping cream
   shortcrust pastry   5 Tblsp. milk
2 eggs, well beaten   1 (12 oz.) can apaaragus spears
Salt and pepper

Preheat oven to 400° F. Roll the pastry out, and use it to line a 8 inch
pie tin. Trim the edges, and lightly prick the base. Bake blind at 400°
for 20 minutes until lightly browned. Remove from the oven, and reduce heat to 350°. Beat the eggs, salt, pepper, cream, and milk together.
Drain the asparagus carefully. Pour the egg mixture into the pastry
shell, and arrange the spears of asparagus in a wheel shape on top.
Cook for 20 - 30 minutes until the mixture has set. *Serve hot or cold
with a mixed salad.*

TOMATO SOUFFLES

Preparation Time: 45 minutes   *Sarah Sheets*
Cooking Time: 20 minutes   *Royono*
Serves: 6

2 Tblsp. butter   Salt and pepper, to taste
2 Tblsp. flour   1 cup grated Swiss cheese
½ cup heavy cream   4 egg whites, stiffly beaten
3 egg yolks, plus   6 large ripe tomatoes
    3 egg yolks

Preheat oven to 350° F. Cut the tops from the tomatoes, and hollow
out the flesh. Set aside to drain on paper towels. Melt butter, add flour,
cream, 3 beaten egg yolks, salt, and pepper. Cook over low heat,
stirring constantly, until thickened. Cool to lukewarm. Stir in cheese
and remaining 3 beaten egg yolks. Fold in stiffly beaten egg whites.
Season tomatoes with salt, pepper, and basil. Fill tomatoes ¾ full with
souffle. Bake 15-20 minutes. Souffle should be puffed and brown.
Serve immediately with spinach salad, French bread, and champagne.

CAROL'S SHRIMP MOLD

Preparation Time: 15 minutes   *Candice Carson*
Chilling Time: Several hours   *Freight Train*
Serves: 8

1 (10¾ oz.) can tomato soup   1 cup mayonnaise
2 (8 oz.) packages cream cheese,   ¾ cup chopped celery
    softened   ¾ cup chopped green onion
1½ envelopes unflavored gelatin   2 (6½ oz.) cans shrimp - drained
1/3 cup cold water

Heat soup in saucepan, and stir in cream cheese. Dissolve gelatin in water, and add to soup mixture. While mixture cools, chop celery and green onions. Drain shrimp. Add the rest of the ingredients, and mix throughly. Place in ring mold, jell in refrigerator, unmold, and serve on a bed of lettuce. *I usually fill the center of the mold with lobster salad, and decorate the plate with flowers, either red Hibiscus or pink Oleander. Carol Nelson gave me this recipe when she was cook on the Heatherwind. Serve with Spinach Salad, French bread, and chilled white wine.*

SALMON-STUFFED ACORN SQUASH

Preparation Time: 20 minutes   *Fiona Baldrey*
Cooking Time: 40 minutes   *Promenade*
Serves: 6

3 acorn squash   1 cup mushrooms, thinly sliced
6 tsp. + 2 Tblsp. butter   15 oz. can red salmon
Salt and ground black pepper   1 cup sour cream
1 cup onions, thinly sliced   2 tsp. ground cumin

Preheat oven to 375° F. Halve the squash across the equator, and scoop out seeds. Place 1 tsp. butter in each cavity and salt and pepper Arrange halves, cut side up, on a baking pan. Bake for 20 minutes. Melt butter in skillet, and saute onions for 2 - 3 minutes. Add mushrooms, and cook further for 2-3 minutes. Remove and cool. Break up large pieces of salmon, and mix with onions, mushrooms, sour cream, and cumin. Stuff squash halves, and bake 20 minutes. *Serve with crusty bread and salad.*

SALMON TIMBALES

Preparation Time: 35 minutes
Cooking Time: 30 minutes
Serves: 4 - 6

Jacklyn Johnson Rabinowitz
Almost Heaven

2 (16 oz.) cans red salmon,
    drained and flaked
1 medium onion, chopped
1 small green pepper, chopped
½ cup chopped celery
½ cup plain dry bread crumbs
¼ cup plain yogurt
¼ cup mayonnaise
1 egg, slightly beaten
¼ tsp. pepper

CUCUMBER DILL SAUCE:
½ cup mayonnaise
¼ cup sour cream
¼ cup plain yogurt
¾ cup finely chopped seeded
    cucumber
¼ cup finely chopped onion
1 Tblsp. fresh chopped dill
Sprigs of dill, for garnish

Preheat oven to 325° F. Generously grease 6 oz. custard cups (2 per serving or use greased scallop shells). Combine ingredients, and pack in cups. Prepare sauce while timbales bake about 30 minutes. To unmold, run small knife around cup and invert. Drizzle sauce over timbales. Garnish with sprigs of dill. Cucumber sauce: assemble ingredients in saucepan, heat until warmed through. *Serve with a tomato and Mozzerella platter, alternate slices of each, and drizzle with olive oil and fresh snipped basil.*

HINT: When substituting canned mushrooms for fresh sauteed ones, the contents of one six-ounce can is equivalent to one pound of fresh cooked mushrooms.

FROSTED TUNA MOUSSE

Preparation Time: 20 minutes
Chilling Time: 2 hours
Serves: 10

Kathy Rodrigues
Valdivia

2 (8 oz.) cans tuna
2 Tblsp. lemon juice
2 tsp. ketchup
1 Tblsp. parsley, finely chopped
Salt and pepper, to taste
Garnish: lettuce, cucumber

4 Tblsp. cold water
1 Tblsp. unflavored gelatin
1 (12 oz.) can evaporated milk,
  chilled
2 egg whites

Mash the fish to a fine paste. Stir in lemon juice, ketchup, parsley, salt and pepper. Sprinkle gelatin over cold water, stir once, and leave to go spongy. Place in pan of hot water. Stir over low heat until gelatin is dissolved. Remove from heat, and strain into tuna mixture. Mix well. Whisk chilled evaporated milk until twice its volume. Add to tuna. Whisk egg whites until standing in peaks. Fold into tuna mix. Turn into an oiled 2 pint (or 1.2 litre) mold and chill well for about 2 hours. Serve mousse with chopped lettuce and cucumber garnish. *A Tomato and Onion Vinegarette Salad is a good accompaniment.*

SALMON MOUSSE

Preparation Time: 20 minutes
Chilling Time: 2 hours
Serves: 10 - 12

Fiona Baldrey
Promenade

1 (14 oz.) can red salmon
2 envelopes unflavored gelatin
½ cup whipping cream
8 oz. cream cheese
1 heaped Tblsp. mayonnaise
1 finely chopped green onion

1 Tblsp. finely chopped bell pepper
1 tsp. anchovy paste
Salt and ground black pepper
Dash tabasco sauce
Garnish: cucumber curls or lime
    wedges

Lightly grease mold. Empty contents of 2 gelatin envelopes into a small saucepan. Drain juice from red salmon on top - in the immortal words of 007 *"shaken NOT stirred"* - set aside. Whip cream and set aside. Cream salmon together with all other ingredients. Melt gelatin on a very low heat, do not boil. Pour into mixture and stir. Fold in whipped cream, and pour into mold. Chill at least 2 hours to set. To free mousse from mold, dunk upside down in boiling water for a couple seconds, and run a sharp knife around the rim. Turn out and garnish. *A copper fish mold is most effective for this dish. Otherwise, experiment with what's on board - cake tins, loaf pans, and bowls, or make individual molds.*

SALADS AND APPETIZERS

NOTES

HONEYMOON SALAD

Preparation Time: 5 minutes   *Jane Glancy*
Serves: 4   *Truant*

¼ cup oil
Juice of ½ lemon

½ head lettuce
¼ cup Parmesan cheese, more if
　　desired

Whisk together oil and lemon juice in bottom of salad bowl. Tear lettuce into bite size pieces, and place in bowl. Toss. Sprinkle Parmesan on top.

Why a honeymoon salad? Let-us alone!

SWEET AND SOUR SPINACH SALAD

Preparation Time: 10 minutes   *Donna Jaggard*
Serves: 6   *Thorobred*

4 egg yolks
1 tsp. dry mustard
1 tsp. salt
¼ tsp. white pepper
½ cup olive oil
¼ cup sugar

3 Tblsp. wine vinegar
Juice of ½ lemon
Spinach
½ lb. cooked, crumbled bacon
Mushrooms

Beat yolks until light and lemony colored. Add mustard, salt, and pepper. Blend well, whisking constantly. Add oil, drop by drop, then in a steady stream. Stir in sugar, vinegar, and lemon juice. Pour this dressing over spinach, and top with bacon and mushrooms.

HINT: Submerging a lemon in hot water for 15 minutes before squeezing will yield almost twice the amount of juice.

ZESTY ITALIAN SALAD

Preparation Time: 10 minutes
Marinating Time: 1 hour
Serves: 8

Jean Thayer
Finesse 60

1 head Romaine lettuce
1 head Iceberg lettuce
1 red onion, thinly sliced
1 can artichoke hearts, drained,
    chopped

1 jar pimento, drained, chopped
¾ cup fresh grated Parmesan
1 bottle Zesty Italian dressing

Wash and thoroughly dry lettuces. Tear lettuces and place in large salad bowl. Add onion, artichokes, pimento, Parmesan and pour salad dressing over all. Do not toss the salad. Refrigerate salad 1 hour. To serve, toss well.

SMOKED MARLIN SALAD

Preparation Time: 15 minutes
Chilling Time: 1 hour
Serves: 6 - 8

Casey Miller
Fancy Free

1 lb. smoked Marlin
2 ribs celery, finely chopped
1 medium onion, finely chopped
1 cup mayonnaise
2 Tblsp. country Dijon

1 Tblsp. honey
Juice of 1 lemon
Salt, pepper to taste
1 Tblsp. chopped fresh dill

Flake Marlin in large bowl and add onion and celery. Mix dressing and next 4 ingredients. Pour over Marlin and mix well. Add salt, pepper and dill and chill until serving time. Serve on a lettuce leaf and garnish.

NOTE: For lunch, serve on small soft rolls, 2 per person with lettuce. For Hors d'oeuvres, serve with crackers or use to stuff mushrooms. Garnish with lemon wedge and parsley flowers.

HINT: Grate and freeze lemon and orange rinds. Use when needed.

BAMBI'S SHRIMP SALAD

Preparation time: 30 minutes　　　　　　　*Gunilla Lundgren*
Chilling Time: 1 - 2 hours　　　　　　　　　　　　*Bambi*
Serves: 4

1 lb. small shrimp, cooked and
　　shelled
½ lb. mushrooms, cut in halves
1 avocado
Lettuce
2 lemons, cut in thin slices and
　　twisted
Dill sprigs (or parsley)

SAUCE:
1 cup sour cream
1/3 cup chili sauce
1/3 cup mayonnaise
1 tsp. curry

Mix shrimp and mushrooms. Peel, seed & slice the avocado and sprinkle with lemon juice. In individual glass dishes (if you have) make a bed of lettuce, then put in shrimp and mushroom mixture. Garnish with avocado slices, lemon wedges, and dill or parsley sprigs. Make sauce by mixing all ingredients. Chill and serve sauce on the side.

LAZY DAY SHRIMP SALAD

Preparation Time: 20 minutes　　　　　　　　*Liz Thomas*
Serves: 6　　　　　　　　　　　　　　　　*Raby Vacluse*

1 cup cooked rice
2 (4½ oz.) cans shrimp, rinsed
　　and drained
½ green pepper, chopped
1 small onion, chopped
1½ cups cauliflower, chopped
　　finely

8 stuffed olives, sliced
Juice of ½ lemon
Dash tabasco
½ cup mayonnaise
Garnish: cherry tomatoes
　　and avocado

Combine rice, shrimp, green pepper, onion, cauliflower, and olives. Toss lightly, then add lemon juice, tabasco, and mayonnaise. Serve on a large platter on a bed of green lettuce leaves, and garnish with cherry tomatoes and avocado, if desired.

HORIATIKI

Preparation Time: 20 minutes *Lisa Ferry*
Serves: 6 - 8 *Tefra*

2 green peppers
3 tomatoes
1 white onion
½ English cucumber
¼ lb. Feta cheese

½ can black olives
1 Tblsp. oregano leaf
1 Tblsp. sweet basil
¼ cup olive oil
3 Tblsp. lemon juice

Seed and slice green peppers into rings. Thinly slice tomatoes, onions, and English cucumber into rounds. Place layer of green pepper on platter, and repeat in order layering tomato, onion, and English cucumber. Crumble Feta cheese over top, and garnish with olives. Crush and sprinkle seasonings over all. Finally pour olive oil over all followed by lemon juice. Serve immediately.

AVOCADO FROSTED CAULIFLOWER SALAD

Preparation Time: 5 minutes *Margo Ann Muckey*
Cooking Time: 5 minutes *Tuff*
Chilling Time: overnight
Serves: 8

1 head cauliflower

MARINADE:
6 Tblsp. salad oil
3 Tblsp. white vinegar
Salt and pepper
Garnish: cherry tomatoes

SAUCE:
3 medium avocados
1 small onion, minced
3 Tblsp. marinade
Dash nutmeg
Salt
Toasted almonds

Steam cauliflower until tender, but firm. Place in a bowl. For marinade, combine ingredients, and pour over cauliflower while still warm. Chill overnight. For sauce, mash avocados with fork. Add onion, marinade, nutmeg, salt, and pepper. Mix well, Frost caulifower completely. Cover with toasted almonds. *Serve on a bed of lettuce, and garnish with cherry tomatoes.*

MUSHROOM SALAD

Preparation Time: 10 minutes　　　　　　　　　　*Emily Welch*
Marinating Time: 15 - 20 minutes　　　　　　　　*Wind's End*
Serves: 6

1½ lb. mushrooms, sliced　　　　1½ Tblsp. fresh lemon juice
9 Tblsp. olive oil　　　　　　　　¾ tsp. salt
3 Tblsp. red wine vinegar　　　　Freshly ground pepper
3 Tblsp. chopped parsley

Wipe mushrooms with a damp towel, and trim and thinly slice. In medium bowl, whisk oil, vinegar, parsley, lemon juice, and salt until blended. Add mushrooms, and toss gently to coat evenly. Let marinate at room temperature, tossing occasionally for 15 - 20 minutes for added flavor before serving. Pass around the pepper at the table. *Great served with Veal, Artichokes and Lemon Sauce and Italian Peas - Onions.*

CHERRY TOMATO SALAD

Preparation Time: 15 minutes　　　　　　*Margo Ann Muckey*
Chilling Time: 1 - 2 hours　　　　　　　　　　　　*Tuff*
Serves: 8

1 cup olive oil　　　　　　　　　　3 green onions, chopped
½ cup red wine vinegar　　　　　　1 clove garlic
2 Tblsp. chopped fresh parsley　　Salt and fresh pepper
1½ Tblsp. Dijon mustard　　　　　2 pints cherry tomatoes
1 Tblsp. fresh lemon juice　　　　Garnish: 1 hardboiled egg
1 Tblsp. fresh dill

Combine the first 8 ingredients with salt and pepper, to taste, in a blender. Pour over tomatoes, toss, cover, and chill for 1 - 2 hours. Sprinkle with grated egg before serving.

HINT: By adding lemon juice to a bowl of cold water, a soggy head of lettuce will become crisp, if soaked for an hour in the refrigerator.

TOMATO AND CUKE SALAD

Preparation Time: 5 minutes   *Pat Rowley*
Chilling Time: 30 minutes   *Calypso*
Serves: 6

5 - 6 ripe tomatoes	**Dash dillweed**
3 cucumbers	**Red wine vinegar**
Salt and pepper	

Cut tomatoes in wedges, and cucumbers in slices. Mix with spices in bowl with seal lid. Pour wine vinegar over tomato and cucumber mix and chill. Before serving, shake bowl to mix. *Nice easy side dish for picnic lunches on the beach.*

CUCUMBER AND DILL SALAD

Preparation Time: 10 minutes   *Jacklyn Johnson Rabinowitz*
Chilling Time: 2 hours   *Almost Heaven*
Serves: 4

1 - 3 cucumbers	**2 Tblsp. chopped fresh dill or**
1 Tblsp. sugar	**2 tsp. dried dillweed**
Salt, to taste	**Freshly ground pepper,**
¼ cup white vinegar	**preferably white, to taste**

Peel, halve, seed, and slice cucumber (if "gourmet" cucumbers are used, just slice). There should be 3 - 4 cups. Put in bowl. Add remaining ingredients to taste. Chill for 2 hours, but overnight is best.

HINT: Wash and dry wooden salad bowls, then rub well inside and out with waxed paper. Prevents stickiness.

CUCUMBERS IN SOUR CREAM

Preparation Time: 10 minutes   *Betsi Dwyer*
Chilling Time: 2 hours   *September Morn*
Serves 6 - 8

½ tsp. salt
1 scant Tblsp. sugar
2 Tblsp. cider vinegar
1 cup sour cream

2 Tblsp. chopped scallion
1 tsp. celery seed
2 medium cucumbers

Dissolve salt and sugar in vinegar. Add sour cream. Stir until smooth. Add scallions and celery seed. Slice cucumbers paper thin and combine. Chill at least 2 hours for best results. *Serve on individual beds of Boston lettuce and garnish with a touch of leftover green onion for color.*

CUCUMBER SALAD

Preparation Time: 5 minutes   *Dawn Drell*
Serves: 6   *Helios*

4 cucumbers, peeled and sliced
5 Tblsp. mayonnaise

4 Tblsp. herb vinegar
Salt and pepper, to taste

Combine sliced cucumbers, mayonnaise, and herb vinegar in a small bowl. Toss, and season with salt and pepper. You might want to add or subtract some of the mayonnaise depending on personal preference. *The salad is easy to prepare with little time, and there is virtually no clean-up! Guests love it.*

HINT: Place an inverted saucer in the salad bowl to let excess liquid drain. Keeps salads fresh and crisp!

ISLAND FRUIT SALAD

Preparation Time: 20 minutes   *Jacqui Hoop*
Chilling Time: 1 hour   *Mary Denise*
Serves: 4

4 lettuce leaves, any type   Juice from orange and other fruits
3 medium sized oranges   2 tsp. soy sauce
Kiwi fruit, pears, or any other   2 Tblsp. vegetable oil
   available fruit, sliced   ¼ tsp. salt
1 medium red onion, thinly sliced   ½ tsp. sugar (optional)
1 Tblsp. vinegar

Peel and remove white membrane from oranges. Slice in a bowl reserving juice. Add other fruits as available and the sliced onion. Marinate in the remaining ingredients in refrigerator for an hour. To serve, place lettuce leaf on each individual plate, and arrange drained fruit and onion slices on top. *Can be a luncheon serving by adding 6 oz. shrimp pieces and accompanying with whole wheat crackers.*

"EASY STARTER" SHERRIED GRAPEFRUIT

Preparation Time: 1 hour and 5 minutes   *Jan Burnes*
          (1 hour soaking time)   *Adaro*
Cooking Time: 5 - 10 minutes
Serves: 4

2 grapefruits   2 Tblsp. sherry (or brandy,
2 Tblsp. brown sugar   rum, hic, etc.)

May be done under a broiler in an oven. Halve the grapefruits, and cut around segments. Leave the segments in the skin. Add ½ Tblsp. of sugar and sherry to each half. Leave to soak in (1 hour). Broil in a hot oven for 10 minutes.

WATERCRESS SALAD WITH PEARS AND BLUE CHEESE

Preparation Time: 10 minutes   *Carol Lowe*
Serves: 4   *Natasha*

Handful of watercress,   **RASPBERRY VINAIGRETTE:**
   (about 1 cup) per person   **1/8 cup raspberry vinegar**
2 ripe pears, cored and sliced   **1/3 cup olive oil**
½ cup crumbled Blue cheese   **Salt and pepper**

Arrange watercress on each plate. Top with pears and cheese. Make vinaigrette, and pour over salad. *Note: you should toss the pears in lemon juice to prevent discoloration if not serving immediately.*

PEARS IN BLUE CHEESE DRESSING

Preparation Time: 15 minutes   *Fiona Baldrey*
Chilling Time: 1 hour or more   *Promenade*
Serves: 8

DRESSING: **4 dessert pears**
1½ cups sour cream   **8 lettuce leaves**
½ lb. Blue cheese
Juice of 1 lemon
Freshly ground black pepper
½ tsp. Worcestershire sauce
Pinch of garlic salt

First make up the dressing. Combine all ingredients except for the pears and lettuce in a bowl, mashing any larger pieces of Blue cheese with a fork. Cover and refrigerate. Place a washed lettuce leaf on 8 small plates. Peel and halve pears, rub with a little lemon juice as you go to prevent browning. Core and place pear half, cut side down, on each lettuce leaf. Cover each pear with 1 heaped Tblsp. of Blue cheese dressing. This dressing can be made ahead of time, and stored for up to 10 days.

CANE GARDEN CREPES

Preparation Time: 30 minutes   *Sue Griffin*
Cooking Time: 10 minutes   *Endless Summer I*
Serves: 6

6 crepes   **FILLING:**
1 cup cheese sauce   **1 (8 oz.) package cream cheese**
                                          1 (10 oz.) package frozen spinach
                                          ½ cup hazelnuts
                                          Seasoning

Make the crepes and cheese sauce. Strain spinach, and put all other filling ingredients in a blender. Spread mixture over crepes and roll up. Cover with sauce, and sprinkle with cheese. Brown under the grill.

FIVE MINUTE SLAW

Preparation Time: 5 minutes   *C. J. Burns*
Chilling Time: 30 minutes (best overnight)   *Grace*
Serves: 8

CARROT SLAW: **CAULIFLOWER/RADISH SLAW:**
1 small package carrots   **(Men especially like this)**
1 small can crushed pineapple,   **1 small head cauliflower**
   drained   **1 package radishes**
1 small 6 pack box raisins   **1 bunch spring onions,**
¾ cup mayonnaise   **cut lengthwise**
1 Tblsp. brown sugar   **¾ cup mayonnaise**
1 tsp. nutmeg   **Dash salt**
Dash salt

For both recipes, clean vegetables. Discard the ends, and cut into 1½ inch chunks. Put pieces in blender (not spring onions) and cover with water so that chunks are not crowded, but float. Zap on high or grate speed 2 or 3 times depending on desired coarseness. Pour into wire strainer or vegetable steamer or noodle strainer. Push water out with fingers, and mix in remaining ingredients. *Great with fruit-stuffed Cornish Hens and whole wheat rolls.*

SUMMER SLAW

Preparation Time: 15 minutes
Chilling Time: 30 minutes
Serves: 10

Rosalind Rice
Endless Summer II

1 small red cabbage
Approx. 2 Tblsp. Thousand
    Island dressing
1 small white cabbage
4 Tblsp. Hellman's mayonnaise

1 lb. carrots
1 cup raisins
1 cup walnuts

Grate cabbages and carrots. Put in a large salad bowl. Add raisins and walnuts. Mix well. Add enough mayonnaise and Thousand Island dressing to bind salad together. Chill for about 30 minutes before serving. *This salad is a good accompaniment to grilled cheeseburgers.*

DATE SLAW

Preparation Time: 15 minutes
Chilling Time: 30 minutes
Serves: 6 - 8

Shannon Webster
Chaparral

4 cups shredded cabbage
2 oranges, peeled and sectioned
1 (8 oz.) package pitted dates,
    chopped
½ cup walnuts, chopped
½ cup sour cream

¾ tsp. salt
¼ tsp. paprika
2 Tblsp. sugar or honey
1 Tblsp. white vinegar
Garnish: orange wheels

Toss cabbage with oranges, nuts and dates. Refrigerate. In a small bowl, combine sour cream with remaining ingredients, and chill. When ready to serve, pour dressing over cabbage. *Serve with orange wheels for garnish.*

HINT: To keep lettuce fresh in the refrigerator, place lettuce in a plastic bag with a dry paper towel inside to absorb any moisture.

SQUID SAUTEED IN GARLIC

Preparation Time: 15 minutes
Cooking Time: 10 minutes
Serves: 4

Jan Robinson
Vanity

Flour
Salt and pepper
2 lbs. squid, cleaned, tenderized
    and sliced in 1" rounds

6 scallions, chopped
4 oz. butter
2 Tblsp. chopped chives
4 cloves garlic, crushed

Combine flour, salt, and pepper. Lightly flour the squid. Melt butter and add scallions, chives, and garlic. Saute until garlic is golden. Add squid and saute for 5 to 7 minutes or until squid is done. Do not overcook. *A scrumptious, spicy appetizer!*

CREAMY TOPPED SCALLOPS

Preparation Time: 15 minutes
Cooking Time: 15 minutes
Serves: 4

Fiona Baldrey
Promenade

8 scallops
1 small onion
½ pint white wine
1 oz. butter
1 oz. flour

¼ pint milk
Salt and pepper
¼ pint whipping cream
2 oz. Cheddar cheese, crumbled

Wash scallops thoroughly. Put scallops, onion, and wine into a saucepan. Simmer until scallops become opaque (about 4 minutes). Remove scallops and onion with a draining spoon and chop. Reduce wine to ¼ pint. Melt butter in a pan, stir in flour, and cook for 1 minute. Remove from the heat, and gradually stir in the milk and wine. Return to heat, and bring to a boil stirring all the time until mixture thickens. Mix in scallops and onion, season to taste. Turn into 4 small dishes. Lightly whip cream, and stir in cheese. Spread on top of scallop mixture. Cook in broiler until golden and bubbling.

ARTICHOKE SURPRISE

Preparation Time: 20 minutes
Cooking Time: 30 minutes
Serves: 10

Barbie Haworth
Ann-Marie II

1 large artichoke
½ cup mayonnaise

½ tsp. curry powder
1 (4½ oz.) can tiny shrimp

Steam artichoke for about 30 minutes until done. Drain. Refrigerate. Combine mayonnaise and curry powder. Remove all artichoke leaves. Dab each leaf with curry and mayonnaise mixture. Place shrimp on top (rinse shrimp thoroughly with ice water.) Arrange on a platter with Romaine lettuce in a sunburst shape and serve. Can be made ahead and chilled.

ARTICHOKE APPETIZER

Preparation Time: 15 minutes
Cooking Time: 10 minutes
Serves: 6

Kimberly Foote
Oklahoma Crude II

2 cans artichoke hearts marinated
½ cup Parmesan cheese, grated
½ cup butter, melted

Paprika
Parsley
Tomato wedges, 1 to 2 tomatoes

Preheat oven to 400° F. Drain can and place artichoke hearts right side up in a small baking pan. Sprinkle with Parmesan cheese. Dab with melted butter. Bake for 10 minutes at 400°. To serve, place approximately three artichoke hearts on each small plate, sprinkle with parsley and paprika, and arrange tomato wedges between each artichoke heart. *An elegant first course!*

HINT: To prevent crying while chopping onions, cut the end root of the onion off last.

SOUFFLES AUX TOMATOES

Preparation Time: 30 minutes   *Sue Griffin*
Cooking Time: 35 minutes   *Endless Summer I*
Serves: 6

6 tomatoes	2 eggs, separated
½ oz. butter, melted	1 oz. Cheddar Cheese
½ oz. flour	½ oz. Parmesan cheese
¼ pint milk	Salt and pepper
Garnish: watercress	

Preheat oven to 350° F. Blanch for 30 seconds, skin and empty tomatoes. Make souffle: Mix the melted butter with the flour, then add the milk. Beat in the egg yolks, seasoning, and cheeses. Whisk the egg whites, and fold into the mixture. Fill tomatoes to the top and bake about 30 minutes. *Serve surrounded with watercress.*

SHRIMP COCKTAIL

Preparation Time: 15 minutes   *Alison Briscoe*
Chilling Time: 2 hours   *Ovation*
Cooking Time: 5 minutes
Serves: 6

6 Romaine lettuce leaves	4 drops Worcestershire sauce
36 medium/jumbo shrimp	½ onion, chopped
SAUCE:	½ tsp. parsley
1 cup mayonnaise	½ tsp. chervil
1 Tblsp. vinegar	½ tsp. tarragon
½ tsp. sugar	Salt and pepper
½ tsp. dry mustard	Garnish: Lemon wedge

Place Romaine lettuce leaves in the bottom of glass cocktail dishes (or wine glasses). Steam for 2 minutes, and de-shell the shrimp. Do not overcook the shrimp - they become rubbery. Combine the sauce ingredients and mix thoroughly. Arrange shrimp attractively in glasses. Cover with sauce, and chill for 2 hours. Serve with a wedge of lemon. *Follow with Turkey Treat, Sesame Broccoli, Zucchini Noodle Casserole, and a peach cobbler.*

SOUPS AND SAUCES

NOTES

PEACH BRANDY SOUP

Preparation Time: 15 minutes
Chilling Time: 4 hours
Serves: 8

Lisa Hawkins
Ariguani

6 large or 8 small peaches
2 tsp. Fruit Fresh
½ cup water

1/3 cup peach brandy
½ cup sugar
Garnish: sliced peaches, sprigs
of mint

Slice peaches, and puree in food processor or blender. Combine Fruit Fresh and water, and add. Add brandy and sugar, mix well. Taste for sweetness as fruit varies. Add more sugar if needed. *Serve ice cold with a slice of peach and a sprig of mint. I do not recommend substituting canned peaches.*

CHILLED RASPBERRY SOUP

Preparation Time: 15 minutes
Chilling Time: overnight
Serves: 8

Jan Robinson
Vanity

1 Tblsp. unflavored gelatin
¼ cup cold water
½ cup hot water
2 (10 oz.) packages frozen
    raspberries, thawed
2¼ cups sour cream

1 cup pineapple juice
1 cup Half and Half (light cream)
1 cup dry sherry
¼ cup grenadine
1 Tblsp. lemon juice
Garnishes: mint and
    whole raspberries

Soak gelatin in cold water for 5 minutes. Stir in hot water and dissolve over low heat. Push raspberries through a strainer to remove seeds, then puree. Combine all ingredients and place in a glass bowl. Cover and refrigerate overnight. *Garnish with mint and/or whole raspberries. NOTE: Great served as a first course for a luncheon. Leftover soup can be frozen for a yogurt-like snack.*

CARIBBEAN CREAM OF PUMPKIN SOUP

Preparation Time: 20 minutes
Cooking Time: 40 - 45 minutes
Serves: 8 - 10

Rosalind Rice
Endless Summer II

3½ lbs. pumpkin
1 large onion, chopped
2 Tblsp. butter
2 (10 oz.) cans condensed
    chicken broth

1 cup water
1½ - 2 cups milk
Salt and pepper
Grated nutmeg
Garnish: chopped parsley

Lightly fry onion and peeled, seeded, and chopped pumpkin in melted butter until soft, but not brown. Add chicken broth and water. Simmer until cooked. Allow to cool slightly. Put in blender, and blend until smooth. Return soup to pan, and add milk to required consistency. Add salt, pepper, and nutmeg to taste. Just before serving, garnish with chopped parsley.

NATIVE PUMPKIN SOUP

Preparation Time: 40 minutes
Cooking Time: 20 minutes
Serves: 6 - 8

Kimberly Foote
Oklahoma Crude II

1 small pumpkin
¼ cup soy sauce
3 Tblsp. chopped chives
3 Tblsp. curry
Garnish: parsley

Generous amounts of:
    garlic powder
    pepper
    nutmeg

Cut pumpkin (by using a large knife) in quarters. Scoop out seeds and cut skin off. Chop in 1 inch cubes, and put to boil for about 20 minutes until soft. Drain water, and let cool completely. Place in blender adding enough water for right consistency. Blend, and place in soup pot. Add the rest of ingredients. Reheat and serve topped with a sprig of parsley.

TWO MELON SOUP

Preparation Time: 10 minutes   *Sarah Sheets*
Chilling Time: 3 hours   *Royono*
Serves: 6

1 very ripe cantaloupe
1 very ripe honeydew melon
2 Tblsp. lemon juice, or
    to taste
2 Tblsp. lime juice, or
    to taste

2 tsp. chopped mint leaves, or to
    taste
Garnish: whipped cream, mint leaves

Peel, seed, and chop cantaloupe. Puree in blender with lemon juice.
Chill. Peel, seed, and chop honeydew melon. Puree with lime juice
and mint. Chill. To serve: pour equal amounts, at same time, into soup
bowls. *Garnish with whipped cream and mint sprigs.*

GREEN GARDEN SOUP

Preparation Time: 15 minutes   *Donna Jaggard*
Cooking Time: 30 minutes   *Thorobred*
Serves: 6

2 Tblsp. butter
3 leeks, sliced
1 cup watercress, chopped
2 cups diced, unpeeled cucumber
½ cup diced raw potatoes

2 cups chicken broth
½ tsp. salt
¼ tsp. pepper
1 tsp. dry mustard
2 cups Half & Half (light cream)
Garnish: watercress sprig

Melt butter, and cook onion until soft. Add remaining ingredients
except for Half & Half, and bring to a boil. Simmer 15 minutes until
potatoes are cooked. Puree. Chill. Blend in Half & Half before serving.
Garnish with a sprig of watercress.

HINT: Sprinkle poppy seeds and sprig parsley on bland colored soups.

CURRIED PEA SOUP

Preparation Time: 10 minutes　　　　　　　　*Wendy Smith*
Cooking Time: 20 minutes　　　　　　　　　　　*Stampede*
Serves: 6

2 cups frozen peas
1 large onion, chopped
2 stalks celery and leaves
2 carrots, diced
2 potatoes, sliced

2 tsp. curry powder
2 cups Half & Half (light cream)
4 cups chicken stock
½ tsp. salt, optional

Cook vegetables in half of the stock. Blend and puree. Add remaining stock and milk. Can be served hot or cold. If reheating, simmer pot over water. It depends on the stock whether or not you need to add the salt. Start by adding 1 tsp. curry powder, and adjust according to taste.

CARROT SOUP

Preparation Time: 15 minutes　　　　　　　*Renie Mousek*
Cooking Time: 20 minutes　　　　　　　　　　*Bon Vivant*
Serves: 6

1 large onion
2 Tblsp. chopped bacon
2 cloves minced garlic
¼ lb. butter
¼ cup cream (optional)

1½ lbs. carrots, peeled and chopped
5 cups chicken bouillon
Salt and pepper, to taste
Note: may substitute zucchini
　　for the carrots

Chop the onion, and saute in butter until translucent with bacon and garlic. Add bouillon and carrots. Cook until carrots are tender. Put all ingredients in blender and puree. *Serve hot with French bread.*

RED PEPPER SOUP

Preparation Time: 5 minutes   *Wendy Smith*
Cooking Time: 50 minutes   *Stampede*
Serves: 4

4 large red bell peppers   ½ cup heavy cream
4 small onions, sliced   2 Tblsp. lemon juice
¾ stick butter (6 Tblsp.)   ½ potato, grated and peeled
2½ cups chicken stock   Garnish: 2 Tblsp. chopped dill

Saute onions and peppers in butter over low heat in covered pan for
30 minutes. Add potato and stock. Bring to a boil, and simmer covered
for 15 minutes. Puree . Return to the pan, add cream, lemon, salt, and
pepper. *Serve hot, garnished with dill.*

FRENCH ONION SOUP

Preparation Time: 20 minutes   *Jan Robinson*
Cooking Time: 1 hour   *Vanity*
Serves: 4

1 lb. onions   4 slices French bread, ½ inch thick
4 - 6 Tblsp. unsalted butter   1 cup grated Gruyere cheese
5 cups chicken or beef stock

Peel and thinly slice the onions. Melt 2 Tblsp. of the butter in a large
saucepan. Add the onions and stir well. Cover with a lid and cook over
low heat for about 15 minutes, or until the onions are soft and transparent. Remove the lid and continue cooking the onions, stirring occasionally, until they are golden brown. Stir in the chicken or beef
stock. Taste. Replace the lid and simmer the soup for 30 minutes.
Meanwhile, spread the remaining butter on both sides of each slice
of French bread. Sprinkle half the cheese over one side of the bread
slices. Bake the bread on a baking sheet in a preheated oven at 350° F
until the bread is crisp and the cheese has melted. Arrange the slices of
bread in individual bowls and pour in the hot onion soup. Serve the
remaining grated cheese in a separate bowl.

WATERCRESS SOUP

Preparation Time: 5 minutes   *Jane Glancy*
Cooking Time: 10 minutes   *Truant*
Serves: 4

4 cups chicken broth
2 bunches watercress, cut into 1 inch lengths including stems
1 tsp. soy sauce

Bring broth to a boil, and add soy sauce. Add watercress. Stir until boiling again. Remove from heat at once.

CREAM OF WATERCRESS SOUP

Preparation Time: 10 minutes   *Chris Balfour*
Cooking Time: 25 minutes   *Stowaway*
Serves: 4

¼ cup minced onion	**4 cups chicken stock, boiling**
2 Tblsp. butter	**2 egg yolks**
2 bundles watercress	**1 cup heavy cream**
2 Tblsp. flour	**Pepper to taste**

In a large saucepan, cook onion in butter until tender. Trim, wash, and dry watercress (save a few leaves for garnish). Add leaves to the onions. Cover and cook for 5 minutes. Stir in flour, and cook for 5 minutes. Add boiling stock, and cook for 5 minutes longer. Puree mixture (can be done day ahead to this point). To serve, reheat soup to simmer. Beat yolks with cream. Add the soup to the cream, and whisk a lot. Return to heat, but do not boil or it will curdle. *Garnish with reserved watercress leaves.*

HINT: For soups and sauces that are too salty, cut up a raw potato and place in the soup. It will absorb the salt once it has cooked.

CREAM OF BROCCOLI SOUP

Preparation Time: 10 minutes   *Shannon Webster*
Cooking Time: 15 minutes   *Chaparral*
Serves: 6 - 8

1 bunch broccoli   1/8 tsp. nutmeg
2 Tblsp. butter   1/8 tsp. ginger
1 medium onion, chopped   3 cups chicken broth
1 - 2 Tblsp. flour   1 cup or pint of heavy cream
1 tsp. salt   Garnish: croutons

Trim broccoli as necessary, and chop into pieces. Melt butter in Dutch
oven. Add onion and spices. Let cook over low heat until onions are
clear. Add flour, stirring well. Cook 1 - 2 minutes longer, and add
chicken broth, chopped broccoli stalks and flowers. Cook over medium
heat until broccoli is tender. Transfer to blender, and puree . Return
to Dutch oven. Add cream, and heat thoroughly just before serving.
Garnish with croutons.

COOL CUCUMBER SOUP

Preparation Time: 10 minutes   *C.J. Burns*
Chilling Time: 30 minutes   *Grace*
Serves: 4

1 large burpless/seedless   ½ tsp. dill weed, parsley, or celery
   cucumber, grated   seed
½ onion, chopped   ½ tsp. thyme
1 (10 ¾ oz.) can chicken broth   1 (16 oz.) container sour cream
   soup   1 tsp. salt
2 Tblsp. butter   Dash tabasco
                                    Garnish: parsley, sliced cucumber

Saute onion in butter until clear. Peel skin off cucumber, and grate.
Add cucumber, chicken broth, dill, thyme, salt, and tabasco. Refrigerate. When ready to serve, stir in sour cream. Float sliced cucumber or
parsley on top. *Serve on hot days with a fresh salad.*

CUCUMBER-DILL SOUP

Preparation Time: 10 minutes
Chilling Time: several hours
Serves: 4 - 6

Barbie Haworth
Ann-Marie II

1 pint Half & Half
2 cups plain yogurt
2 medium cucumbers, peeled,
    seeded, and diced
3 Tblsp. minced fresh dillweed
    or 1 Tblsp. dried dillweed

2 Tblsp. lemon juice
2 Tblsp. scallions, chopped
½ tsp. salt
1/8 - ¼ tsp. white pepper
Garnish: sliced cucumber and
    dill sprigs

Combine all ingredients, and stir well (may use blender). Chill thoroughly. *Serve with sliced cucumber and dill sprig on top.*

AVOCADO LIME SOUP

Preparation Time: 20 minutes
Chilling Time: 1 hour
Serves: 8

Emily Welch
Wind's End

4 ripe avocados, peeled, pitted,
    and chopped coarsely
4 cups canned chicken broth
2 Tblsp. fresh lime juice

1 tsp. salt
¼ tsp. cayenne pepper
2 cups Half & Half
Garnish: 8 very thin slices of lime

Puree avocado and broth in processor in 2 batches, and transfer to a large bowl. Stir in lime juice, salt, cayenne, and Half & Half. Cover and chill for 1 hour. *Serve immediately, and garnish with lime slices.*

AVOCADO OCCASION

Preparation Time: 15 minutes
Chilling Time: 3 - 4 hours
Serves: 8

Alison Pamela Briscoe
Ovation

4 ripe avocados
3 pints chicken stock
½ pint heavy cream

Juice of 1 lemon
Salt and freshly ground pepper
Chopped chives, fresh if possible

Halve the avocados, and remove the stones. Scoop out the flesh into an electric blender. Add chicken stock. Cover and blend for a few moments until smooth. Pour into a bowl, and stir in cream, lemon juice, salt, and pepper. Chill well for 3 - 4 hours. Stir in the chives just before serving.

CHILLED AVOCADO GAZPACHO

Preparation Time: 25 minutes
Chilling Time: 3 hours
Serves: 4

Sharon Strong
Promises

1 Tblsp. mild green jalapena
    pepper, seeded
2 Tblsp. green onion
1 green pepper, chopped and
    seeded
2 large garlic cloves
1 celery stalk, chopped
1 cucumber, peeled

1 (28 oz.) can whole tomatoes
1 cup chicken stock
5 Tblsp. olive oil
3 Tblsp. red wine vinegar
3 large avocados, halved
Garnish: sour cream, chopped chives
    chopped tomatoes, onions,
    olives, and croutons

With spoon, scoop out avocado flesh leaving ½ inch shell in each. Use the shells to serve the avocado gazpacho soup in. Take the flesh from the six halves, and add the above ingredients to a blender for one minute. Chill for at least 3 hours. To serve: spoon into avocado shells, and add 1 tsp. dollop sour cream sprinkled with chopped chives. Pass around the small bowls of chopped tomatoes, onions, olives, and croutons.

ZESTY GAZPACHO

Preparation Time: 10 minutes   *Shannon Webster*
Chilling Time: several hours   *Chaparral*
Serves: 4 - 6

4 large ripe tomatoes, peeled
    and chopped
1/3 green bell pepper
1/3 cucumber, peeled
¼ onion, chopped
2 garlic cloves

3 Tblsp. red wine vinegar
2 Tblsp. olive oil
1 Tblsp. salt
3 cups French bread, (crust re-
    moved), soaked in water
Garnish: minced onion, green pep-
    per, cucumber, sour cream

In processor/blender puree tomatoes, green pepper, cucumber, onion, and garlic. Blend in vinegar, oil, salt, and bread crumbs in batches. Transfer to a bowl, thin it to desired consistency with ice water. Chill covered. Garnish with minced onion, green pepper, cucumber, and a dollop of sour cream with black olive curls. Makes 6 cups. *Yum!*

QUICK SHE CRAB SOUP

Preparation Time: 5 minutes   *D. Stetson*
Cooking Time: 5 minutes   *Fantasy*
Serves: 6

1 (10¾ oz.) can condensed
    tomato soup
1 (10 ¾ oz.) can condensed split
    pea soup
2 cups whole milk or 1 cup whole
    milk and 1 cup Half & Half

½ - ¾ lb. crab flakes
4 Tblsp. butter
1 small onion, minced
Salt and pepper
Sherry

Blend together tomato soup, split pea soup, and milk. Heat on the stove. Saute crab flakes in butter with minced onion, salt, and pepper. Add this to the soup after browning. Add a few drops of sherry while soup is cooking. Before serving, add 1 Tblsp. of sherry to each bowl.

EASY VICHYSSOISE

Preparation Time: 15 minutes
Cooking Time: 30 minutes
Chilling Time: several hours
Serves: 6 - 8

Joan Della Dora
Bluewater

2 - 3 leeks
2 - 3 medium potatoes
4 Tblsp. chicken stock base
   (Spice Islands)
½ pint heavy cream, whipped

4 Tblsp. butter or margarine
4 cups water
¼ tsp. salt and white pepper, to taste
1 tsp. curry powder
3 Tblsp. snipped chives

Cut away most green part from the leeks. Cut the white part in half lengthwise. Riffle leek as you would a deck of cards to wash away all dirt. Cut leeks crosswise into ½ inch sections. Melt butter, and saute leeks over low heat until limp (10 minutes). Peel potatoes, and slice crosswise ¼ inch slices. Add to the pot along with water, chicken stock base, salt, pepper, and curry powder. Bring mixture to a boil, then simmer 20 minutes or until potatoes are tender. Puree the mixture in blender, a portion at a time. Taste and season with salt and pepper. Over season, as chilling will dull the seasonings. Press some plastic wrap onto the surface of the soup to prevent skin from forming. Serve in chilled bowls. Top with dollop (2 Tblsp.) of cream, and sprinkle with chives.

JELLIED CONSOMME WITH CAVIAR

Preparation Time: 5 minutes
Chilling Time: 4 hours
Serves: 6

Sarah Sheets
Royono

2 (10¾) cans consomme (gelatin added)
Garnish: sour cream, red caviar, and parsley

Chill consomme for 4 hours or more. Divide equally among six small bowls or plates lined with lettuce. Garnish with a dollop of sour cream, sprinkling of red caviar, and parsley sprigs. *Serve immediately, Easy!! But very elegant!!*

ZUCCHINI BISQUE

Preparation Time: 15 minutes
Cooking Time: 45 minutes
Serves: 8 - 10

Rosalind Rice
Endless Summer II

3 lbs. zucchini, thinly sliced
1 large onion, chopped
4 Tblsp. butter
¾ - 1 tsp. curry powder,
    depending on individual taste

2 (10¾ oz.) cans chicken broth
1½ cups milk
Salt and pepper

Melt butter in large saucepan. Add onion and zucchini. Simmer until almost tender. Add milk, broth, and seasonings. Bring to a boil, and simmer until cooked. Allow to cool slightly before putting in blender. Blend until smooth. *This soup can be served either hot or cold, it is delicious either way. If serving cold, allow to chill at least 4 hours in the refrigerator.*

ASPARAGUS LEEK BISQUE

Preparation Time: 10 minutes
Cooking Time: 40 minutes
Serves: 6 - 8

Barbie Haworth
Ann-Marie II

¼ cup butter
1 lb. fresh asparagus tips or 1 can
    white drained
5 - 6 medium leeks, thinly sliced
    (white part only)

1 quart chicken broth
1 tsp. sugar
Freshly ground pepper
2 cups whipping cream
Garnish: fresh chopped parsley

In a large heavy saucepan, melt butter, and add asparagus and leeks. Cook until slightly softened for about 10 minutes, stirring occasionally. Add stock, and simmer until vegetables are tender, about 15 minutes. Puree mixture in blender or food processor. Strain through fine sieve or cheese cloth into saucepan. Stir in sugar and pepper. Simmer over medium heat for about 10 minutes. Blend in cream, and simmer for another 5 minutes. *Serve hot with fresh chopped parsley as garnish.*

CHEESE SAUCE

Preparation Time: 5 minutes   *Terrie Thornbjornson*
Cooking Time: 10 minutes   *Western Star*

½ cup butter   1 (12 oz.) can evaporated milk
4 Tblsp. flour   Cheese of your choice
2 Tblsp. dry sherry

Melt butter in small saucepan. Blend flour, and cook until bubbles.
Slowly add milk when sauce thickens. Add cheese (type and amount
depends on your taste), then add sherry. *Excellent on fish, asparagus,
broccoli, cauliflower, etc.*

BECHAMEL SAUCE

Preparation Time: 10 minutes   *Fiona Baldrey*
Chilling Time: 10 minutes   *Promenade*

1 pint milk   ¼ tsp. mace
1 small onion   Salt
1 small carrot   6 peppercorns
2 inch celery stick   Small bunch of herbs
1 bay leaf   2 oz. butter
1 clove   2 oz. all-purpose flour
1/8 pint cream (optional)

Warm the milk with vegetables, herbs, salt, and spices. Bring it slowly
to simmering point. Stand in warm place for ½ hour. Strain the milk.
Melt butter, and add the flour. Cook this roux for a few minutes.
Gradually stir in flavored milk. Bring sauce to boiling point, stirring
constantly. If cream is used, add it to sauce just at boiling point, and
do not reboil.

*HINT: Store garlic in a basket at room temperature. If refrigerated,
the garlic peel becomes moist and the head tends to dry out.*

HORSERADISH SAUCE

Preparation Time: 5 minutes   *Louise Brendlinger*
Serves: 6   *Ring-Andersen*

1 Tblsp. freshly grated horseradish   2 Tblsp. mayonnaise
2 Tblsp. premixed hot horseradish   2 Tblsp. sour cream
   sauce   Seasonings

Combine all ingredients. Season to taste and serve.

VEGETABLE SPAGHETTI SAUCE (OR LASAGNA)

Preparation Time: 10 minutes   *Marion Vanderwood*
Cooking Time: 30 minutes   *Ocean Voyager*
Serves: 4

2 large onions, chopped   ¼ tsp. cayenne
6 oz. mushrooms, chopped   1 (6 oz.) can tomato paste
2 large tomatoes, peeled and   2 Tblsp. red wine
   chopped   2 - 3 bay leaves
2 (16 oz.) cans no salt tomatoes   1 tsp. Italian seasoning
                                     3 celery stalks, chopped

For heart patients no salt or oil used. Dry saute onions and celery for 5 minutes. Add all other ingredients and simmer for 30 minutes. *Serve over wholemeal spaghetti boiled in unsalted water or layered with wholemeal lasagna noodles.*

HINT: To peel a tomato, place it on the end of a fork and turn it over a gas burner. Remove the skin when it starts to darken and peel. You can also plunge the tomato in boiling water, remove and let sit for a minute, then put in a bowl of cold water. The skin will be easily lifted.

HOMEMADE CROUTONS

Preparation Time: 10 minutes
Cooking Time: 40 minutes
Makes: about 2 cups

Fiona Baldrey
Promenade

PLAIN:
1/3 loaf French bread
¼ cup butter

HERB & ONION:
1 tsp. onion powder
½ tsp. of each: basil, chervil,
    and oregano

ITALIAN HERB & CHEESE:
½ tsp. Worcestershire sauce
1 tsp. Italian seasoning
1 Tblsp. Parmesan cheese

GARLIC:
1 large clove garlic
1 tsp. parsley flakes

Preheat oven to 300° F. Cut day old French bread into ½ inch cubes. Evenly spread cubes on a rimmed baking sheet. Bake in oven 300° for 10 minutes. Remove and reset oven temperature to 275°. In a wide skillet over medium heat, melt ¼ cup butter (or margarine). Stir in your choice of seasoning mixes described above or leave them quite plain. Add toasted bread cubes to seasoned butter, and toss to coat as evenly as possible. Spread cubes out on baking sheet again, and return to the oven. Bake for 30 minutes or until cubes are crisp and lightly brown. *Note: When cool, they can be stored in a covered jar for several weeks.*

AVOCADO BUTTER

Preparation Time: 10 minutes
Serves: 8

Jill Cooper
Kestral

3 Tblsp. minced shallots
2 Tblsp. white wine
1 ripe avocado

1 lb. butter, cubed
Salt and pepper

Saute shallots in 1 Tblsp. butter and white wine until transparent. When cooled, drop shallots, skinned avocado, butter cubes, and seasoning into food processor. Run just until all ingredients are combined. Scrape butter onto one end of tin foil, and roll up tightly pressing out air bubbles. Keep in freezer until needed. Place thin slices of avocado butter over tenderloin fillets just before serving.

SAUCE MARINARA

Preparation Time: 5 minutes
Cooking Time: 15 minutes

2 Tblsp. olive oil
2 minced garlic cloves
1 (28 oz.) can tomato puree
1 Tblsp. sugar
1 Tbslp. freshly minced parsley

1 tsp. oregano
1 tsp. basil
1 tsp. salt
¼ tsp. pepper

In a 3 quart saucepan, heat olive oil, and saute garlic until golden brown. Add remaining ingredients, and simmer for 15 minutes.

*MEATS

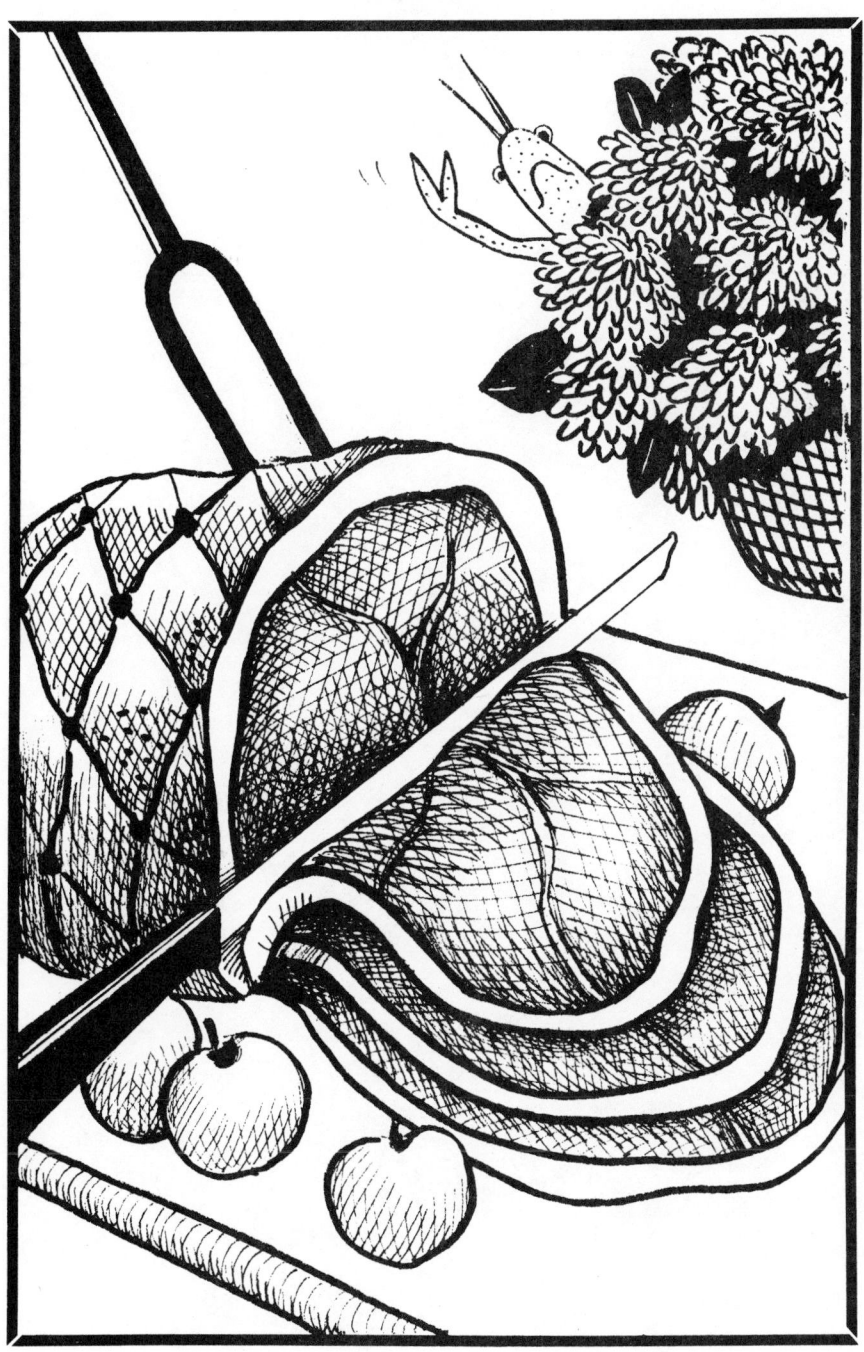

NOTES

DEVILED STEAK THOROBRED

Preparation Time: 15 minutes   *Donna Jaggard*
Marinating Time: 2 hours   *Thorobred*
Cooking Time: 15 - 20 minutes (on BBQ grill)
Serves: 6

2½ lbs. London broil	¼ cup oil
2 Tblsp. mustard	2 Tblsp. wine vinegar
2 tsp. lemon juice	2 Tblsp. soy sauce
Seasoned salt	3 Tblsp. plum or cherry jam
¼ cup ketchup	3 Tblsp. brown sugar
Few drops tabasco	1/8 tsp. pepper

Combine mustard and lemon juice. Spread on both sides of meat.
Sprinkle with seasoned salt. Combine other ingredients in a saucepan,
and heat until boiling. Pour over meat. Allow to stand for 2 hours.
Grill over charcoal.

MENU:

SWEET & SOUR SPINACH SALAD p. 63

. . .

DEVILED STEAK THOROBRED p. 97
BAKED STUFFED POTATOES p. 222
CONFETTI SQUASH SAUTE p. 224

. . .

MIGHTY MOUSSE p. 253

. . .

RED GRAVES : CABERNET SAUVIGNON

BEEF GOULASH

Preparation Time: 10 minutes   Louise Brendlinger
Cooking Time: 2¼ hours   Ring-Anderson
Serves: 6

2 lbs. stewing beef   1 Tblsp. cornflour or cornstarch
¼ cup flour, seasoned   1 Tblsp. chili powder
2 oz. butter   3 onions, finely chopped
1 can tomatoes   3 tsp. paprika
½ cup sour cream or yogurt   Garnish: parsley

Cube the meat, and toss in flour. Fry the finely chopped onion, then fry the meat. Add the paprika, chili, and tomatoes. Bring to a boil, and simmer for 2 hours or until meat is tender. Remove the meat. Strain and thicken the sauce with cornflour mixed with sour cream. Mix in the meat. *Serve with a side dish of sour cream or yogurt.*

MENU:

MIXED GREEN SALAD

· · ·

BEEF GOULASH p. 98
BUTTERED NOODLES WITH PARSLEY

· · ·

PUFFS OF MOUNTAIN AIR p. 248

· · ·

FLEURIE : GAMAY

TENDERLOIN DELUXE

Preparation Time: 10 minutes   *Jean Thayer*
Cooking Time: 45 minutes   *Finesse 60*
Serves: 8

4 lbs. beef tenderloin	2 Tblsp. soy sauce
2 Tblsp. butter, softened	1 Tblsp. Dijon mustard
¼ cup scallions, chopped	Freshly ground pepper
2 Tblsp. butter	¾ cup dry sherry

Preheat oven to 400° F. Meat should be at room temperature. Place meat on a rack in a shallow baking pan and spread meat with the softened butter. Bake, uncovered, for 20 minutes. In a small saucepan, saute the scallions in butter. Add soy sauce, Dijon, pepper, and sherry. Bring to a simmer. After the meat has baked for 20 minutes, baste occasionally with the sherry sauce and continue baking for another 25 minutes. Remove meat from oven and let rest for 5 minutes before carving in ½ inch slices. Meat will be rare to medium rare. Accumulated basting juices may be served on the side or a Bearnaise sauce may be served separately.

MENU:

ZESTY ITALIAN SALAD p. 64

. . .

TENDERLOIN DELUXE p. 99
PARMESAN MASHED POTATOES p. 222
MINTY CARROTS p. 213

. . .

CHOCOLATE ALMOND FLUFF p. 249

. . .

CHIANTI : ZINFANDEL

GERMAN ROULLADON

Preparation Time: 30 minutes   *Jan Stoughton*
Cooking Time: 2½ hours   *Lady Columbo*
Serves: 6

6 slices, thinly sliced roast beef
Beef bouillon
Use dill pickles, mushrooms, onions, tomatoes, Dijon mustard, paprika,
salt and pepper and any other vegetable plus garlic can be substituted
or added. Roulladon can be prepared in the morning or day before.

Lay out beef, sprinkle with paprika, salt and pepper - a generous amount.
Spread a teaspoon or so of Dijon mustard on beef. Lay out vegetable
slices on beef. Dill pickle adds nice flavor. Roll up beef stuffed with
vegetables and secure with toothpicks. Slow cook for about 2 hours
in a Dutch oven. Keep adding water, so meat does not dry out. Thirty
minutes before serving, add beef boullion and hot water to make gravy.
Add cornstarch to thicken.

MENU:

CHILLED RASPBERRY SOUP p. 79

. . .

GERMAN ROULLADON p. 100
ASPARAGUS
PARSLEY NOODLES

. . .

ULTIMATE CHOCOLATE SEX CAKE p. 239

. . .

BORDEAUX ROUGE : CABERNET

CHINESE BEEF AND TOMATO

Preparation Time: 20 minutes　　　　　　　　*Jane Glancy*
Marinating Time: 15 - 30 minutes　　　　　　　*Truant*
Cooking Time: 20 minutes
Serves: 4

2 cups beef sliced thin (1 lb.)
1½ cups celery, sliced diagonally
1 onion, cut in 2" segments
2 cups green peppers, cut in strips
2 stalks green onion, in 1" pieces
2 cups tomatoes, quartered

GRAVY:
2 Tblsp. cornstarch
¼ cup ketchup
1 tsp. sugar
2 Tblsp. soy sauce
1 Tblsp. vinegar
1 tsp. Worcestershire sauce
¼ cup water

MARINADE:
1 Tblsp. oil
3 Tblsp. soy sauce
1 tsp. ginger, chopped
1 clove garlic, crushed
1 Tblsp. cornstarch
2 Tblsp. sherry
1 Tblsp. sugar
Dash of pepper

Combine marinade ingredients, and add beef. Marinate for 15 minutes or longer. Combine gravy ingredients, and set aside. Heat large pan or wok, and add some oil. Quickly stir-fry all vegetables except for the tomato, about 2 minutes. Remove from pan. Reheat, and add oil. Stir-fry beef. Add gravy, and cook while stirring until thickened. Add tomato, and cook for 30 seconds. Add vegetables, and mix well. Spoon over white rice.

MENU:

WATERCRESS SOUP p. 84

. . .

CHINESE BEEF AND TOMATO p. 101
WHITE RICE

. . .

RUM CAKE p. 242

. . .

SANCERRE ROUGE : PINOT NOIR

DADDY'S BEEF BOURGUIGNONNE

Preparation Time: 30 minutes   *Sylvia Dabney*
Cooking Time: 1 hour   *Native Sun*
Serves: 4 - 6

2 lbs. sirloin or round in 1½ x 2"
   cubes
4 Tblsp. butter
2 Tblsp. Brandy
2 Tblsp. flour
1 tsp. tomato paste
1 tsp. Kitchen Bouquet
16 mushroom caps
3 - 5 bay leaves

½ Tblsp. thyme
¾ cup beef broth
¾ cup dry red wine
½ tsp. pepper
12 small frozen pearl onions or 1
   medium onion sliced in
   eighths lengthwise and thirds
   widthwise
Salt to taste
Curled noodles or rice

In a large skillet (will need a lid), brown meat in 2 Tblsp. butter. Heat brandy, ignite and pour over meat. Stir until flame dies. Sprinkle flour over, stir in tomato paste, Kitchen Bouquet, and slowly blend in broth, wine and seasonings. Bring to boil. Reduce heat to slow simmer. In a small fry pan, brown onions in remaining butter, add mushrooms, cook three minutes. Add to meat mixture, cover and simmer 1 hour. *Looks best served over spiral noodles.*

MENU:

CUCUMBER AND DILL SALAD p. 68

. . .

DADDY'S BEEF BOURGUIGNONNE p. 102
SPIRAL NOODLES

. . .

MINT CHOCOLATE CHIP CAKE p. 240

. . .

GEUREY CHABERTIN : PINOT NOIR

BEEF STROGANOFF OVATION

Preparation Time: 15 minutes
Cooking Time: 15 minutes
Serves: 8

Alison Briscoe
Ovation

2 lbs. sirloin steak
2 onions
1 lb. button mushrooms
4 oz. butter

Salt and freshly ground black pepper
1 (16 oz.) carton sour cream
Fresh chopped parsley

Trim fat off steak, and cut into thin strips. Peel and finely chop onion. Slice mushrooms. Melt 2 oz. butter in frying pan, and add onion. Saute until softened, and add mushrooms and saute for 2 - 3 minutes. Drain and keep warm. Add remaining butter to pan, and add steak. Fry on high flame stirring with spoon for 3 minutes or to taste. Put onion and mushrooms in pan, and season with salt and pepper. Lower heat, and stir in sour cream. Reheat and sprinkle with chopped parsley.

MENU:

GREEN SALAD

. . .

BEEF STROGANOFF OVATION p. 103
RICE PARISIENNE p. 234
EGGPLANT AND TOMATO CASSEROLE p. 229
MUSHROOMS A LA GRECQUE p. 216

. . .

PEAR TART p. 267

. . .

BORDEAUX ROUGE : CABERNET SAUVIGNON

VIENNESE STRUDEL

Preparation Time: 35 minutes
Chilling Time: 30 minutes
Cooking Time: 30 - 35 minutes
Serves: 6

Barbara Lowe
My Way

1 small onion, finely chopped
4 Tblsp. butter
1½ lbs. ground beef
¼ lb. mushrooms, chopped
¼ tsp. pepper
½ tsp. oregano
2 cloves minced garlic

12 sheets filo dough or 1½ sheets
       puff pastry dough
3 eggs
1½ cups shredded Swiss cheese
¼ cup chopped parsley
¼ cup dry bread crumbs
2 tsp. curry powder

Preheat oven to 375° F. Saute onions in 2 Tblsp. butter until transparent. Add mushrooms and meat, and cook until crumbly. Turn into bowl, and season with salt, pepper, oregano, garlic, and curry. Let cool. Add eggs, and mix lightly. Mix in cheese, parsley, and crumbs. Chill. If using filo dough, form a 15x24 inch rectangle with the 12 sheets, brushing with butter to make them stick or roll pastry to that size. Cover dough with meat mixture leaving enough edge to tuck in, and roll up jelly roll style. Bake at 375° for 30 - 35 minutes. I like to top this roll with the boat's name cut out of leftover dough. *This can be served with side dishes of sour cream and chutney as toppings.*

MENU:

TOMATO & CUKE SALAD p. 68

. . .

VIENNESE STRUDEL p. 104
SPINACH WITH BUTTER

. . .

CREAMY COCONUT PIE p. 264

. . .

GWERTZ TRAMINER : DRY CHENIN BLANC

PORK TENDERLOIN IN CASSIS SAUCE

Preparation Time: 10 minutes   *Carol Lowe*
Cooking Time: 35 minutes   *Natasha*
Serves: 4

2 pork tenderloins   Salt and freshly ground black pepper
¼ cup black currant preserves   1/3 cup white wine vinegar
1½ Tblsp. Dijon mustard   Garnish: watercress

Mix preserves and mustard together, and set aside. Brown tenderloins slightly on all sides in a skillet. Season with salt and pepper. Spoon currant/mustard mixture over. Cover pork, reduce heat, and cook for 20 minutes. Remove pork, and keep warm. Remove excess fat from skillet. Add vinegar, set pan over medium heat, and bring to a boil stirring up any brown bits. Slice pork on the diagonal. When the sauce is reduced by 1/3, pour it over the chops, and serve garnished with watercress. *This was adapted from a Silver Palate recipe.*

MENU:

WATERCRESS SALAD WITH PEARS AND BLUE CHEESE p. 71

. . .

PORK TENDERLOIN IN CASSIS SAUCE p. 105
BUTTERED NOODLES
PUREED BUTTERNUT SQUASH p. 226

. . .

APPLE CLAFOUTI p. 258

. . .

TAVEL ROSE : ZINFANDEL WHITE

PORK VERONIQUE

Preparation Time: 30 minutes　　　　　　　　　　　*Alison Briscoe*
Cooking Time: 1½ hours　　　　　　　　　　　　　　　*Ovation*
Serves: 8

4 lbs. pork tenderloin
2 dozen seedless grapes, green
4 oz. butter
½ pint white wine
½ pint chicken stock
2 onions, chopped
2 carrots, chopped

2 bay leaves
2 sprigs thyme or ½ tsp. dried
Salt and freshly ground pepper
2 oz. flour
2 oz. butter
2 egg yolks

Preheat oven to 350° F. Cut the pork tenderloin down the middle about ½ way through and open out. Stuff with 12 grapes which have been halved. Put 2 oz. butter in knobs on the grapes. Tie the fillet with string, and saute with butter in frying pan until brown (you can cut tenderloin in half and fry each, if hard to manage). Transfer to a casserole dish. Add wine, stock, salt, pepper, onions, carrots, bay leaves, and thyme. Cover and cook in the oven for 1 hour. Heat butter, add flour, and saute, stirring. Add strained liquid from casserole. Mix egg yolks with some of sauce. Return all to heat, and cook gently to thicken. Pour over pork, remove string. *Garnish with remaining grapes, halved.*

MENU:

SMOKED MARLIN SALAD p. 64

. . .

PORK VERONIQUE p. 106
BROWN RICE
STEAMED BRUSSEL SPROUTS

. . .

GRAND MARNIER CHOCOLATE COVERED PEARS p. 245

. . .

WHITE GRAVES : CABERNET BLANC

PORK TENDERLOIN IN A FESTIVE SAUCE

Preparation Time: 10 minutes   *Gunilla Lundgren*
Cooking Time: 15 minutes   *Bambi*
Serves: 4

1½ lbs. pork tenderloin, cut into   4 Tblsp soy sauce
    1 inch slices   1 cup whipping cream
Salt and pepper   ½ cup brandy
Butter

Fry tenderloin slices in butter, 5 - 7 minutes on each side. Add salt, pepper, soy sauce, and cream. Saute for 1 - 2 minutes, then add brandy. *So easy and so very delicious!*

MENU:

BAMBI'S SHRIMP SALAD p. 65

. . .

PORK TENDERLOIN IN A FESTIVE SAUCE p. 107
POTATOES AU GRATIN
PAPRIKA-BUTTERED BROCCOLI p. 211

. . .

STRAWBERRY CAKES p. 241

. . .

WHITE BORDEAUX : FUME BLANC

CHA-CHIU (pronounced Chow-Shoe)

Preparation Time: 5 minutes
Marinating Time: at least 4 hours
Cooking Time: 45 minutes
Serves: 4

Jan Burnes
Adaro

2 pork tenderloins

MARINADE:
3 cloves garlic, crushed
1 tsp. salt

½ tsp. ginger
1 Tblsp. soy sauce
1 Tblsp. honey
1 Tblsp. sherry
½ tsp. 5-spice powder
Red food coloring (cochineal)

Preheat oven to 372° F. Mix all the marinade ingredients. Place tenderloins in a plastic (spill proof) container, and pour the marinade over the tenderloins. Leave for 24 hours if possible but at least for a minimum of 4 hours, turning occasionally. Heat oven to high setting (350° - 400°). Place tenderloins on a wire rack above a baking dish of hot water. Cook for 30 minutes. Turn the pork over, baste with marinade, and cook further for 15 minutes. Slice very thinly. *Serve hot or cold.*

MENU:

"EASY STARTER" SHERRIED GRAPEFRUIT p. 70

. . .

CHA-CHIU p. 108
WHITE RICE
SNOW PEAS AND TOMATOES p. 217

. . .

LEMON SYLLABUB p. 252

. . .

VOUVRAY : JOHANNISBERG RIESLING

ROAST STUFFED PORK TENDERLOIN

Preparation Time: 20 minutes   *Barbie Haworth*
Cooking Time: 2 hours   *Ann-Marie II*
Serves: 6 - 8

2 large pork tenderloins
2 cups Pepperidge Farm stuffing
   (or seasoned breadcrumbs)
½ cup onion, chopped
½ cup celery, sliced crosswise
1 egg, lightly beaten

¼ cup butter
2/3 cup hot water
Salt, pepper, and paprika
Poultry seasoning or sage
2 (16 oz.) cans whole potatoes
2 Tblsp. fresh parsley

Preheat oven to 325° F. Saute onion and celery in butter. Add sauteed vegetables, butter, and hot water to stuffing, and blend. Add egg and seasoning (to taste) and mix thoroughly. Cut both loins ¾ way through lengthwise (like butterflying pork chops). Open and lay flat. Season both sides with salt and pepper. Spread stuffing over one loin and lay the other on top. Roll and tie. Sprinkle salt, pepper, and paprika on top. Bake in an oblong pan at 325° for 1 hour covered, and baste as needed. Remove cover and bake for another hour. Make gravy from droppings. Drain and rinse potatoes twice. Add to the roast for the last 45 minutes and baste. Sprinkle parsley over potatoes at serving time.

MENU:

HOT CURRIED FRUIT

. . .

ROAST STUFFED PORK TENDERLOIN p. 109
FRENCH CUT GREEN BEANS ALMONDINE p. 216
PARSLEY POTATOES p. 223

. . .

PRALINE PARFAIT p. 246

. . .

BEAUJOLAIS (CHILLED) : GAMAY (CHILLED)

PORK CHOPS SERENDIPITY

Preparation Time: 15 minutes
Cooking Time: 40 minutes
Serves: 6

Marilyn Stenberg
Champagne

6 pork chops
Salt and freshly ground black
   pepper
1 oz. butter
1½ oz. breadcrumbs
½ tsp. ground mace

½ tsp. dried thyme
1 Tblsp. parsley, finely chopped
1 oz. shelled walnuts, chopped
1 cup brown stock
Garnish: lemon wedges and
   parsley sprigs

Preheat oven to 400° F. Trim the chops, and season with salt and pepper. Brown the chops in the butter on both sides. Transfer to a shallow ovenproof dish large enough to take them in one layer. Mix together the breadcrumbs, mace, thyme, parsley, and walnuts. Season to taste, and spoon evenly over the chops. Add stock, and cover with lid or foil. Cook in moderately hot oven at 400° for 20 minutes. Remove lid or foil, and cook further for 20 minutes until chops are tender and topping crispy. *Garnish with lemon wedges and parsley sprigs.*

MENU:

CREAM OF BROCCOLI SOUP p. 85

. . .

PORK CHOPS SERENDIPITY p. 110
DAVE LOVES CARROTS p. 214
GREEN HERBED RICE p. 231

. . .

SOUFFLE DANNON p. 256

. . .

BORDEAUX BLANC : SAUVIGNON BLANC

PORK CHOPS PROVENCAL

Preparation Time: 40 minutes
Cooking Time: 1 hour
Serves: 8

Rosalind Rice
Endless Summer II

8 pork chops
Salt and pepper
Garlic powder
Oil
1 large onion, sliced
½ lb. mushrooms, sliced
1 lb. carrots, sliced

4 large celery stalks, sliced
2 red peppers, chopped
3 cups orange juice
1 tsp. grated orange rind
½ tsp. cayenne pepper
1 tsp. rosemary

Preheat oven to 350° F. Rub the chops on both sides with salt, pepper, and garlic powder, and fry lightly in hot oil until brown. Transfer to casserole dish. Fry vegetables slightly, and add to chops. Add orange rind, cayenne pepper, and rosemary to orange juice. Pour over the chops. Cook in the oven at 350° until tender for about 1 hour. Remove chops and vegetables, and keep warm on a serving platter. If necessary, thicken sauce with cornstarch, and spoon over chops before serving.

MENU:

CARIBBEAN CREAM OF PUMPKIN SOUP p. 80

. . .

PORK CHOPS PROVENCAL p. 111
JACKET POTATOES

. . .

WALNUT PIE p. 265

. . .

CABERNET D'ANJOU : GRENACHE ROSE

SAUTEED PORK WITH ARTICHOKES

Preparation Time: 20 minutes
Cooking Time: 50 - 60 minutes
Serves: 4 - 6

Margo Ann Muckey
Tuff

4 large artichokes
1 lemon, halved
2 quarts water
Oil
2 lbs. pork sirloin, cut into
    1 inch cubes
1 medium onion, minced
4 garlic cloves

1 - 1½ cup chicken stock
2 Tblsp. minced fresh Italian
    parsley
1 Tblsp. tomato paste
¼ tsp. salt
1/8 tsp. pepper
Garnish: lemon wedges, sprigs
    of parsley

Snap off coarse outer leaves. Cut off top fourth of each artichoke and discard. Quarter each artichoke starting at the bottom. Cut away choke and purple-tinged leaves. Squeeze lemon halves into large bowl, and add water and artichokes. Set aside. Heat oil over medium-high heat, and add pork in batches. Saute until brown. Remove from skillet. Increase heat to high, add onion, and brown quickly. Add drained artichokes, garlic, and toss until artichokes begin to color. Stir in stock, 2 Tblsp. parsley, tomato paste, salt, and pepper. Blend well, and return pork to skillet. Reduce heat, cover, and simmer until pork is tender, about 50 minutes, adding more stock if mixture seems too dry. Taste and adjust seasoning. Place on heated platter, and sprinkle with parsley. *Garnish with lemon wedges.*

MENU:

TOSSED GREEN SALAD

. . .

SAUTEED PORK WITH ARTICHOKES p. 112
LINGUINE AND MARINARA SAUCE

. . .

STRAWBERRY ICE CREAM

. . .

MACON BLANC : PINOT BLANC

PORK AND APPLE CASSEROLE

Preparation Time: 5 minutes   *Sheila Smith*
Cooking Time: 1 hour   *Victorious*
Serves: 4

1 lb. pork, chopped   1 large onion, sliced
3 apples, sliced   Tomato, optional
Seasonings and bay leaf

Preheat oven to 350°F. In a casserole, place pork, then onion rings, then sliced apples, and then top with tomato rings, if you wish. Almost cover with water, season, and cover. Cook in oven for an hour, check seasonings, remove some liquid, thicken, and return to casserole. *This is always delicious, always popular - try it and see!*

MENU:

AVOCADO LIME SOUP p. 86

. . .

PORK AND APPLE CASSEROLE p. 113
PARSLEY RICE
HERBED SPINACH p. 219

. . .

FLAMING PLANTAINS p. 251

. . .

SANCERRE ROSE : ZINFANDEL BLANC

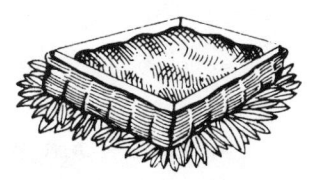

CHEESY TOPPED PORK CHOPS

Preparation Time: 10 minutes
Cooking Time: 25 minutes
Serves: 4

Fiona Baldrey
Promenade

4 thick pork chops
1 Tblsp. olive oil
1 Tblsp. butter
Salt and black pepper

½ lb. Gruyere cheese, finely grated
2 level tsp. strong mustard
Whipping cream

Trim the excess fat from 4 good-sized pork chops, and saute them gently with a little oil and butter in a thick bottomed skillet. Season to taste with salt and pepper. When cooked, spread with a pomade made of finely grated Gruyere (about 6 Tblsp.) mixed with mustard and just enough cream to make a smooth mixture of spreading consistency. Spread chops generously with cheese pomade, and glaze quickly in the broiler until sauce is golden. Serve immediately.

MENU:

GREEN SALAD

. . .

CHEESY TOPPED PORK CHOPS p. 114
HARVARD BEETS p. 212
CAULIFLOWER NEOPOLITAN p. 215

. . .

BANANAS GOMEZ p. 250

. . .

BEAUJOLAIS BLANC : FUME BLANC

CARIBBEAN PORK ROAST

Preparation Time: 20 minutes   *Tom Martin*
Cooking Time: 2 hours   *Mischief*
Serves: 5

3 to 5 lbs. pork loin, boneless   3 cloves garlic
5 stalks of celery   1 Tblsp. oregano
1 potato per person   1 tsp. basil leaves
2 large limes   Pepper to taste

Preheat oven to 350° F. Place pork in pan with ½ inch water. Squeeze limes over meat. Season with oregano, garlic, basil, and pepper. Add vegetables in chunks. Cook covered for 1 hour at 350°, uncover for the last hour, basting the meat and turning the vegetables so they can brown, and not dry out on one side.

MENU:

CUCUMBER-DILL SOUP p. 86

· · ·

CARIBBEAN PORK ROAST p. 115
SWEET AND SOUR CABBAGE p. 213

· · ·

CHOCOLATE BANANA PIE p. 264

· · ·

WHITE GRAVES : DRY CHENIN BLANC

FILET MARSALA

Preparation Time: 10 minutes   *Lisa Hawkins*
Marinating Time: several hours   *Ariguani*
Cooking Time: 15 - 20 minutes
Serves: 8

1 tenderloin, trimmed or   2 Tblsp. olive oil
    8 fillets   Freshly ground pepper
2 cups Marsala wine   1 cup sliced fresh mushrooms
1 tsp. garlic powder   2 Tblsp. butter
2 cloves garlic

In a dish big enough to hold fillets, pour 1 cup of wine or enough to cover bottom of dish. Add garlic powder and 1 Tblsp. olive oil. Place fillets in dish, and cover with ground pepper. Be generous. Marinate for several hours in refrigerator, turning once. Before cooking, allow meat to reach room temperature. In heavy skillet, saute garlic in remaining oil. Brown fillets on each side according to personal taste. Keep fillets warm while making the sauce. Deglaze pan with remaining wine on high heat until it begins to reduce. Add any meat juices and 2 Tblsp. chilled butter in small pats. Add mushrooms, and continue cooking on high heat until sauce thickens. Spoon sauce over fillets.

MENU:

COCONUT FRIED SHRIMP

. . .

FILET MARSALA p. 116
BAKED STUFFED POTATO p. 222
ASPARAGUS IN LEMON BUTTER p. 209

. . .

E-Z APPLE PIE p. 266

. . .

RED BORDEAUX : CABERNET SAUVIGNON

ESCALLOPS CHANTECLER

Preparation Time: 40 minutes   *Rosalind Rice*
Cooking Time: 45 minutes   *Endless Summer II*
Serves: 8

8 veal escallops (4 - 6 oz. each)
Seasoned flour
2 Tblsp. butter
½ lb. mushrooms, cut in quarters
2 finely chopped shallots
2 Tblsp. brandy
1½ cups dry white wine
1½ cups chicken broth
1 Tblsp. finely chopped parsley

1 tsp. Dijon mustard
½ tsp. Worcestershire sauce
8 Tblsp. heavy cream

Garnish:
8 small round croutons of fried
   bread
1 - 2 tomatoes, sliced
8 artichoke hearts
Chopped parsley

Preheat oven to 350° F. Beat the escallops well, and coat with seasoned flour. Brown them quickly on both sides in the hot butter. Add the mushrooms and shallots. Cook together for a few minutes, then add the brandy and flame. Transfer to a casserole dish. Pour in the wine, and cook in a medium oven (350°) until reduced by half. Add the chicken stock, and continue cooking for a further 10 minutes. Remove the escallops to a serving dish and keep warm. Add the parsley, mustard, and Worcestershire sauce to the liquid. Then add the cream, and stir the sauce until it thickens. Add a little lemon juice, and check the seasoning. *To serve: Put a crouton on top of each escallop, then a slice of tomato and an artichoke heart, both warmed in a little butter. Sprinkle with chopped parsley, and serve the sauce separately.*

MENU:

SHRIMP SALAD p. 76

. . .

ESCALLOPS CHANTECLER p. 117
NEW BOILED POTATOES

. . .

PINEAPPLE SURPRISE p. 251

. . .

ST. VERAN : CHARDONNAY

STUFFED VEAL ROLLS

Preparation Time: 30 minutes
Cooking Time: 45 minutes
Serves: 4

Carol Lowe
Natasha

4 veal scallops
8 thin slices of cooked ham,
    proscuitto, or bacon
1 oz. crustless bread
3 Tblsp. seedless white raisins
¼ cup pine nuts

¼ cup Parmesan cheese
2 Tblsp. fresh parsley, chopped
Salt and freshly ground black
    pepper
1 Tblsp. olive oil
2/3 cup white wine

Lay scallops flat between wax paper, and beat thin, but not broken. Cut in half to make 8. Lay slice of ham on each. Soak bread in water, and squeeze dry. Add raisins, nuts, cheese, parsley, salt, and pepper to taste, and mix well. Divide stuffing between the 8 veal scallops, roll up, and secure with toothpicks. Heat oil in saucepan, and fry rolls briskly, turning until lightly browned all over. Pour wine over rolls, cover tightly, and simmer gently for 20 - 25 minutes until tender, turning once or cook in preheated 350° oven. Transfer rolls to serving dish. Boil pan juices until reduced by ½ and thickened. Remove picks and pour sauce over.

MENU:

MUSHROOM SALAD p. 67

. . .

STUFFED VEAL ROLLS p. 118
BUTTERED NOODLES
BASIL TOMATOES p. 220

. . .

STRAWBERRY MOUSSE p. 255

. . .

BEAUJOLAIS (CHILLED) : GAMAY

PICCATINE AL LIMONE

Preparation Time: 10 minutes
Cooking Time: 10 minutes
Serves: 6

Paola Taglia
Stormvogel

6 very thin veal cutlets
1/3 cup flour
1 tsp. salt
1 tsp. pepper
¼ lb. butter

2 cloves garlic, crushed
2 lemons
¼ cup water
Oregano
Garnish: lemon slices

Combine flour and pepper, and dredge the cutlets in the mixture. In a skillet, saute the cutlets with butter and garlic until they are brown. Add the juice of one lemon mixed with water and the salt. Cover and simmer for 5 minutes. *Garnish with lemon slices.*

<u>MENU:</u>

RED PEPPER SOUP p. 83

. . .

PICCATINE AL LIMONE p. 119
GREEN BEANS SAUTEED IN BUTTER AND GARLIC
WHITE RICE

. . .

CHOCOLATE DIPPED STRAWBERRIES p. 245

. . .

POUILLY FUISSE : SAUVIGNON BLANC

VEAL MALTESE

Preparation Time: 10 minutes   *Cherie Hughes*
Cooking Time: 30 minutes   *Skopbank of Finland*
Serves: 6

2 Tblsp. unsalted butter
4 Tblsp. oil
12 veal scallops, lightly pounded
Flour for dredging
Salt and pepper
Chopped parsley
SAUCE:
4 egg yolks
½ lb. butter, softened

REDUCTION:
One sprig of thyme
6 peppercorns
Rind and juice of 1 orange
1 Tblsp. basalmic vinegar
½ cup red wine
2 Tblsp. Grand Marnier
Garnish: orange slices, parsley

Prepare reduction, and reduce to 2 Tblsp. Strain and reserve. Mix together flour, salt, pepper, and parsley. Dredge, then saute veal in butter and oil. Sauce: In a small saucepan over high flame, whisk together 4 egg yolks with 2 Tblsp. water. Remove from heat, and keep whisking: Add butter in bits. Add reduction. Pour some sauce over veal. Pass remaining sauce. *Garnish with sliced oranges and parsley.*

MENU:

QUICK SHE CRAB SOUP p. 88

· · ·

VEAL MALTESE p. 120
GREEN BEANS ALMONDINE p. 216
SWEET POTATOES ANNA p. 220

· · ·

SOUFFLE GRAND MARNIER p. 256

· · ·

VIENNESE COFFEE
CHATEAUNEUF DU PAPE BLANC : PINOT CHARDONNAY

VEAL CHOPS FOUR SEASONS

Preparation Time: 10 minutes
Cooking Time: 20 minutes
Serves: 4

Jacklyn Johnson Rabinowitz
Almost Heaven

½ cup all purpose flour
1½ tsp. fresh chopped rosemary or ½ tsp. dried, crumbled
1½ tsp. fresh chopped sage, or ½ tsp. dried crumbled
½ tsp. salt

¼ tsp. pepper
4 veal chops (about 3 lbs.), cut 1 inch thick
¼ cup vegetable oil

Combine flour and spices on wax paper. Lightly coat chops. Saute chops, turning occasionally in oil in a large, heavy skillet for 15 - 20 minutes or until meat next to bones loses pink color.

MENU:

VEAL CHOPS FOUR SEASONS p. 121
ARTICHOKE BOTTOMS STUFFED WITH MUSHROOMS p. 209
PARSLEY POTATOES p. 223

. . .

CALEDONIAN CREAM p. 262

. . .

SANCERRE BLANC : PINOT CHARDONNAY

VEAL SCALLOPINI

Preparation Time: 20 minutes
Cooking Time: 45 minutes
Serves: 6

Michelle Mitchell
Madam

6 veal scallopini cuts
¾ cup flour
2 tsp. paprika
1 (3 oz) can mushrooms, sliced

1 tsp. beef flavored gravy base
½ cup tomato sauce
2 Tblsp. chopped green pepper

Preheat oven to 350° F. Season veal with flour and paprika. Add pepper and salt to taste. Brown in hot fat. Place in oven dish with preheated mushroom juice and gravy base. Cover and place in oven at 350° for 30 minutes. Mix mushrooms, tomato sauce, and green peppers. Coat veal with sauce, and bake uncovered for 15 minutes more.

MENU:

VEAL SCALLOPINI p. 122
FETTUCCINI ALFREDO p. 230
ZUCCHINI IN GRAND MARNIER p. 227

. . .

CHEESECAKE p. 244

. . .

COTE DU RHONE BLANC : DRY CHENIN BLANC

VEAL A LA VICTORIOUS

Preparation Time: 5 minutes
Cooking Time: 10 minutes
Serves: 4

Sheila Smith
Victorious

2 slices scallopini per person
1 slice Genoa salami per person
Mozarella cheese
Tomato

Olive oil
Lemon juice
Seasoning

Layer veal, salami, cheese, tomato, and top with veal. Do it individually per person, not a whole dish. Place in frying pan with olive oil, lemon juice, and a good splash of vermouth. Season, cover pan, and cook for about 10 minutes. Serve on parsley noodles. *I made up this dish in desperation one night, and we all loved it.*

MENU:

ONION SOUP

. . .

VEAL A LA VICTORIOUS p. 123
PARSLEY NOODLES
GREEN BEANS WITH ALMONDS

. . .

BAKED ALASKA p. 261

. . .

BORDEAUX ROUGE : PINOT NOIR

VEAL FRANCISCAN

Preparation Time: 10 minutes
Cooking Time: 5 minutes (on BBQ grill)
Serves: 8

Sue Griffin
Endless Summer I

8 (6oz.) veal escallops
Parsley butter
Wedge of lemon

Lemon juice
Capers

Marinate veal in lemon juice. Make parsley butter by mixing parsley and butter. Roll in tin foil, and chill. Cut lemon wedges, slice at end, and insert piece of parsley. Barbeque veal for 5 minutes on a very hot grill. *Serve immediately with a pat of butter, lemon, and capers.*

MENU:

SOUFFLES AUX TOMATOES p. 76

• • •

VEAL FRANCISCAN p. 124
FETTUCCINI PESTO p. 231
GREEN BEANS

• • •

ICE CREAM PIE p. 257

• • •

WHITE GRAVES : FUME BLANC

ESCALLOP DE VEAU ANCHOIS

Preparation Time: 10 minutes   *Marilyn Stenberg*
Cooking Time: 10 minutes   *Champagne*
Serves: 6

6 escallops of veal	**Garnish:**
Butter	**1 lemon**
Flour	**12 rolled anchovy fillets**
1 beaten egg	**Parsley**
Breadcrumbs to coat	

Flatten the escallops if necessary, and coat with flour, egg, and bread-crumbs. Saute in butter until golden brown and cooked through. *Serve garnished with a good slice of lemon and 2 anchovies per portion and parsley sprig. The anchovies give a delightfully piquant contrast to the escallops.*

MENU:

GREEN SALAD

. . .

ESCALLOP DE VEAU ANCHOIS p. 125
RICE PILAF
SPINACH MOUNDS p. 219

. . .

PEACH AND MARSHMALLOW DESSERT CAKE p. 241

. . .

POUILLY FUISSE : FUME BLANC

SAUTE DE VEAU MARENGO

Preparation Time: 30 minutes
Cooking Time: 1 - 1¾ hours
Serves: 6 - 8

Laura Greces
Mistral

3 lbs. boneless veal for stew, cut into cubes
4 Tblsp. vegetable oil
1 tsp. thyme
1 tsp. salt
Freshly ground black pepper
2 Tblsp. flour
2 Tblsp. butter
1 cup onions, finely chopped

1 clove garlic, finely chopped
½ cup dry white wine
2 cups beef bouillon
1 cup canned tomatoes, drained
2 Tblsp. fresh parsley
1 bay leaf
3 Tblsp. butter
1 (16 oz.) can whole mushrooms
Garnish: parsley

Preheat the oven to 500° F. Dry veal with paper towels. In a skillet, heat oil. Saute veal a few chunks at a time until golden brown. Transfer veal to a 4 - 5 quart casserole dish. Discard cooking oil, and set aside pan. Sprinkle veal with thyme, salt, pepper, and flour tossing to coat meat evenly. Place casserole in oven, and cook for about 10 minutes. Remove from oven. Reduce heat to 325°. Meanwhile, melt 2 Tblsp. butter in skillet, and cook onions and garlic until soft and lightly browned. Add wine and bouillon, and bring to a boil. Boil for 1 - 2 minutes, then pour into casserole. Stir in tomatoes, parsley, and bay leaf. Place casserole in oven for 1 - 1¼ hour or until veal is tender. Add the mushrooms, and continue cooking for 10 - 15 minutes. Remove casserole from oven. Season to taste. Garnish with chopped parsley.

MENU:

TOSSED SALAD

· · ·

SAUTE DE VEAU MARENGO p. 126
SPINACH NOODLES

· · ·

PINA COLADA SOUFFLE p. 257

· · ·

CHIROUBLES : PINOT NOIR

GIGOT D'AGNEAU BOMBARD

Preparation Time: 20 minutes
Cooking Time: 2 - 2½ hours
Serves: 8

Judith Meyers Vegiard
Ruach

8 lb. leg of lamb
1½ cups Dijon mustard
6 garlic cloves, chopped

2 Tblsp. crumbled dried rosemary
 leaves
6 Tblsp. butter, melted
Garnish: rosemary

Preheat oven to 375° F. Trim fat from lamb (mustard mixture will keep meat moist while cooking. In a bowl, mix mustard, garlic, and roesemary. Coat flat side of leg with ½ mustard paste. Roast at 375° for 1 hour. Drizzle with melted butter to brown. Remove lamb from oven. Turn and coat other side with remaining mustard paste. Continue roasting at 375° for another hour (rare to medium) or an hour and a half (medium to well done) drizzling with butter to brown. *Garnish with sprigs of rosemary.*

MENU:

GREEN SALAD

· · ·

GIGOT D'AGNEAU BOMBARD p. 127
HOT POTATOES VINAIGRETTE p. 221
MINTED CARROTS p. 214

· · ·

SOUR CREAM CREPES WITH CHOCOLATE SAUCE p. 259

· · ·

COTE DU RHONE : PINOT NOIR

WHITE WINE LEG OF LAMB

Preparation Time: 20 minutes
Cooking Time: 20 minutes
Serves: 6

Paola Taglia
Stormvogel

4 - 5 lbs. boneless leg of lamb
6 Tblsp. corn oil
4 cloves garlic, minced
2 Tblsp. butter
4 onions, sliced

2 tsp. salt
1 tsp. sugar
3 Tblsp. soy sauce
½ cup white wine

Put the oil in a pot, and saute the garlic and the lamb until brown. Add the butter. When it's melted, add the onions. Stir for 2 minutes, then add salt, sugar, soy sauce, and wine (all mixed into the same cup). Cover and simmer for about 20 minutes (turn the lamb on both sides every 10 minutes). Check the meat inside; when it is pink, it's ready.

MENU:

CARROT SOUP p. 82

. . .

WHITE WINE LEG OF LAMB p. 128
POTATOES "PUREE"
SPINACH SAUTEED WITH BUTTER AND PEPPER

. . .

VANILLA ICE CREAM WITH CREME DE MENTHE

. . .

POUILLY FUISSE : PINOT CHARDONNAY

BARBEQUED MARINATED LEG OF LAMB

Preparation Time: 30 minutes
Chilling Time: 12 - 24 hours
Cooking Time: 25 minutes (on BBQ grill)
Serves: 8

Jacklyn Johnson Rabinowitz
Almost Heaven

6 lb. leg of lamb, boned and butterflied
1 tsp. coarsely cracked pepper
4 cloves garlic, sliced
2 Tblsp. vinegar

½ cup red wine
½ cup olive oil
2 bay leaves
½ tsp. dried tarragon
2 tsp. salt

Spread lamb flat in glass container. Sprinkle with pepper and garlic. Add remaining ingredients, and marinate in refrigerator 12 - 24 hours. Remove meat from marinade, and cook over very hot coals for 6 minutes on each side. Meat should be well browned and crusty. Spread out coals, and cook for 6 - 7 minutes longer on each side. Slice as you would steak.

MENU:

JELLIED CONSOMME WITH CAVIAR p. 89

. . .

BARBEQUED MARINATED LEG OF LAMB p. 129
RICE PARISIENNE p. 234
MUSHROOM CAPS WITH PETIT POIS p. 218

. . .

SILKY APRICOT MOUSSE p. 255

. . .

ST. EMILION : CABERNET SAUVIGNON

RACK OF LAMB

Preparation Time: 15 minutes
Marinating Time: overnight
Cooking Time: 25 minutes
Serves: 8

Lisa Hawkins
Ariguani

4 racks of lamb, trimmed and
   bone cracked
Olive oil
Red wine
Minced garlic or garlic in a jar

Dijon mustard
Honey
Fresh mint and parsley, chopped
   fine
Freshly ground pepper

Preheat oven to 475° F. In a large roasting pan, combine red wine and
¼ cup olive oil. Rub each rack with garlic and mustard. Spoon honey
generously on each rack and pat with fresh herbs. Grind pepper over
racks, and place in marinade. Let meat marinade overnight in refrigerator. Before cooking, let meat reach room temperature. Drain off
marinade, and roast meat side up. You may want to spoon more
honey and herbs on the racks before roasting. Roast in hot oven at
475° for 25 minutes, for medium rare. *To serve, slice racks, and
arrange on plates.*

MENU:

PEACH BRANDY SOUP p. 79

. . .

RACK OF LAMB p. 130
GLAZED SNOW PEAS AND CARROTS p. 218
"WILD" RICE p. 235

. . .

DECADENT CHOCOLATE MOUSSE p. 253

. . .

MOULIN A. VENT : GAMAY BEAUJOLAIS

CAP'N BARKY'S LAMB CHOPS

Preparation Time: 5 minutes   *Lisa Ferry*
Cooking Time: 6 - 8 minutes (on BBQ grill)   *Tefra*
Serves: 6

12 lamb chops
1 Tblsp. ground thyme
¼ cup rosemary leaves

MINT JELLY:
¾ cup apple mint jelly
2 Tblsp. plain vinegar
2 Tblsp. chopped fresh mint or
    1 Tblsp. mint flakes
1 Tblsp. white sugar, or to taste
1/8 cup mint syrup

Separate lamb chops, and rub ground thyme over all surfaces. Sprinkle rosemary over hot barbeque coals, and cook chops for 3 - 4 minutes per side with barbeque cover on. Serve with mint jelly. Mint Jelly: Blend all ingredients in small saucepan over low heat. Transfer to serving dish and table. *Note: Mint Jelly can ruin good red wines. Ask your wine cellar for advice.*

MENU:

PEARS IN BLUE CHEESE DRESSING p. 71

. . .

CAP'N BARKY'S LAMB CHOPS p. 131
BAKED POTATO
GLAZED CARROTS p. 215

. . .

ORANGE SHERBET

. . .

RED GRAVES : PINOT NOIR

RACK OF LAMB WITH ZINFANDEL SAUCE

Preparation Time: 5 minutes
Marinating Time: 1 hour
Cooking Time: 30 minutes
Serves: 6

Chris Balfour
Stowaway

3 racks of lamb, boned

1 cup Zinfandel wine

MARINADE:
½ cup soy sauce
½ cup olive oil
½ cup sesame oil
½ cup parsley
½ tsp. mace

2 garlic cloves
1 Tblsp. thyme
1 tsp. rosemary
1 tsp. dry mustard
½ tsp. oregano

Combine marinade in food processor. Transfer ½ cup to a small sauce-pan. Pour remaining marinade over lamb, and let sit for 1 hour. Turn often. Transfer lamb to racks in pan, and bake for 20 - 25 minutes basting often. 10 minutes before serving, combine wine with ½ cup reserved marinade and simmer, stirring. Serve in a sauceboat. *Garnish with parsley or watercress.*

MENU:

CREAM OF WATERCRESS SOUP p. 84

· · ·

RACK OF LAMB WITH ZINFANDEL SAUCE p. 132
POMMES DAUPHINE p. 221
SAUTEED LEEKS p. 217

· · ·

STRAWBERRY ICE p. 263

· · ·

ST. JULIEN : ZINFANDEL

ROAST LEG OF LAMB

Preparation Time: 15 minutes   *Rosalind Rice*
Cooking Time: 2½ - 3 hours   *Endless Summer II*
Serves: 8

1 New Zealand leg of lamb   2 tsp. dried rosemary
   (6 - 7 lbs.)   Oil
1 large clove garlic, sliced

Preheat the oven to 350° F. Insert slices of garlic into the joint of meat.
Rub the surface with oil, and sprinkle with rosemary. Cover the meat
with foil, and cook in the oven for 2½ - 3 hours. Baste regularly.
Halfway through cooking time, remove the foil in order for the joint
to brown. Use pan juices to make gravy.

MENU:

CHICKEN LIVER PATE

. . .

ROAST LEG OF LAMB p. 133
ROAST POTATOES
CAULIFLOWER WITH CHEESE
GLAZED CARROTS p. 215

. . .

PINEAPPLE UPSIDE DOWN CAKE p. 240

. . .

CHATEAUNEUF DU PAPE : ZINFANDEL

POSSUM DELIGHT

Preparation Time: Could take days   *LeAnn Cline*
Cooking Time: 24 hours   *Vanity*
Serves: Whoever will try it

1 possum, freshly run over   **Salt and pepper**
1 medium board   **Butter**
                                                         Garnish: fresh flowers

Preheat oven to 600° F. Wait by the road until a possum comes along and gets run over. Scrape up and skin. Place on a medium board. Butter, salt, and pepper to taste. Place in a hot oven and bake for 24 hours. Remove from oven. Garnish with fresh flowers. Discard possum and eat the board!

MENU:

FRESH FLOWERS

. . .

POSSUM DELIGHT
SLOW COOKED RAMPS

. . .

SUNFLOWER SEEDS

. . .

MAD DOG 151

*POULTRY

NOTES

FLAMED CHICKEN WITH MUSHROOMS

Preparation Time: 10 minutes
Cooking Time: 20 Minutes
Serves: 6 - 8

Jan Robinson
Vanity

5 Tblsp. butter
¼ cup minced shallots
1 clove garlic, crushed
½ lb. fresh mushrooms, sliced
1 Tblsp. fresh marjoram, chopped,
    or 1 tsp. dried
2 Tblsp. fresh chives, chopped or
    2 tsp. freeze-dried

Black pepper, freshly ground
¼ cup dry white wine
8 skinless, boneless chicken breast
    halves
¼ cup brandy
Garnish: 2 Tblsp. chopped fresh
    parsley

Melt 3 Tblsp. of the butter in skillet large enough to hold chicken in one layer. (It may be necessary to use two skillets to cook chicken.) Stir in shallots and garlic and cook over low heat for about a minute. Add mushrooms and continue cooking for another minute. Stir in herbs, seasonings, and wine. Cook over moderately high heat about 3 minutes, or until wine has reduced to an essence. Remove mushroom mixture and set aside on warm plate. Cover and keep warm. Put chicken between sheets of waxed paper and pound until breasts are about ½ inch thick. Season with pepper. Add the remaining 2 Tblsp. butter to skillet over medium-high heat. When butter is hot, saute chicken breasts, without crowding pan, 3 to 4 minutes on 1 side until lightly browned. Reduce heat slightly, turn each breast and brown other side--adding more butter if necessary. Place some mushroom mixture on top of each breast and turn off heat. Slightly warm brandy in small saucepan. Standing back, hold a match just above brandy and set it aflame. Pour flaming brandy over chicken. Shake pan gently until flames have subsided. Remove to platter and garnish with parsley, if desired.

MENU:

ISLAND FRUIT SALAD p. 70

. . .

FLAMED CHICKEN WITH MUSHROOMS p. 137
BULGAR WITH AROMATIC VEGETABLES p. 232
BASIL-TOMATOES p. 220

. . .

PAPAYA CREAM p. 259

. . .

BOURGOGNE ALIGOTE : CHARDONNAY

ASPARAGUS BREASTS

Preparation Time: 20 minutes   *Denise Wright*
Cooking Time: 45 minutes   *Parandah*
Serves: 6

6 boneless chicken breasts Butter
18 fresh asparagus stalks 1 (10¼ oz.) can cream of asparagus
1 cup cream cheese   soup
¼ - ½ cup cream   Garnish: chopped parsley and pap-
          rika

Preheat oven to 400° F. Cut asparagus into spears 4 inches in length, blanche or steam lightly. Set aside. Pound breasts to an even thickness with mallet. Spread each with cream cheese, then place 3 asparagus spears in center, and wrap to make roll, turn over. Dot with butter. Cover with cream of asparagus soup saving a little soup. Place in a 400° F. oven for 45 minutes. Add cream and heat, use as a sauce immediately before serving. Sprinkle with paprika and chopped parsley. (To serve as an hors d'oeuvres, omit the cream of asparagus soup and cream, and place in the oven for 45 minutes after placing the pats of butter on. When done, cool and refrigerate. To serve, slice each breast into 4 or 5 coins. Place on lettuce leaf with twisted lemon slice, parsley, and a few cherry tomatoes.

MENU:

SMOKED MARLIN SALAD p. 64

. . .

ASPARAGUS BREASTS p. 138
STEAMED WHITE RICE
SWEET AND SOUR CARROTS p. 214

. . .

LEMMON BARS p. 244

. . .

ST. VERAN : CHARDONNAY

CHICKEN "DUKE OF ELBA"

Preparation Time: 15 minutes
Cooking Time: 30 minutes
Serves: 6

Fiona Baldrey
Promenade

6 split chicken breasts
2 medium onions, finely chopped
2 garlic cloves, crushed
4 ozs. butter
½ cup dry Vermouth

6 slices Swiss cheese
¼ cup toasted almond flakes
Salt and ground black pepper
Garnish: almonds

Fry chicken pieces, using large skillet, in butter for 15 minutes, turning once. Remove and set aside. When cool, remove skin. Fry onions in remaining fat for 5 minutes, adding crushed garlic for last minute. Add Vermouth, season, and return chicken to pan. Cook for 5 minutes to reduce sauce, and top each portion with a slice of Swiss cheese. Cook 5 minutes more. Toast almond flakes in broiler (about 2 - 3 minutes). *Serve with almond garnish on top.*

MENU:

ZUCCHINI BISQUE p. 90

• • •

CHICKEN "DUKE OF ELBA" p. 139
GREEN BEANS WITH BUTTER
GLAZED CARROTS p. 215

• • •

JAN'S KEY LIME PIE p. 262

• • •

WHITE BORDEAUX : DRY SAUVIGNON

LEMON CHICKEN

Preparation Time: 10 minutes
Cooking Time: 30 minutes
Serves: 6

Lisa Ferry
Tefra

6 chicken breasts
Salt and freshly ground pepper
   to taste
2 Tblsp. butter
¼ cup shallots (or onions),
   finely chopped
1 Tblsp. garlic, finely minced

Grated lemon rind from one lemon
2 lemons, sliced and seeded
¾ cup dry white wine
1 Tblsp. finely chopped parsley
Garnish: Fresh lemon slices and
   parsley

Sprinkle chicken on both sides with salt and pepper. Melt butter in heavy skillet. Cook chicken skin side down until nicely browned about 5 minutes. Turn chicken pieces, and add shallots and garlic. Cook for 1 minute, add grated lemon rind, and cook for 2 minutes more. Place lemon slices over breasts, and pour the wine over. Scrape bottom of pan with wooden spoon to deglaze. Cover and reduce heat to low. Let simmer 10 - 15 minutes until done. *Garnish with fresh lemon slices and parsley.*

MENU:

COOL CUCUMBER SOUP p. 85

. . .

LEMON CHICKEN p. 140
STUFFED SUMMER SQUASH p. 225
ITALIAN PEAS AND ONIONS p. 218

. . .

E-Z APPLE PIE p. 266

. . .

MACON BLANC VILL : FUME BLANC

CHICKEN SUPREME

Preparation Time: 20 minutes   *Laura Greces*
Cooking Time: 1 hour 15 minutes   *Mistral*
Serves: 6

6 split chicken breasts
½ tsp. Caribbean seasoning (or
    your choice)
Dash pepper
1 chicken bouillon cube, dissolved
    in 1 cup boiling water

1/3 cup dry white wine
½ tsp. instant minced onion
½ tsp. curry powder
2 Tblsp. flour
¼ cup cold water
1 (3 oz.) can sliced mushrooms,
    drained
Paprika

Preheat the oven to 350°F. Sprinkle breasts with seasoning and pepper. Place in a baking dish. Mix dissolved bouillon cube in water with wine, onion, and curry powder, and pour over the chicken. Cover with foil, and bake at 350° F. for 30 minutes. Uncover and bake for 30 minutes or until tender. Remove chicken, and place in a platter. Reserve pan juices. Blend 2 Tblsp. flour and ¼ cup cold water into saucepan. Slowly stir in pan juices. Cook and stir over low heat until sauce thickens. Boil 2 - 3 minutes. Add sliced mushrooms. Pour sauce over chicken. Sprinkle on paprika.

MENU:

ONION SOUP

. . .

CHICKEN SUPREME p. 141
PARSLEY POTATOES p. 223
MINTED PEAS
STEAMED CARROTS

. . .

NO CRUST CRANBERRY PIE p. 265

. . .

CHABLIS : PINOT CHARDONNAY

PUNISHED POULTRY, RATHER ROMANTIC

Preparation Time: 1 hour　　　　　　　　　　　　*Kim Turk*
Cooking Time: 30 minutes　　　　　　　　　　　*Antipodes*
Serves: 10

10 boneless chicken breasts, beaten and skinned	**SAUCE:**
Flour	**Dry white wine**
Seasoning	**Salt and pepper**
Oil	**Tarragon, to taste**
	Basil, to taste
	Heavy cream
	Garnish: Tomato Rose

Separate breasts, dip in flour, shake off excess, and saute. Place in an oven proof dish. To make the sauce, pour enough wine in a small pan to let reduce. Add seasonings, tarragon, and basil to taste. When reduced sufficiently, heat the cream, and add to sauce. Reduce the heat, and cook until it thickens. Pour over the chicken and reheat in oven or keep warm. *Serve with a tomato rose (rather romantic).*

MENU:

CURRIED PEA SOUP p. 82

. . .

PUNISHED POULTRY, RATHER ROMANTIC p. 142
STEAMED RICE
DAVE LOVES CARROTS p. 214
CORGETTES A LA FRITZ p. 227

. . .

BLACK CHERRY AND ALMOND CREAM p. 261

. . .

WHITE GRAVES : SAUVIGNON BLANC

CHICKEN A LA VICTORIOUS

Preparation Time: 10 minutes　　　　　　　　　　*Sheila Smith*
Marinate: 30 minutes　　　　　　　　　　　　　　*Victorious*
Cooking Time: 40 minutes
Serves: 4

4 chicken breasts, sliced in half

MARINADE:	**FILLING:**
¼ cup lemon juice	**8 oz. tub Ricotta**
½ cup olive oil	**Handful walnuts, chopped**
	Handful dried apricots, chopped
	Salt and pepper, to taste
	Flaked almonds

Preheat oven to 350° F. Slice breasts lengthwise, and marinate for ½ hour. In a bowl, combine cheese with fruit and nuts, salt and pepper. In a round dish, layer chicken, then filling, then chicken (you can serve it in slices like a cake). Cook at 350° F. for ½ hour, then check (cooling time depends on whether you made 2 or 3 chicken layers). Cover top with almonds, and cook for 10 more minutes. Be careful not to over-cook because cheese will lose its flavor.

MENU:

CREAM OF WATERCRESS SOUP p. 84

. . .

GREEN SALAD WITH GARLIC DRESSING
CHICKEN A LA VICTORIOUS p. 143
STUFFED TOMATOES
BUTTERED ASPARAGUS

. . .

STRAWBERRY ICE p. 263

. . .

BEAUJOLAIS BLANC : PINOT BLANC

WEST INDIAN CURRY CHICKEN

Preparation Time: 20 minutes
Marinating Time: overnight
Cooking Time: 2 hours
Serves: 6 - 8

Shannon Webster
Chaparral

6 - 8 chicken breasts, boneless
3 Tblsp. butter or oil
1 green pepper
3 large onions
1 fresh coconut with milk
1 pint chicken stock (canned bouillon)
½ cup raisins

5 Tblsp. mild curry powder
4 Tblsp. chutney
3 Tblsp. raspberry jam
2 Tblsp. tumeric
Dash or two of tabasco
Salt and pepper to taste

Sear chicken in 3 Tblsp. oil or butter. Saute onions and green pepper. Add curry powder, shredded coconut with milk, raisins, chutney, jam, salt, pepper, tabasco, and herbs. Add 1 pint chicken stock, and simmer for ½ hour (let sit overnight if possible). Heat 1 hour before serving adding chopped chicken breasts 15 - 20 minutes before done. Serve with sliced apple, bananas, pineapple, nuts, etc. *This is a wonderful dish for those who don't think they like curry.*

MENU:

WEST INDIAN CURRY CHICKEN p. 144
WHITE RICE
TOASTED GARLIC PITA BREAD TRIANGLES

. . .

ICE CREAM PIE p. 257

. . .

WHITE BORDEAUX : SAUVIGNON BLANC

BARBEQUED TANDOORI CHICKEN

Preparation Time: 15 minutes
Marinating Time: 4 hours
Cooking Time: 30 minutes (on BBQ grill)
Serves: 6

Fiona Baldrey
Promenade

6 split chicken breasts
1 cup plain yogurt
1 large onion, grated
3 cloves garlic, crushed
2 tsp. grated fresh ginger
2 tsp. ground cumin
2 tsp. ground coriander

2 tsp. ground paprika
2 tsp. ground tumeric
2 tsp. salt
1 tsp. tabasco sauce
Juice of 2 lemons
Dash of each, red and yellow food
    coloring

TANDOORI SAUCE:
1 cup plain yogurt
2 tsp. dried mint
¼ cucumber, grated

Garnish: onion rings and lemon
    wedges, shredded lettuce

Skin, wash, and dry chicken. Prick all over with a very sharp knife point. Mix yogurt with all other ingredients, this should be a bright orange color. Marinate chicken in yogurt mixture for at least 4 hours (this can be done the day before). Barbeque chicken pieces ½ hour approximately or just until tender. NOTE: frequent turning prevents burning in a breeze. Serve on a bed of lettuce, and garnish with onion rings and lemon wedges. Serve Tandoori sauce separately. Also serve a platter of warmed whole wheat pita bread. *Tandoori in India denotes the method of cooking. Tandoori is food cooked on the spit in a clay oven. This particular recipe tastes just as good cooked on the barbecue.*

MENU:

SPINACH SALAD
. . .
BARBEQUED TANDOORI CHICKEN p. 145
OVEN BROWNED POTATOES
CORN ON THE COB
. . .
MIGHTY MOUSSE p. 253
. . .
VOUVRAY : CALIFORNIA RIESLING

CHICKEN SAUTE IASCANA

Preparation Time: 30 minutes
Cooking Time: 15 minutes
Serves: 8

Shannon Webster
Chaparral

8 boneless chicken breasts
2 Tblsp. butter
Salt and pepper
½ cup olive oil
2 - 3 cloves fresh chopped garlic
½ lb. fresh mushrooms, quartered
Dash soy sauce

1 onion, chopped coarsely
2 Tblsp. chopped parsley
2 Tblsp. lemon juice
½ cup dry white wine
½ tsp. Italian seasoning mix
1 - 2 jars artichoke hearts
Garnish: parsley, toasted almonds
(sliced), and lemon wheel

Brown chicken in butter and olive oil. Add garlic, onion, and mushrooms. Pour wine over all. Add lemon juice, herbs, a dash of soy sauce, and pepper. Add artichoke hearts, cover, and simmer on low heat for 10 - 15 minutes. Serve over wild brown rice, and sprinkle with sliced toasted almonds. Garnish with lemon wheel and parsley. *A quick dish when you are running behind.*

MENU:

ZESTY GAZPACHO p. 88

• • •

CHICKEN SAUTE IASCANA p. 146
BROCCOLI MOLD p. 211
WILD BROWN RICE

• • •

RUM CAKE p. 242

• • •

COTE DU RHONE BLANC : DRY CHENIN BLANC

CHICKEN MUSHARTI

Preparation Time: 30 minutes   Jan Robinson
Cooking Time: 1 hour 15 minutes   *Vanity*
Serves: 8 - 10

2 3lb. chickens cut up or 10 bone- ½ lb. mushrooms, sliced
    less chicken breasts   5 Tblsp. flour
4 tsp. pepper   1½ cup chicken broth
4 tsp. paprika   ½ cup dry sherry
2 Tblsp. oil   ½ tsp. rosemary
8 Tblsp. butter or margarine   ½ tsp. oregano
1 (14 oz.) can artichoke hearts, 4 Tblsp. chopped parsley
    drained and halved   10 spring onions, chopped

Preheat the oven to 375° F. Rinse chicken, and pat dry. Sprinkle with
pepper and paprika. In a frying pan, brown chicken pieces in melted
butter and oil. Transfer chicken to a shallow 3 - quart casserole, and
arrange artichokes in between. Set aside. Drain all but 3 Tblsp. drippings from frying pan. Add mushrooms, and cook until golden. Stir
flour into mushrooms, and cook for 1 minute. Then add broth, sherry,
rosemary, and oregano. Cook, stirring until thickened. Add chopped
parsley and spring onions. Pour sauce evenly over chicken and artichokes. Cover and bake in oven for 40 minutes.

MENU:

CHERRY TOMATO SALAD p. 67

. . .

CHICKEN MUSHARTI p. 147
PLAIN RICE
BRUSSEL SPROUTS
(wrapped in bacon and sprinkled with cheese)

. . .

CREPES A LA PECHE p. 260

. . .

BOURGOGNE ALIGOTE : CHARDONNAY

CHICKEN VALENTINE

Preparation Time: 20 minutes
Marinating Time: 2 hours
Cooking Time: 15 minutes
Serves: 6

Cherie Hughes
Skopbank of Finland

1 Tblsp. olive oil
3 Tblsp. clarified butter
6 whole, boneless, skinless
    breasts of chicken,
    slightly pounded
2 large red bell peppers
2 cloves garlic

Garnish: watercress

MARINADE:
½ cup olive oil
¼ cup raspberry vinegar
½ tsp. fennel seeds, chopped
2 tsp. basil
2 tsp. tarragon
Pepper, freshly ground
1 Tblsp. cornstarch mixed with
    2 Tblsp. water

Over a gas flame, roast the peppers (whole) until they turn black. Place in a paper sack to sweat. Peel and rinse off skins. Slice into julienne. Also roast the garlic, and add to it the combined ingredients of the marinade except for cornstarch. Let the chicken rest in marinade at least 2 hours. Remove chicken, pat dry, and saute in clarified butter and 1 Tblsp. olive oil, being careful not to overcrowd the pan. Return the breasts to skillet. Add marinade and peppers, reduce sauce, and add cornstarch mixture. Pour sauce over warm "hearts" of chicken. *Garnish with watercress.*

MENU:

TWO MELON SOUP p. 81

. . .

CHICKEN VALENTINE p. 148
SAUTEED SNOW PEAS
MUSHROOMS AND YELLOW SQUASH
SAFFRON RICE PILAF p. 233

. . .

PLUM MERINGUE TART p. 266

. . .

BOURGOGNE ALIGOTE : CHARDONNAY

CHICKEN FLORENTINE

Preparation Time: 20 minutes   *Margo Muckey*
Cooking Time: 60 minutes   *Tuff*
Serves: 6

6 (8 oz.) chicken breast halves
1½ cups boiling chicken stock
1 cup seasoned breadcrumbs
1 cup uncooked long grain rice
2 Tblsp. olive oil
2 Tblsp. butter
½ cup dry red wine
2½ oz. sliced black olives
2 Cups Sauce Marinara
    (See recipe, p. 94)

2 (10 oz.) packages frozen chopped
    spinach
1 cup Ricotta or cottage cheese
2 beaten eggs
½ tsp. ground marjoram
½ tsp. salt
¼ tsp. nutmeg
¼ cup grated Parmesan cheese

Preheat the oven to 350°F. Coat chicken with breadcrumbs. Heat oil and butter in skillet. Add chicken breasts, and saute until brown. Remove from pan, and set aside. Combine Sauce Marinara and wine. Place 1 cup of sauce-wine mixture in skillet. Add chicken stock, rice, and olives, stir thoroughly, scraping bottom of skillet. Place in lightly oiled 3 quart casserole dish. Arrange the chicken skin side down on top of rice. Cover tightly with foil, and bake for 20 minutes. Turn chicken, recover with foil, and bake for another 25 minutes. While chicken is baking, combine spinach (thawed and pressed dry) with Ricotta, eggs, marjoram, salt, and nutmeg. Spoon mixture around edge of baking dish. Pour remaining sauce-wine mixture over chicken. Sprinkle with Parmesan, and bake uncovered for 15 - 20 minutes more.

MENU:

CHERRY TOMATO SALAD p. 67

. . .

CHICKEN FLORENTINE p. 149

. . .

PINEAPPLE PUDDING p. 252

. . .

WHITE BORDEAUX : DRY CHENIN BLANC

CHICKEN DIVAN

Preparation Time: 45 minutes
Cooking Time: 35 minutes
Serves: 4 - 6

Jacklyn Johnson Rabinowitz
Almost Heaven

4 chicken breasts
1 small head broccoli
1 small onion, finely chopped
1 celery stalk, finely chopped
¼ tsp. pepper
½ tsp. garlic powder
½ lb. Monteray Jack cheese
1 (10½ oz.) can cream of celery
   soup
½ cup mayonnaise

TOPPING:
½ cup Pepperidge Farm Stuffing
   Mix, or seasoned
   breadcrumbs
½ tsp. snipped parsley
¼ tsp. paprika
2 oz. butter

Garnish: parsley, paprika

Partially cook chicken, cool, and slice. Lightly steam broccoli. Mix soup, mayonnaise, onion, celery, pepper, and garlic powder. Arrange chicken slices in casserole dish in a spiral pattern. Layer broccoli in spiral on top, then cheese. Pour soup mixture over this. Top with dry stuffing mix, dot with butter. *Garnish with parsley and paprika.*

MENU:

GREEN SALAD

. . .

CHICKEN DIVAN p. 150
SPINACH FETTUCINI

. . .

PRALINE PARFAIT p. 246

. . .

BEAUJOLAIS BLANC : PINOT BLANC

CHICKEN IN CHAMPAGNE SAUCE

Preparation Time: 20 minutes
Cooking Time: 25 minutes
Serves: 4

Joan Della Dora
Bluewater

4 whole chicken breasts,
    boned and skinned
¼ cup flour
1 tsp. salt
½ tsp. pepper
6 Tblsp. butter
2 Tblsp. oil

½ lb. mushrooms, quartered
½ pint heavy cream
¼ cup chopped parsley
¼ cup champagne
Salt and pepper, to taste

Garnish: fluted mushroom caps

Place breast between wax paper, and pound with side of a mallet to flatten slightly. Place flour, salt, and pepper in a bag. Shake breasts in this mixture, shaking off excess flour as completed. Melt butter with oil over medium heat, and lightly brown the floured breasts. When breasts are lightly browned, add cleaned mushrooms to pan. Cover the pan, and cook over low heat for about 5 minutes. Uncover pan, and remove most of the excess butter. Add the cream, parsley, and champagne, and simmer slowly, uncovered, for 5 minutes more. Remove from heat. To serve, remove breasts to a warm platter. Season with salt and pepper, to taste. If sauce has become too thick, thin with a little milk or cream. Pour sauce over breasts, and top with fluted mushroom caps as garnish. Fluted mushroom caps: While breasts are cooking, flute mushroom caps. Saute mushroom caps slowly in 1 Tblsp. butter and lemon juice for 2 - 3 minutes.

MENU:

EASY VICHYSSOISE p. 89

. . .

CHICKEN IN CHAMPAGNE SAUCE p. 151
PAPRIKA-BUTTERED BROCCOLI p. 211
CROISSANTS

. . .

! SPECIAL CHRISTMAS RUM CAKE! p. 242

. . .

CHAMPAGNE

CHICKEN IN CHABLIS

Preparation Time: 10 minutes   *Jane Glancy*
Cooking Time: 30 minutes   *Truant*
Serves: 4

2 whole chicken breasts   ¼ lb. mushrooms, quartered
Salt   2/3 cup chablis
Nutmeg   1 tsp. cornstarch mixed with
2 Tblsp. butter   2 tsp. chablis
2 Tblsp. minced onion

Bone, skin, and halve the chicken breasts. Sprinkle with salt and nutmeg on both sides. Brown in a skillet with butter. Add the onion,
mushrooms, and wine. Bring to a boil, reduce heat, and simmer for 15
minutes. Remove the chicken, and keep warm. Bring pan juices to a
boil, and cook until slightly reduced. Stir in cornstarch mixed with
chablis, cook, and stir until thickened. Spoon sauce over chicken.

MENU:

HONEYMOON SALAD p. 63

. . .

CHICKEN IN CHABLIS p. 152
RICE BROWNED IN BOUILLON
GREEN BEANS

. . .

DECADENT CHOCOLATE MOUSSE p. 253

. . .

CHABLIS : PINOT CHARDONNAY

CHICKEN IN MUSTARD SAUCE

Preparation Time: 30 minutes
Cooking Time: 40 minutes
Serves: 6

Louise Brendlinger
Ring-Anderson

6 chicken breasts, boned
½ cup white wine
2 bay leaves
2 ginger slices
2 oz. butter

2 oz. flour
2 Tblsp. sour cream
2 Tblsp. whole grain Dijon mustard
Salt and pepper
Garnish: chopped parsley

Poach the chicken in the white wine with water, bay leaves, and ginger slices. Cook for 20 minutes. Retain cooking juices, and skin breasts. Melt the butter in a pan. Add the flour and stir. Then add some of the cooking liquid, adding as much as necessary to reach desired thickness. Add the sour cream, mustard, season to taste, and add chicken. Heat thoroughly and serve. *Garnish with chopped parsley.*

MENU:

CHEF'S SALAD p. 36

. . .

CHICKEN IN MUSTARD SAUCE p. 153
SUCCOTASH STUFFED BAKED GREEN PEPPERS p. 225

. . .

PANANA POUNDS p. 249

. . .

BORDEAUX BLANC : DRY SAUVIGNON

CHICKEN BREASTS
WITH BRANDY CREAM SAUCE

Preparation Time: 10 minutes
Cooking Time: 20 minutes
Serves: 4

Jacklyn Johnson Rabinowitz
Almost Heaven

¼ cup butter
4 chicken breasts, boned and
  skinned
2 Tblsp. chopped fresh basil or
  2 tsp. dried

1/3 cup brandy
¼ cup heavy cream
½ tsp. salt
Garnish: basil or watercress

In a large skillet over medium heat, melt butter. Add chicken, and lightly brown on both sides. Add basil, cover, and cook for 10 - 12 minutes until juices run clear when chicken is pierced. Remove to covered warm platter. Add brandy to skillet. Heat for 1 minute. Add cream and salt, and cook, stirring constantly for 1 minute. Pour over chicken. *Garnish with basil.*

MENU:

CHICKEN BREASTS WITH BRANDY CREAM SAUCE p. 154
BROCCOLI WITH WALNUT BUTTER p. 210
NOODLES WITH CARROTS AND POPPY SEEDS p. 229

. . .

FROZEN STRAWBERRY MARGARITA PIE p. 263

. . .

MACON BLANC VILL : PINOT BLANC

CHICKEN BREAST WITH CRABMEAT STUFFING

Preparation Time: 1 hour
Cooking Time: 30 minutes (on BBQ grill)*
Serves: 6

Margo Hall
Winji

6 boneless chicken breasts
1 (6½ oz.) can lump crabmeat, drained
1 cup herb seasoned stuffing mix
¼ cup chopped green pepper
1 small onion, chopped
2 - 3 stalks celery, chopped

2 Tblsp. butter
1 (10½ oz.) can cream of mushroom soup
1/3 cup white wine
2 tsp. Worcestershire sauce
1 tsp. dry mustard
1 Tblsp. lemon juice

Saute pepper, onion, and celery in butter. Add crab, stuffing mix, ½ can soup, 2 Tblsp. white wine, lemon juice, mustard, Worcestershire sauce. Fill chicken breast with stuffing mixture, skewer, or sew closed. Broil over hot coals for 30 minutes turning frequently. Combine the rest of the soup and wine, and pour over breast last 10 minutes. Can also be dusted with flour and paprika, and baked in 350° oven for 1 hour.

MENU:

FIVE MINUTE SLAW p. 72

. . .

CHICKEN BREAST WITH CRABMEAT STUFFING p. 155
WILD RICE
STEAMED ASPARAGUS

. . .

PINEAPPLE CHOCOLATE FONDUE p. 246

. . .

MUSCADET : RIESLING DRY

HENS WITH CHINESE BASTING SAUCE

Preparation Time: 15 minutes
Marinating Time: overnight
Cooking Time: 1 hour
Serves: 4

Margo Ann Muckey
Tuff

4 Cornish hens
¼ cup soy sauce
2 Tblsp. honey

2 Tblsp. cider vinegar
½ tsp. grated fresh ginger
½ tsp. minced garlic

Preheat oven to 350° F. Place hens in a large bowl that holds snugly. Combine remaining ingredients in blender and puree. Pour over hens, cover, and refrigerate overnight. Drain, reserve sauce, and roast at 350°F. for 1 hour. After hens have cooked 20 minutes, pour sauce over, and continue to roast basting every 20 minutes.

MENU:

CREAMY TOPPED SCALLOPS p. 74

. . .

HENS WITH CHINESE BASTING SAUCE p.156
SNOW PEAS AND TOMATOES p. 217

. . .

CHOCOLATE MOUSSE p. 254

. . .

POUILLY FUME : PINOT BLANC

FLAMBE'D CORNISH HENS A L' ORANGE

Preparation Time: 15 minutes　　　　　　　　　*Sharon Strong*
Cooking Time: 1½ hours　　　　　　　　　　　　*Promises*
Serves: 4 - 6

4 Cornish game hens
Salt and pepper
½ cup chicken stock
2 Tblsp. butter
¼ cup Grand Marnier
¼ cup dry white wine
1½ Tblsp. 151 rum

2 oranges
1 lemon
1 cup orange marmalade
3 Tblsp. butter
Garnish: twisted orange slices,
　　　　parsley sprigs, orange flowers

Preheat the oven to 350°F. Rub the inside cavity and exterior of hens with salt and pepper. Tie legs with utility string so their legs are together when served (be sure to remove at end of roasting time). Place foil around the feet, so that they don't burn. Drizzle butter over the hens before placing in the oven. Baste occasionally for 1¼ hours or until nearly done. 15 minutes before taking out, use a pastry brush, and lightly coat hens with ¼ cup marmalade, heated. This gives a wonderful golden brown color. While the hens are cooking, peel 1 orange and the lemon. Cut the peels into thin strips, and boil for about 5 minutes. Drain. Melt the remaining marmalade in pan. Add orange and lemon peel, the juice of the peels, stock, Grand Marnier, and a bit of salt. Boil gently to reduce. After roasting, set the hens on a warm platter. Remove the fat from the roasting pan, and deglaze the pan with the white wine, scraping up the brown bits at the bottom. Add this to the hot orange sauce, and boil for about 5 minutes. Arrange the hens on a platter. Slice 1 orange with the rind to obtain 2 thick slices, cut each in half. Twist each ½ orange slice, and put on top of each hen. Cut an orange flower, and place in the middle of the platter with a sprig of parsley in the center. Serve rice between the hens and the flower. Put the hot orange sauce in a server, and add 1½ Tblsp. rum, gently. Meanwhile, have the hens already served on table before you flambe. *Your guests will rave.*

MENU:

TOMATO JUICE COCKTAIL
. . .
FLAMBE'D CORNISH HENS A L'ORANGE p. 157
SHREDDED ZUCCHINI p. 227
"WILD" RICE p. 235
. . .
EBONY AND IVORY CHEESECAKE p. 243
. . .
ST. VERAN : PINOT CHARDONNAY

MARINATED ROCK CORNISH HENS

Preparation Time: 15 minutes
Marinating Time: overnight
Cooking Time: 45 minutes
Serves: 4 - 6

Jan Robinson
Vanity

4 small Rock Cornish hens, split down breast and flattened

MARINADE:
1 cup soy sauce
Peel of 1 orange
½ tsp. ginger root, chopped
2 cloves garlic
½ tsp. ground coriander
Black pepper, freshly ground
1 small bay leaf
2 Tblsp. honey

SAUCE:
2 tsp. olive oil
1 tsp. minced garlic
1 tsp. minced ginger root
1 Tblsp. minced scallions
¼ tsp. red pepper, crushed
1 Tblsp. soy sauce
1 tsp. vinegar
1½ Tblsp. brown sugar
1 Tblsp. water
1 Tblsp. sesame oil
Garnish: watercress

Flatten hens and combine marinade ingredients in blender or food processor. Blend until smooth. Place hens, skin side down, on 2 baking pans and pour marinade over them. Refrigerate overnight. Remove 1 hour before preparation. Preheat oven to 450°F. Place baking sheets with hens in oven and bake 35 to 40 minutes. Baste often with marinade using bulb baster. To make sauce, heat olive oil in small saucepan over medium-low heat. Stir in minced garlic, ginger root, and scallions; add crushed red pepper. Cook 2 minutes. Add soy sauce, vinegar, brown sugar, and water. Cook, stirring 1 minute. Strain sauce and add sesame oil. Sauce will thicken as it sits. Just before serving, use pastry brush to coat hens with sauce. *Leftover suggestion: Cold hens come in handy for next day's picnic lunch ashore, so you may want to bake an extra couple of hens. Combine the cold meat with slivers of Belgian endive and cherry tomatoes, and toss with a tart, lemony dressing: half olive oil, half lemon juice, and have an easy day on the beach.*

MENU:

SQUID SAUTEED IN GARLIC p. 74
• • •
MARINATED ROCK CORNISH HENS p. 158
GREEN HERBED RICE p. 231
TOMATO & CUKE SALAD p. 68
• • •
BAKED ALASKA p. 261
• • •
ST. VERAN : PINOT CHARDONNAY

TURKEY TREAT

Preparation Time: 15 minutes   *Alison Briscoe*
Cooking Time: 2½ hours   *Ovation*
Serves: 6

1 lb. sliced turkey (white meat)   1 tsp. tarragon
1 onion, sliced   ½ tsp. marjoram
¾ lb. carrots, sliced   1½ tsp. lemon juice
1 Tblsp. oil   1 Tblsp. cornstarch
1 (8 oz.) can tomatoes   1 Tblsp. milk
1 Tblsp. tomato puree   Salt and pepper
1½ cups chicken stock

Preheat oven to 350°F. Saute onion until golden. Add turkey, and saute until brown. Transfer to covered casserole dish. Put carrots over meat and onion. Bring stock to a boil, and add tomatoes, puree, and seasonings. Pour into casserole, and bake for 2½ hours at 350°F. Mix cornstarch with milk and add lemon juice. Add to casserole 15 minutes prior to serving.

MENU:

SHRIMP COCKTAIL

. . .

TURKEY TREAT p. 159
SESAME BROCCOLI p. 210
ZUCCHINI NOODLE CASSEROLE p. 228

. . .

PINEAPPLE UPSIDE DOWN CAKE p. 240

. . .

PULIGNY MONTRACHET : CHARDONNAY

WILDHERN DUCK

Preparation Time: 30 minutes
Cooking Time: 30 minutes
Serves: 8

Sue Griffin
Endless Summer I

2 ducks
2 carrots
1 large onion
3 celery stalks
½ lb. mushrooms

Parsley
1 (28 oz.) can whole tomatoes
Seasonings
Basil

Quarter the ducks, and boil carcasses for stock and reduce. Quickly
fry meat in a Dutch oven to seal it. Dice vegetables and add. Season,
add tomatoes and stock to just cover the meat. Cook for 20 minutes,
and allow to settle. Remove the fat. Put the meat onto a serving dish.
Add the mushrooms to sauce, thicken, pour over duck, and sprinkle
with parsley.

MENU:

CANE GARDEN CREPES p. 72

. . .

WILDHERN DUCK p. 160
JACKET POTATOES
STEAMED VEGETABLES

. . .

WHITE CHOCOLATE MOUSSE p. 254

. . .

CHAT-DU-DUKE RED : CABERNET SAUVIGNON

CHICKEN ROLLS

Preparation Time: 15 minutes   *Didgie Belschner*
Cooking Time: 15 minutes   *Tequila*
Serves: 4

4 chicken breasts, boned	Salt and pepper
and skinned	Garlic, chopped and crushed
Progresso Herbed bread crumbs	Toothpicks
Butter	Garnish: orange slices, parsley

Cut breasts down the middle so you have 8 pieces. Pound flat with a mallet. Mix the butter, garlic, salt, and pepper together, and spread on chicken. Roll up, and secure with toothpicks, 2 in each. Roll in bread-crumbs, and saute in butter until browned. *Garnish with orange slices, twisted, and parsley.*

MENU:

HORIATIKI p. 66

. . .

CHICKEN ROLLS p. 161
LEMON RICE
BROCCOLI WITH WALNUT BUTTER p. 210

. . .

PINEAPPLE SURPRISE p. 251

. . .

ENTREE DEUX MENS : SAUVIGNON BLANC

CHICKEN CABBAGE CASSEROLE

Preparation Time: 25 minutes
Cooking Time: 80 minutes
Serves: 4

Jacqui Hoop
Mary Denise

1 cup medium onion, coarsely
   chopped
1 large apple, diced
1 medium red cabbage,
   coarsely chopped
¼ cup butter, melted

½ bottle dark beer
3 lb. chicken, quartered
½ tsp. cumin
½ tsp. basil
Salt and pepper to taste
¼ cup parsley, chopped

Preheat oven to 375°F. Melt the butter in a large skillet. Add onions, apple, and saute on gentle heat for 10 minutes. Add cabbage. Toss. Add beer. Cover and let simmer for 10 minutes. Transfer to a 3 inch deep baking dish. Place chicken quarters on top. Sprinkle seasonings on top. Cover with foil, and bake for 30 minutes. Uncover and continue to bake 30 minutes more, all at 375°F. Add remaining beer as necessary to keep moist. On serving dish, place chicken in center, and place cabbage around using a slotted spoon. Sprinkle parsley on top. Serve extra sauce on side.

MENU:

WALNUT SPAGHETTI p. 230

. . .

CHICKEN CABBAGE CASSEROLE p. 162

. . .

ISLAND FRUIT SALAD p. 70

. . .

MACON BLANC VILLAGE : PINOT BLANC

SCHEZUAN STIR-FRY

Preparation Time: 45 minutes   *Norma Trease*
Cooking Time: 15 minutes   *Caroline*
Serves: 6

½ lb. chicken, pork, or beef,
   cut in strips
4 Tblsp. flour
Lots of pepper
1 head broccoli, florets
½ head red and/or green cabbage
1 cup snow peas, stringed
2 - 3 carrots, cut diagonally

2 tomatoes, quartered
1 bunch scallions, sliced (or best
   fresh vetetables available)
½ tsp. hot dried peppers
Peanut oil, Hot!
½ cup ketchup
1 Tblsp. fresh ginger
1 tsp. curry powder

Mix meat with 4 Tblsp. flour, and lots of pepper. Brown in a large pan
or wok with peanut oil and hot oil, as needed. Add carrots and broccoli. After 2 - 3 minutes, add sauce of ½ cup ketchup, 1 Tblsp. fresh
ginger, 1 tsp. hot oil, 1 tsp. curry powder, ½ tsp. hot dried peppers,
to taste. Add other vegetables, cover, and steam until cabbage is limp
(not too limp!). Stir together, and serve with hot sauce on the side.

MENU:

EGG DROP SOUP

. . .

SCHEZUAN STIR-FRY p. 163
MIXED, MASHED, SWEET WHITE POTATOES (with skins)

. . .

VANILLA ICE CREAM
and
FORTUNE COOKIES

. . .

COTE DU RHONE (Red or White) : ZINFANDEL (Red or White)

CHICKEN CHOW MEIN

Preparation Time: 15 minutes   *Marilyn Stenberg*
Cooking Time: 20 minutes   *Champagne*
Serves: 6

10 oz. linguini roll

1 medium onion

6 oz. mushrooms

8 oz. small broccoli

1 sweet red pepper

5 boned chicken legs

1 chicken bouillon cube

1 ½ cups water

MARINADE:

5 Tblsp. dry sherry

5 Tblsp. light soy sauce

5 tsp. cornstarch

Slice chicken into bite-size slices, and mix well with marinade of soy sauce, sherry, and cornstarch. Cook linguini according to directions. Meanwhile, roughly chop the onion, pepper, and mushrooms. Quickly stir-fry along with the broccoli (a skillet will do if no wok). Add to linguini (warm). Stir-fry chicken until thoroughly cooked. Add water and bouillon cube stirring constantly. A nice sauce will result from the marinade. Mix with linguini and vegetables, making sure the dish is thoroughly warmed without being overcooked.

MENU:

COTTAGE CHEESE - PEAR SALAD

. . .

CHICKEN CHOW MEIN p. 164
FLUFFY WHITE RICE

. . .

KIWI-BANANA TARTLETS p. 268

. . .

BEAUJOLAIS BLANC : PINOT BLANC

*SEAFOOD

NOTES

FISH FILLETS IN CUCUMBER SAUCE

Preparation Time: 10 - 15 minutes　　　　　*Shirley Dorn Burroughs*
Cooking Time: 40 minutes (18 - 20 minutes　　　　　　　　*Odyssey*
Serves: 4　　　　　　　*in microwave)*

2 lbs. frozen fish fillets (4-5 fillets)　1 (10¾ oz.) can condensed cream
　I use King or Dolphin, thawed　　　of mushroom soup
1 medium cucumber, unpeeled　　1/3 cup sour cream
　and chopped　　　　　　　1 medium tomato, chopped
½ tsp. dill weed　　　　　　2 Tblsp. butter or margarine, melted
2 Tblsp. butter or margarine　　½ tsp. salt

Preheat oven to 350°F. Combine cucumber, dill weed, and 2 Tblsp. butter in saucepan. Heat until butter is melted. Stir in soup, sour cream, and tomato and set aside. Combine melted butter and salt in 2 quart glass baking dish. Arrange fish with thick edges toward outside of the dish. Pour sauce over the fish. If lucky enough to have a microwave, cover with plastic wrap, and microwave on roast for 18 - 20 minutes. If using an oven, cover with foil, and bake for 30 - 40 minutes at 350° until fish flakes easily. Let stand for 5 minutes before serving. *Very delicious!*

MENU:

"EASY STARTER" SHERRIED GRAPEFRUIT p. 70

. . .

FISH FILLETS IN CUCUMBER SAUCE p. 167
RICE

. . .

CHEESECAKE p. 244

. . .

WHITE BORDEAUX : SAUVIGNON BLANC

FILLETS A LA MOUTARDE

Preparation Time: 5 minutes
Cooking Time: 15 minutes
Serves: 8

Cindy Harhen
Impervious Cover

3 lbs. Turbot, Flounder, or
   Sole fillets
½ cup mayonnaise
4 Tblsp. imported mustard
   (the more grain the better)

3 tsp. finely chopped dill, fresh
   or dried
8 lemon wedges
Parsley
Garnish: lemon & parsley

Preheat oven to 350°F. Place fillets in a baking dish, skin side down.
Sprinkle with salt and pepper. Blend the mayonnaise, mustard, and dill.
Brush it evenly over the fillets. Place the fillets in the oven, and bake
for about 15 minutes or until meat flakes when checked with a fork.
Garnish with lemon and parsley. *One of my easiest and best received
dishes.*

MENU:

GRAPEFRUIT SECTIONS

· · ·

FILLETS A LA MOUTARDE p. 168
PARSLEY RICE
BROCCOLI WITH LEMON BUTTER

· · ·

LEMMON BARS p. 244

· · ·

WHITE COTE DU RHONE : CHARDONNAY

POACHED FISH

Preparation Time: 5 minutes
Cooking Time: 20 minutes
Serves: 4

Jacklyn Johnson Rabinowitz
Almost Heaven

4 fillets or steaks
   (Snapper, Grouper, Dorado)
1 cup dry white wine
2 Tblsp. butter plus 1 Tblsp.

1 Tblsp. fresh parsley
1 tsp. dried chives
1 tsp. Vegit (no salt seasoning)
Garnish: 1 orange, lemon and
   lime, sliced

Put butter and wine in large heavy skillet. Cover and boil to reduce to 1/3 cup. Reduce flame to low, and add herbs and fillets, skin side down. Add 1 Tblsp. butter and enough water to create ½ inch liquid. Cover tightly and cook over low heat (approximately 8 - 12 minutes depending on the thickness of fish) until fish is slightly underdone (flesh is almost opaque, and flakes to a fork). Remove from heat and let sit for a few moments. Serve with liquid poured over fish. *Garnish with overlapping slices of citrus.*

MENU:

DATE SLAW p. 73

. . .

POACHED FISH p. 169
HOT WHITE RICE
SHREDDED ZUCCHINI p. 227

. . .

STRAWBERRY ICE p. 263

. . .

ENTRE DEUX MERS : FUME BLANC

STUFFED FISH FILLETS

Preparation Time: 30 minutes
Cooking Time: 35 minutes
Serves: 6

Laura Greces
Mistral

¼ cup chopped onion
¼ cup butter
1 (3 oz.) can mushrooms, drain
    and reserve liquid
1 (7½ oz.) can crabmeat
½ cup breadcrumbs
2 Tblsp. chopped parsley
½ tsp. salt
Pepper

6 thin fish fillets (Flounder,
    Snapper, etc.)
3 Tblsp. butter
3 Tblsp. flour
¼ tsp salt
Milk
1/3 cup dry white wine
4 oz. shredded Swiss cheese
Paprika

In skillet, cook onion in ¼ cup butter until tender. Stir in mushrooms, crab, breadcrumbs, parsley, salt, and pepper. Spoon mixture onto fillets. Roll fillets, secure with toothpicks, and place seam side down in baking pan. In saucepan, melt 3 Tblsp. butter. Blend flour and ¼ tsp. salt. Add enough milk to mushroom liquid to make 1½ cups. Add with wine to saucepan. Cook and stir until mixture thickens and bubbles. Pour over fillets. Bake at 400° for 25 minutes. Sprinkle with cheese and paprika. Return to oven, and bake for 10 minutes longer, or until fish flakes easily with fork.

MENU:

LETTUCE AND TOMATO
. . .
STUFFED FISH FILLETS p. 170
LONG GRAIN AND WILD RICE
SAUTEED ZUCCHINI
. . .
SHERBET
. . .
MUSCADET : PINOT BLANC

FLOUNDER ROLL-UPS

Preparation Time: 10 minutes　　　　　　　*Barbie Haworth*
Cooking Time: 25 minutes　　　　　　　　　*Ann-Marie II*
Serves: 6

½ cup butter
¼ cup fresh parsley, minced
1 medium fresh tomato, chopped
½ cup celery, minced
2 Tblsp. scallions, chopped
¼ cup blue cheese, crumbled

3 cups Italian breadcrumbs
1 egg, well beaten
2 Tblsp. white wine
½ tsp. salt
1½ lbs. Flounder fillets
1 lemon, juice only

Preheat oven to 350° F. In a skillet, melt ¼ cup butter. Saute parsley, tomato, celery, and scallions for 5 minutes. Remove from heat. Stir in blue cheese. Add crumbs, egg, wine, and salt. Mix well. On waxed paper, lay out 6 fillets, spread mixture on top, roll up each fillet, and fasten with toothpicks. Butter a baking dish, and place fish in pan. In the same skillet, melt ¼ cup butter, and add lemon juice. Pour over fish. Bake in oven until fish flakes; about 20 minutes.

MENU:

ARTICHOKE SURPRISE p. 75

. . .

FLOUNDER ROLL-UPS p. 171
BROCCOLI SPEARS
RISOTTO MILANESE p. 232

. . .

BANANA POUNDS p. 249

. . .

MOUITRE BORDEAUX : CABERNET BLANC

FISH BAKED IN FOIL

Preparation Time: 15 minutes
Cooking Time: 15 minutes
Serves: 4

Gunilla Lundgren
Bambi

1½ lbs. fish fillets (Trout, Flounder or Sole)
Salt
Juice from 1 lemon
2 tomatoes, peeled and cut in cubes

4 Tblsp. fresh chopped dill or 2 tsp. dry dill weed
4 tsp. butter
Garnish with sprigs of dill or parsley and lemon wedges

Preheat oven to 500° F. Place fish on 4 pieces of buttered foil. Salt the fish and sprinkle with lemon juice. Mix tomatoes and dill, and put on top of fish. Top with butter. Seal foil. Place packets sealed side up in a shallow baking pan. Bake at 500° for about 15 minutes or until the fish flakes. Give everybody a packet garnished with dill or parsley and lemon.

MENU:

CONSOMME WITH SHERRY

. . .

TOSSED GREEN SALAD
FISH BAKED IN FOIL p. 172

. . .

MANGOES AU GRATIN p. 250

. . .

ENTRE DEUX MERS : ZINFANDEL BLANC

GROUPER BONNE FEMME

Preparation Time: 20 minutes
Cooking Time: 20 minutes
Serves: 6

Sarah Sheets
Royono

8 oz. mushrooms, sliced
¼ cup green onion, chopped
2 Tblsp. butter
6 Grouper fillets
¾ cup dry white wine
1 Tblsp. lemon juice

2 Tblsp. butter
2 Tblsp. flour
½ cup heavy cream
¼ cup grated Swiss cheese
Salt and pepper to taste
Garnish: twisted lemon slice, parley

Melt 2 Tblsp. butter in a 10 inch skillet. Saute mushrooms and onions until tender. Remove. Add grouper to skillet with wine, lemon juice, and water to cover. Cook until fish flakes easily. Remove fish to baking pan saving liquid. Melt 2 Tblsp. butter in skillet, and stir in flour. Remove from heat, and stir in heavy cream and one cup of reserved liquid. Heat to boiling, stirring constantly. Add mushrooms, onions, salt, and pepper. Spoon over fish. Sprinkle with cheese. Broil in oven about 3 minutes until cheese melts. *Garnish with twisted lemon slice and parsley.*

MENU:

JELLIED CONSUMME WITH CAVIAR p. 89

• • •

GROUPER BONNE FEMME p. 173
VEGETABLE MELANGE
POTATO BALLS

• • •

KIWI - BANANA TARTLETS p. 268

• • •

MACON BLANC VILLAGES : CHARDONNAY

GROUPER RUSSIAN STYLE

Preparation Time: 30 minutes
Cooking Time: 30 minutes
Serves: 6

Jean Thayer
Finesse 60

6 Grouper fillets
1 lb. medium shrimp, shelled
    and deveined
½ pint heavy cream
8 Tblsp. butter
¼ cup minced shallots
1 cup dry white wine
2 oz. Black Icelandic Caviar

FISH VELOUTE:
2 Tblsp. butter
2 Tblsp. flour
1 cup bottled clam juice
Salt, pepper to taste

Prepare fish veloute - in small sauce pan, melt butter, add flour, blending well. Whisk in bottled clam juice, stirring constantly. Cook until slightly thickened. Set aside for later use.

Preheat oven to 350° F. In an ovenproof skillet, melt 4 Tblsp. butter and lightly saute shallots. Add fillets and cook 1 minute on each side. Pour in wine, cover and bake in oven 10 to 15 minutes until done and fish flakes. While fish is baking, heat cream in a medium sized skillet and poach shrimp. Remove shrimp with slotted spoon and continue heating cream until slightly thickened. Add veloute to cream along with remaining 4 Tblsp. butter and simmer sauce. *To serve, top each fillet with sauce, reserved shrimp and a heaping teaspoon of caviar.*

MENU:

AVOCADO FROSTED CAULIFLOWER SALAD p. 66

. . .

GROUPER RUSSIAN STYLE p. 174
YELLOW RICE

. . .

BANANAS GOMEZ p. 250

. . .

SANCERRE BLANC : PINOT CHARDONNAY

DOLPHIN POLYNESIAN

Preparation Time: 30 minutes
Cooking Time: 40 minutes
Serves: 4

Mardy Array
Emerald Lady

2 large Dolphin fillets
Salt and pepper
1 cup cooked rice
1 cup seasoned breadcrumbs
1 cup crushed pineapple, drained
2 Tblsp. blanched almonds

1/8 tsp. tarragon
1/8 tsp. dill
1/8 tsp. cayenne
2 Tblsp. melted butter
2 slices bacon, halved crosswise

Preheat oven to 350° F. Season fillets with salt and pepper. Place 1 fillet in buttered baking dish. Combine cooked rice, breadcrumbs, drained pineapple, almonds, and seasonings. Spoon on fillet in dish pressing stuffing to make compact. Top with second fillet. Press sides of fillet together, and secure with toothpicks if necessary. Sprinkle with additional breadcrumbs, a light dusting of cayenne, and lay bacon strips diagonally over top. Bake at 350° for 40 minutes.

MENU:

LEAFY GREEN SALAD

. . .

DOLPHIN POLYNESIAN p. 175
BREADFRUIT CHIPS p. 212

. . .

HELIOS BROWNIES p. 248

. . .

ST. VERAN : CHARDONNAY

DOLPHIN ON THE GRILL

Preparation Time: 5 minutes   *Kimberly Foote*
Cooking Time: 30 minutes (on BBQ grill)   *Oklahoma Crude II*
Serves: 6

6 fillet steaks Dolphin   2 tomatoes, sliced
2 medium onions, sliced in rings   1 cup Italian dressing
2 limes, sliced   Garnish: paprika and parsley leaves

Place Dolphin pieces in foil. Pour small amount of salad dressing over, enough to cover (this is the key that keeps the fish from drying out). Place slice of lime, onions, and tomato on top. Wrap in foil, each piece separately. Place on grill for 15 minutes on each side. *To serve, sprinkle with paprika and parsley leaves on each piece.*

MENU:

NATIVE PUMPKIN SOUP p. 80

. . .

DOLPHIN ON THE GRILL p. 176
CHRISTOPHENE CASSEROLE
PEAS AND ONIONS

. .

CHOCOLATE BANANA PIE p. 264

. . .

BOURGOGNE ALIGOTE : PINOT CHARDONNAY

FILLET OF SOLE STUFFED WITH CRABMEAT

Preparation Time: 20 minutes
Cooking Time: 45 minutes
Serves: 6

Jan Stoughton
Lady Columbo

4 fillets of Sole (or any other
    white fish)
½ cup Ritz crackers, crushed
2 - 3 Tblsp. Miracle Whip
2 cups crabmeat

White pepper
Butter
Lemon juice
Salt and pepper
Paprika

Preheat oven to 350° F. Smash up crisp Ritz crackers or any other buttery crackers. Add 2 - 3 Tblsp. of Miracle Whip. Do not make it with mayonnaise. Add crabmeat. Mix well. Adjust proportions until you have nice semi-firm stuffing. Add white pepper to taste. Place two slices of fish in a shallow dish or pan. Coat lightly in butter and lemon juice, salt and pepper. Place crabmeat stuffing on top of first slices. Place second piece of fish on top. Double the amount of butter, lemon juice, and salt and pepper to top. Fold in sides of fish to keep juices in. Sprinkle with paprika. Bake at 350° F. Cook until fish is flaky and done. Best test for readiness is flakiness and smell. Extra crabmeat stuffing can be used as an appetizer. Add more Miracle Whip, lemon juice, and white pepper. Place on Ritz crackers and broil for 2 - 3 minutes.

MENU:

SPINACH SALAD

. . .

FILLET OF SOLE STUFFED WITH CRABMEAT p. 177
STEAMED BROCCOLI

. . .

MINT CHOCOLATE CHIP CAKE p. 240

. . .

WHITE BORDEAUX : FUME BLANC

SOLE VERONIQUE

Preparation Time: 20 minutes   *Annie Scholl*
Cooking Time: 20 minutes   *Bon Vivant*
Serves: 6 - 8

2 lbs. Sole	Butter
Flour	2 cups green grapes
Salt	½ pint heavy cream
Nutmeg	Garnish: lemon slices, parsley

Lightly flour and salt each fillet, and sprinkle generously with nutmeg.
Saute each fillet in butter, and keep warm until all are cooked. Saute
grapes in drippings until opaque. Stir in heavy cream and heat
thoroughly. Pour cream and grape mixture over cooked fillets which
you have arranged on a warm platter. Garnish with lemon slices and
parsley. *This recipe never fails to evoke raves from our guests.*

MENU:

ASPARAGUS LEEK BISQUE p. 90

. . .

SOLE VERONIQUE p. 178
BOILED NEW POTATOES

. . .

GRAND MARNIER CHOCOLATE COVERED PEARS p. 245

. . .

WHITE BORDEAUX : SAUVIGNON BLANC

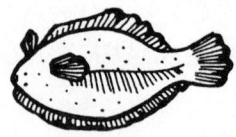

CUCUMBER SOLE

Preparation Time: 10 minutes   *Donna Jaggard*
Cooking Time: 10 - 12 minutes   *Thorobred*
Serves: 4

1 cup peeled, seeded, coarsely
    chopped cucumber
½ sliced green onion
¼ cup coarsely chopped celery
1 Tblsp. fresh parsley, chopped
1 tsp. dried dill, crumbled

1 cup dry white wine
4 - 6 oz. Sole fillets
1 cup whipping cream
2 tsp. prepared horseradish
Salt and pepper, to taste

Combine cucumber, green onion, celery, parsley, and dill in 12 inch skillet. Pour wine over. Set fish fillets atop vegetables. Cover and bring to a boil. Reduce heat, and simmer gently until fish is opaque, about 5 minutes. Transfer fish to heated serving platter, and keep warm. Add cream and horseradish to vegetable mixture. Season with salt and pepper.

MENU:

GREEN GARDEN SOUP p. 81

. . .

CUCUMBER SOLE p. 179
PARSLEY NEW POTATOES
SUNSHINE CARROTS p. 212

. . .

SUMMER PUDDING

. . .

GRAVES : ZINFANDEL BLANC

SALMON STEAKS

Preparation Time: 15 minutes
Marinating Time: 30 minutes
Cooking Time: 15 minutes
Serves: 4

Jan Robinson
Vanity

½ cup vegetable oil
2 Tblsp. lemon juice
2 cloves garlic, finely chopped
   and divided
4 (½ lb.) Salmon steaks,
   1 inch thick

1 cup crushed herb-seasoned
   stuffing
¼ cup grated Parmesan cheese
¼ cup fresh parsley, chopped
Garnish: lemon wedges,
   watercress

Preheat oven to 450° F. Combine oil, lemon juice, and half the chopped garlic. Place salmon steaks in a shallow pan, and pour marinade over steaks. Cover and marinate in the refrigerator for 30 minutes, turning once. Remove salmon from marinade reserving 2 Tblsp. of the marinade. Combine herb-seasoned stuffing, cheese, parsley, and remaining garlic. Dredge salmon in stuffing mixture. Place salmon in a greased 13 x 9 x 2 inch baking dish. Sprinkle reserved marinade over salmon, and bake at 450° for 15 minutes or until fish flakes easily. *Garnish with lemon wedges and watercress.*

MENU:

CHILLED CRISP GREENS

• • •

SALMON STEAKS p. 180
ASPARAGUS IN LEMON BUTTER p. 209
NEW BOILED POTATOES

• • •

ULTIMATE CHOCOLATE SEX CAKE p. 239

• • •

MONTRACHET : CHARDONNAY

RED SNAPPER IN PARCHMENT PAPER

Preparation Time: 20 minutes   *Dawn Drell*
Cooking Time: 15 minutes   *Helios*
Serves; 6

6 Snapper fillets
6 circles, 16 inches in diameter,
    of parchment paper
6 Tblsp. butter
Freshly ground black pepper
12 baby carrots

6 small onions
12 cherry tomatoes
3 baking potatoes, cut in 4ths
Sprigs of fresh dill
Thyme

Preheat the oven to 350° F. Butter each circle of paper, and place snapper fillets on one half. Sprinkle with fresh pepper. Arrange fresh vegetables and herbs over and around fish. Fold the paper over the fillet. Close halves by crimping and folding the edges. Bake on an ungreased cookie sheet for 15 minutes until paper is puffed. Serve closed.

MENU:

CUCUMBER SALAD p. 69

. . .

RED SNAPPER IN PARCHMENT PAPER p. 181
WILD RICE WITH MUSHROOMS

. . .

STRAWBERRY MOUSSE p. 255

. . .

POUILLY FUME : PINOT CHARDONNAY

POACHED OLD WIFE

Preparation Time: 15 minutes
Cooking Time: 30 minutes
Serves: 1

Nancy Wilkinson
Hooter

1 Old Wife (plate size)
2 lemon slices
¼ cup white wine
2 Tblsp. lemon juice

Onions
Green peppers
2 Tblsp. butter

Place the fish in foil. Add lemon slices, lemon juice, wine, and butter. Wrap tightly. Place over a hot grill for 15 minutes on each side, per fish. Fish is done when meat is easily lifted from bones. Served topped with sauteed sliced onions and green peppers.

MENU:

SUMMER SLAW p. 73

. . .

POACHED OLD WIFE p. 182
RICE WITH PEAS

. . .

SOUFFLE GRAND MARNIER p. 256

. . .

CHABLIS : PINOT CHARDONNAY

GRILLED TUNA

Preparation Time: 5 minutes
Marinating Time: 1 hour
Cooking Time: 15 - 20 minutes (on BBQ grill)
Serves: 6

Casey Miller
Fancy Free

6 fresh Tuna steaks
1 cup Teriyaki sauce*

1 clove garlic
Garnish: lemon wedges

* see "Ship to Shore" vol. I pg. 121

Marinate Tuna in Teriyaki and garlic 1 hour. Remove. Drain. Grill over medium coals 7 - 10 minutes each side. *Garnish with lemon wedges.*

MENU:

LEAF LETTUCE WITH POPPY SEED DRESSING

. . .

GRILLED TUNA p. 183
LONG GRAIN RICE
SAUTEED GREEN BEANS AND RED ONIONS

. . .

PEAR TART p. 267

. . .

WHITE BORDEAUX : FUME BLANC

SNAPPER CARIBBEAN STYLE

Preparation Time: 5 minutes
Marinating Time: 2 hours
Cooking Time: 30 minutes
Serves: 6

Jean Thayer
Finesse 60

6 Red Snapper fillets
1 tsp. salt
2 garlic cloves, crushed
¼ cup lime juice
2 Tblsp. olive oil
1 medium onion, thinly sliced
1 (28 oz.) and 1 (14 oz.) can plum
   tomatoes, drained and
   chopped

15 large pimento stuffed olives,
   halved
2 jalapeno chilles, seeded and
   minced
Dash of oregano and thyme
3 Bay leaves
Butter

Make a paste of the garlic and salt, rubbing the mixture into the fish fillets. Place fillets in a glass pan, add lime juice and marinate, covered, at room temperature for 2 hours. Turn fillets occasionally. 30 minutes before serving, heat oil in skillet and saute onion briefly. Add tomatoes, olives, chilles, oregano, thyme, and bay leaves. Simmer, uncovered, 10 minutes. Sauce may be made ahead of time and re-warmed in a smaller saucepan before serving. Remove bay leaves before serving. Over high heat, in a heavy skillet, melt 2 Tblsp. butter. When the butter sizzles, add drained fish fillets. Cook over high heat 4 minutes per side, depending upon the thickness of fillets. As fillets begin to flake, re-move, keep warm, and cook remaining fillets, adding more butter each time. *To serve, top fillets with tomato sauce.*

<u>MENU:</u>

GREEN SALAD

. . .

SNAPPER CARIBBEAN STYLE p. 184
RICE

. . .

CREPES A LA PECHE p. 260

. . .

WHITE COTE DU RHONE : JOHANNISBERG RIESLING

KINGFISH AU POIVRE

Preparation Time: 30 minutes   *Casey Miller*
Marinating Time: 30 minutes   *Fancy Free*
Cooking Time: 25 minutes
Serves: 6

6 fresh Kingfish steaks

1 lemon

Cayenne pepper

Freshly ground black pepper

"Old Bay" seafood seasoning

Salt

Mint flakes, dried

Rosemary leaves, broken

1 shallot, finely chopped

2 Tblsp. butter

Remaining juice of lemon

¼ cup white wine

½ cup chicken stock

Garnish: fresh mint and lemon
wedges

Pat fish dry. Lay steaks in a flat dish and squeeze a few drops of lemon
on each. Season each steak with a generous amount of cayenne and
black pepper. Then a reasonable amount of the next 4 seasonings. Press
finger atop each so seasoning adheres. Turn. Repeat. Let sit for 30
minutes to an hour. High heat a heavy aluminum skillet, large enough
to fit steaks comfortably. Cook steaks 7 - 10 minutes or until seared
brown on each side. Remove to serving plate. Add shallots and butter.
Cook 5 minutes. Keep high heat and add lemon, white wine, and chick-
en stock. Scraping up all brown bits, reduce to half and spoon over
Kingfish. Garnish with fresh mint and lemon wedges. *NOTE: This is
truly a trial and error recipe for knowing how much spice to use. Be
sure to know your guests' degree of spicy hotness first, especially if
your cayenne is new!*

MENU:

HONEYDEW MELON

. . .

KINGFISH AU POIVRE p. 185
HERBED SPINACH p. 219
SWEET AND SOUR CARROTS p. 214

. . .

JAN'S KEY LIME PIE p. 262

. . .

WHITE BORDEAUX : SAUVIGNON BLANC

HALIBUT WITH RASPBERRY VINEGAR

Preparation Time: 20 minutes
Cooking Time: 10 minutes
Serves: 2 - 3

Pamela McMichael
Bon Harbor

2 lbs. Halibut
4 medium leeks
5 carrots
5 stalks celery

SAUCE:
½ cup raspberry vinegar
5 oz. shallots, finely minced
Salt and pepper, to taste
4 oz. heavy cream
12 oz. butter

Preheat oven to 350° F. Cut leeks, carrots, and celery into julienne strips. Cook them in butter for a short period of time allowing them to remain crunchy. Cook shallots with raspberry vinegar until reduced to 1 Tblsp. Season with salt and pepper. Add the heavy cream and stir. Add butter gradually over low heat until blended. Place halibut in oven with some of the julienned vegetables, and cook for 10 minutes at 350°. Remove from oven, and cover the fish and vegetables with the raspberry butter sauce. *An elegant and tasty dish.*

MENU:

SLICED AVOCADO

. . .

HALIBUT WITH RASPBERRY VINEGAR p. 186
BAKED POTATOES

. . .

CHOCOLATE TOFFEE DESSERT p. 247

. . .

ST. VERAN : FUME BLANC

FISH GUADELOUPE

Preparation Time: 10 minutes   *Wendy Smith*
Cooking Time: 30 minutes   *Stampede*
Serves: 6

3 Tblsp. butter
1 medium onion, chopped
¼ cup light rum
¼ lb. mushrooms
1½ lbs. fish (white meat)
Salt and pepper, to taste
2 Tblsp. olive oil

1 clove garlic, crushed
2 cups tomatoes, peeled and
    diced
½ cup dry white wine
1 tsp. curry powder
Juice of 1 lemon

Heat butter and oil. Simmer onions and garlic. Add fish in large chunks, and brown lightly. Spoon rum over fish and flame. When flame dies out, add peeled and diced tomatoes, mushrooms, ½ of the lemon juice, and the wine. Season. Cover and simmer for 15 minutes or until fish is cooked. Dilute curry powder with remaining lemon juice, and add to fish.

MENU:

GREEN SALAD

. . .

FISH GUADELOUPE p. 187
WHITE RICE
PETIT POIS

. . .

SOUFFLE DANNON p. 256

. . .

WHITE BORDEAUX : ZINFANDEL BLANC

CANDLELIGHT BAKED STUFFED SHRIMP

Preparation Time: 30 minutes
Cooking Time: 20 minutes
Serves: 6

Cindy Harhen
Impervious Cover

24 large shrimp (12 to a lb. size)
   uncooked

MORNAY SAUCE: (makes
   1½ cups)
1 Tblsp. grated Swiss cheese
1 Tblsp. grated Parmesan cheese
1 cup medium cream sauce
2 Tblsp. butter
Dash cayenne pepper

STUFFING:
4 cups bread crumbs
½ cup chopped onions
¾ lb. butter (12 oz.)
¼ cup sherry wine
½ cup chopped crab meat
1 clove chopped garlic
4 Tblsp. paprika
Garnish: parsley and lemon wedges
   Butter for dipping

Preheat oven to 400° F. Begin by making Mornay Sauce. Add the grated cheeses to the medium cream sauce enriched with 2 Tblsp. butter and dash of cayenne. Set aside. Mix all stuffing ingredients together. Then remove shrimp from shells, leaving tail section. With a small paring knife, cut from leg (bottom) side toward back. Do not cut all the way through. This is called butterfly. Devein, and wash under cold running water. On a buttered cookie sheet, lay shrimp on its back. Spread butterfly wide, and place about 3 Tblsp. of stuffing over each shrimp. Put 1 Tblsp. Mornay Sauce on each shrimp. When all shrimp are stuffed and marked with sauce, cover with foil, and bake 12 - 15 minutes in 400° oven. Remove foil, and brown 2 - 3 minutes. *Garnish and serve with melted butter.*

MENU:

PEARS IN BLUE CHEESE DRESSING p. 71

· · ·

CANDLELIGHT BAKED STUFFED SHRIMP p. 188
BAKED POTATO
PEAS

· · ·

SHERBET

· · ·

ENTRE DEUX MERS : CABERNET BLANC

SHRIMP SCAMPI SENSATION

Preparation Time: 15 minutes   *Alison Briscoe*
Cooking Time: 10 minutes   *Ovation*
Serves: 8

4 lbs. jumbo shrimp, shelled   SAUCE:
1 cup fresh bread crumbs   4 scallions
4 oz. melted butter   ¾ lb. butter (12 oz.)
                                     1 clove garlic
                                     1 Tblsp. Worcestershire sauce
                                     ¾ cup Dijon mustard
                                     ¾ cup cream sherry
                                     1 cup lemon juice
                                     Salt

Sauce: chop the scallions finely, and press garlic. Add Worcestershire sauce, lemon juice, and sherry. Mix the butter with the mustard until soft and smooth. Add to the rest of the sauce. Boil for 5 minutes, stirring constantly.

Shrimp: split down the middle, and arrange on a baking tray. Brush with butter, and sprinkle with bread crumbs. Broil 5 minutes. Arrange on a platter and pour the sauce over. *This sauce is also excellent over chicken breasts and all fish.*

MENU:

AVOCADO OCCASION p. 87

. . .

SHRIMP SCAMPI SENSATION p. 189
RICE CASSEROLE OVATION p. 228
SCRUMPTIOUS SQUASH p. 226

. . .

CREAMY COCONUT PIE p. 264

. . .

WHITE GRAVES : DRY SAUVIGNON

SHRIMP PARMAGINIA

Preparation Time: 15 minutes　　　　　　　　　*Casey Miller*
Cooking Time: 10 minutes　　　　　　　　　　*Fancy Free*
Serves: 6

5 or 6 large shrimp per person　　2 Tblsp. chopped fresh sweet basil
1½ cups tomato sauce, preferably　½ cup reserved hot tomato sauce
　　homemade　　　　　　　　　Grated Romano cheese
12 oz. good quality Provolone
　　cheese

Preheat oven to 350° F. Peel, devein butterfly fish. Lay flat on a large
sheet pan careful not to crowd. Top each shrimp with 1 Tblsp. tomato
sauce and a slice of Provolone. Bake 10 minutes at 350° or until pink.
Top each shrimp with a teaspoon of reserved tomato sauce, a sprinkle
of basil and a dash of grated Romano.

MENU:

CAESAR SALAD

. . .

SHRIMP PARMIGINIA p. 190
FETTUCCINI ALFREDO p. 230
GARLIC BREAD

. . .

NUTTY CYN! p. 247

. . .

MUSCADET : CHARDONNAY

MICHAEL'S SHRIMP POMEROY

Preparation Time: 20 minutes
Cooking Time: 12 - 15 minutes
Serves: 4

Pat Rowley
Calypso

1 lb. shrimp, peeled and
    deveined
4 Tblsp. butter
1 tsp. dill
1 fresh clove garlic, chopped

Dash oregano
2 oz. Brandy
½ pint heavy cream
Salt and pepper, to taste

Saute shrimp in butter. Add remaining ingredients. Cook on medium heat for about 7 - 10 minutes.

MENU:

LEAFY GREEN SALAD
. . .
MICHAEL'S SHRIMP POMEROY p. 191
SESAME BROCCOLI p. 210
. . .
LEMON SYLLABUB p. 252
. . .
WHITE GRAVES : FUME BLANC

STIR FRY SHRIMP WITH VEGETABLES

Preparation Time: 1 hour   *Margo Hall*
Cooking Time: 30 minutes   *Winji*
Serves: 6

2 lbs. large shrimp, peeled   4 - 5 cloves garlic, minced
    and deveined   8 oz. sharp Cheddar cheese,
1 head cauliflower   grated
1 bunch broccoli   3 Tblsp. soy sauce
1 large red pepper   Cooking oil
1 (6½ oz.) can water chestnuts,
    drained

A good recipe to be creative with. Try adding mushrooms, snow peas, bamboo shoots, or whatever you have around.

Preheat oven to 350° F. Peel and devein shrimp. Break cauliflower and broccoli into florets. Cut the red pepper into strips. Coat the bottom of a large skillet with oil, and add ½ tsp. garlic. Add vegetables and shrimp in a single layer, and stir fry for 2 - 3 minutes over medium high heat. You will have to do several pan loads. Transfer to casserole dish and repeat procedure. Add soy sauce to vegetable and shrimp mixture. Top with grated cheese. Microwave for 3 - 4 minutes or bake in oven at 350° for 15 - 20 minutes until heated through and cheese is melted.

MENU:

PEACH BRANDY SOUP p. 79

. . .

STIR FRY SHRIMP WITH VEGETABLES p. 192
BROWN RICE

. . .

HONEYDEW MELON WITH YOUR FAVORITE LIQUEUR

. . .

COTE DU RHONE BLANC : ZINFANDEL BLANC

STIR FRY VEGETABLES AND PRAWNS

Preparation Time: 20 minutes
Cooking Time: 5 minutes
Serves: 4 - 6

Geli Burrill
Jolie Brise

24 jumbo shrimp
2 Tblsp. coconut oil
1 Tblsp. seasoning salt
1 Tblsp. finely minced fresh ginger
1 clove minced garlic
2 carrots, julienned
4 stalks celery, sliced finely
¼ lb. fresh pea pods
½ onion, thinly sliced

¼ lb. mushrooms, thinly sliced
Juice of 2 lemons
¼ cup vermouth
2 tomatoes, thinly sliced
¼ cup teriyaki sauce
¼ cup chopped green onion
4 Tblsp. toasted sesame seeds
Garnish: lemon wedges

Add coconut oil to wok. When hot, add shrimp and ¾ Tblsp. seasoning salt. Cook, stirring constantly, until shrimp begins to curl. Stir in ginger and garlic. Saute 30 seconds. Stir in carrots, celery, pea pods, onion, and season with remaining salt. Satue for 1 minute. Stir in sliced mushrooms and saute 1 minute. Add lemon juice, vermouth, tomatoes, and saute for 1 minute. Pour in teriyaki sauce and toss. Turn mixture on to a platter and top with toasted sesame seeds and green onion. *Garnish with lemon wedges.*

MENU:

FRENCH ONION SOUP p. 83

. . .

STIR FRY VEGETABLES AND PRAWNS p. 193
HERBED AND WILD RICE

. . .

CHOCOLATE MOUSSE p. 254

. . .

BORDEAUX BLANC : CABERNET BLANC

SHRIMP COCO-LADA

Preparation Time: 30 minutes
Cooking Time: 20 minutes
Serves: 8 - 10

Mardy Array
Emerald Lady

1 lb. shrimp, cleaned and tails
   left intact
½ cup flour
1 tsp. dry mustard
1 tsp. salt
1 egg

½ cup cream of coconut (Coco
   Lopez or may substitute
   cream)
1 cup (or more as needed) flaked
   coconut
2/3 cup breadcrumbs
Oil

A perfect go-together with our frosty Emerald Lady drinks! Combine flour, mustard, and salt in a small dish, and set aside. In a bowl, beat egg, then add cream stirring until blended. Combine flaked coconut with breadcrumbs in 3rd dish. Dredge shrimp in flour mixture, dip in egg/cream, and lastly in coconut. Chill shrimp until ready to fry. Heat oil, 2 inches deep, to 375°. Fry shrimp for 2 - 3 minutes or until golden. Drain on paper towels. Can be kept warm in slow oven.

MENU:

CHILLED AVOCADO GAZPACHO p. 87

. . .

SHRIMP COCO-LADA p. 194
HOT STEAMED RICE

. . .

PINEAPPLE PUDDING p. 252

. . .

BEAUJOLAIS BLANC : CHENIN BLANC

TANGERINE SHRIMP

Preparation Time: 25 minutes   Chris Balfour
Cooking Time: 10 minutes   *Stowaway*
Serves: 6 - 8

2 lb. large shelled shrimp, deveined
2 tsp. Sichuan peppercorns
8 dried chili peppers
4 tsp. peeled minced ginger
2 tsp. Sichuan chili paste with
    garlic
2 Tblsp. Hoisin sauce
3 Tblsp. dark soy sauce
4 Tblsp. tangerine or orange juice

1½ tsp. sugar
3 Tblsp. peanut oil
1 1/3 cup cubed onion
8 scallions, cut in 2" strips
10 narrow strips of tangerine or
    orange peel
2 tsp. white vinegar
2 tsp. sesame oil (Chinese)

Heat wok, add peppercorns, and dry fry for 30 seconds. Remove and crush. Soak chili peppers for 15 minutes in warm water. Combine with chili paste, Hoisin, soy sauce, juice, and sugar. Heat wok with 2 Tblsp. peanut oil. Stir fry shrimp. Remove. Add remaining oil, and add pepper mixture, then peel onion, and then shrimp, and mix. Add liquid mixture. Add vinegar, and then add sesame oil, mix, and serve.

MENU:

EGG DROP SOUP

. . .

TANGERINE SHRIMP p. 195
HOT FLUFFY RICE

. . .

CHOCOLATE TOPPED ICE CREAM

. . .

BORDEAUX BLANC : BLUSH WINE

CURRIED SHRIMP

Preparation Time: 10 minutes
Cooking Time: 15 minutes
Serves: 6

Barbie Haworth
Ann-Marie II

1/3 cup butter or margarine
3 Tblsp. all-purpose flour
1 Tblsp. curry powder (may
    increase to 2 Tblsp.)
½ tsp. salt
¼ tsp. paprika
Dash of nutmeg

Dash of Worcestershire sauce
2 cups Half & Half
3 cups cooked, cleaned shrimp
1 Tblsp. lemon juice
1 Tblsp. sherry
1 tsp. minced onion

Melt butter, stir in flour, and cook for 2 minutes stirring. Add curry, paprika, nutmeg, and salt. Gradually blend in Half & Half. Stir on low heat until thickened and smooth. Add remaining ingredients. Taste for salt, and heat through. *Serve with curry condiments in bowls (chutney, flaked coconut, chopped salted peanuts, chopped fresh parsley, mandarin orange sections, bacon bits, and raisins).*

MENU:

EGG ROLLS

. . .

CURRIED SHRIMP p. 196
STEAMED PEA PODS
FLUFFY RICE

. . .

CALEDONIAN CREAM p. 262

. . .

WHITE BORDEAUX : CHABLIS

SHRIMP LINGUINE

Preparation Time: 10 minutes
Cooking Time: 15 minutes
Serves: 4

Donna Jaggard
Thorobred

1 package white linguine	4 - 6 minced cloves garlic
6 oz. can white clam sauce	1 Tblsp. dried parsley
1/8 cup + 1 Tblsp. olive oil	1 lb. cleaned deveined shrimp
1/8 cup + 1 Tblsp. pure lemon juice, not concentrate	1/8 cup freshly grated Romano cheese
6½ Tblsp butter	1/8 cup freshly grated Parmesan

Heat clam sauce over medium heat in saucepan. Boil linguine in large pan with 1 Tblsp. olive oil and adequate water. In 10 inch skillet, heat olive oil, butter, garlic, lemon juice, and parsley. Add shrimp, turning constantly at medium high heat until shrimp turns white. *To serve: cover linguine with shrimp and its sauce. Spoon clam sauce over, and garnish with grated cheeses.*

MENU:

ANTIPASTO

. . .

SHRIMP LINGUINE p. 197
GARLIC BREAD
BUTTERED BRUSSEL SPROUTS

. . .

APPLE CLAFOUTI p. 258

. . .

MACON BLANC VILLAGES : CHARDONNAY

HONEY-BROILED SCALLOPS

Preparation Time: 5 minutes   *Shannon Webster*
Chilling Time: 3 - 6 hours   *Chaparral*
Cooking Time: 5 minutes
Serves: 4

1 lb. scallops	1 Tblsp. soy sauce
3 Tblsp. lime juice	¼ tsp. ground ginger
2 Tblsp. vegetable oil	¼ tsp. toasted sesame seeds (optional)
1 Tblsp. honey	Garnish: lime and cherry tomatoes

In a 2 quart mixing bowl, combine all ingredients. Cover and chill 3 to
6 hours, stirring frequently. Remove scallops from marinade, reserving
marinade. Thread scallops on skewers. Broil 4 inches from source of
heat, turning occasionally, and basting with reserve marinade for about
3 - 5 minutes until opaque throughout. If desired, place sesame seeds
on wax paper, and roll each skewer to coat scallops. *Garnish with lime
wheels and cherry tomatoes.*

MENU:

WATERCRESS SALAD
· · ·

HONEY-BROILED SCALLOPS p. 198
BUTTERED SPINACH
RICE WITH DICED CARROTS
· · ·

PAPAYA CREAM p. 259
· · ·

WHITE BORDEAUX : CHENIN BLANC

SCALLOPS GEORGETTE WITH BANANAS

Preparation Time: 20 minutes
Cooking Time: 10 minutes
Serves: 10

Georgina Morris
Natasha

5 lbs. scallops	2 bananas, sliced
2 Tblsp. butter	6 oz. cream
1 Tblsp. oil	1 large glass white wine
6 green sweet peppers	3 tsp. mild curry powder
2 red peppers	2 Tblsp. flour
1 carrot, diced	6 bunches scallions
½ lb. mushrooms	Garnish: parsley

Chop scallions, and slice peppers and mushrooms thinly. Dust scallops in flour, and saute in Tblsp. butter mixed with 1 Tblsp. oil in small quantities in frying pan until lightly golden. Set scallops aside. Fry scallions and other vegetables together in butter and oil, and add curry powder (more or less, to taste). Cook until just tender. Add wine and reduce. Add cream and scallops, and heat through gently about 3 minutes. Then add sliced bananas. Decorate with parsley, and serve with rice. *The sweetness of the scallops goes surprisingly well with the sweetness of the bananas.*

MENU:

CHERRY TOMATO SALAD p. 67

· · ·

SCALLOPS GEORGETTE WITH BANANAS p. 199
RICE PILAF

· · ·

CHESS PIE p. 258

· · ·

WHITE BORDEAUX : JOHANNISBERG RIESLING

SCALLOPS IN SAFFRON/LEMON SAUCE

Preparation Time: 25 minutes
Cooking Time: 20 minutes
Serves: 6

Sharon Strong
Promises

¾ cup dry white wine
¾ cup fish stock (clam juice in bottle)
5 Tblsp. fresh lemon juice
4 shallots, minced
1 tsp. mashed garlic

½ tsp. saffron threads
1 large tomato, peeled, and diced (or 3 plum tomatoes)
¼ tsp. ground red cayenne pepper
3 cups heavy cream
Garnish: 1 red pepper and lemon and lemon juice

Melt butter in heavy large skillet over low heat. Add garlic and shallots. Cover and cook until tender, stirring occasionally, about 8 minutes. Add fish stock, wine, lemon juice, red pepper, and simmer until scallops are opaque about 1 - 2 minutes. Remove scallops with slotted spoon and keep warm. Boil liquid until reduced to 1 cup, about 7 minutes. Add 1 Tblsp. mixture to saffron, and let sit for 1 minute. Return to skillet. Add cream and boil until reduced to 2 cups about 10 - 15 minutes. Mix tomato and parsley. Season with salt and pepper to taste. Return scallops to skillet, and stir until just warm. Garnish each plate with 2 small red pepper fans and a twist of ½ lemon slice between them.

MENU:

TOMATOES FLORENTINE

. . .

SCALLOPS IN SAFFRON/LEMON SAUCE p. 200
WHITE RICE

. . .

CREAM PUFFS

. . .

GRAVES WHITE : FUME BLANC

SEA SHELL AU GRATIN

Preparation Time: 5 - 10 minutes   *Shirley Dorn Burroughs*
Cooking Time: 5 - 10 minutes   *Odyssey*
Serves: 4

1 cup white sauce (May use mix or your favorite white sauce recipe).

8 oz. can Crab meat, may use Tuna or Shrimp

Salt and pepper to taste

4 scallop shells

2 oz. butter

3 oz. grated cheese, Swiss

Dash of paprika, tabasco, and Worcestershire sauce

Preheat oven to 350° F. Make a white sauce. Add crab meat to this, and season with salt and pepper. Butter shells and fill with hot mixture. Place a pat of butter on each shell, and sprinkle with cheese. Add a dash of paprika, Worcestershire, and tabasco. Put in a hot oven at 350° for 5 - 10 minutes. May use as an appetizer.

MENU:

CUCUMBERS IN SOUR CREAM p. 69

. . .

SEA SHELL AU GRATIN p. 201
CREAMED MASHED POTATOES
SPINACH WITH BUTTER

. . .

STRAWBERRY CAKES p. 241

. . .

ENTRE DEUX MERS : PINOT BLANC

CURRIED CONCH

Preparation Time: 10 minutes   *Jan Robinson*
Cooking Time: 1 hour   *Vanity*
Serves: 6

2 lbs. cleaned conch   1 cup green pepper, chopped
½ cup cream of coconut   1 cinnamon stick
½ cup of water   4 whole cloves
1½ cups diced onions   1 tsp. flour
1 clove garlic, crushed   3 Tblsp. butter
1 Tblsp. curry powder

Pound conch thoroughly and cut into 1 inch strips. Mix cream of
coconut with water to make 1 cup of coconut milk. Cook onions and
garlic until tender in hot butter. Add curry powder, green peppers.
Cook with lid on low heat 10 minutes. Then stir in conch, cinnamon
stick, cloves and coconut milk. Cook slowly until conch is tender,
about 45 minutes. Blend in flour in water and add to sauce to thicken.
Remove cinnamon and cloves. Serve hot.

MENU:

SWEET AND SOUR SPINACH SALAD p. 63

. . .

CURRIED CONCH p. 202
FLUFFY WHITE RICE

. . .

EBONY AND IVORY CHEESECAKE p. 243

. . .

POUILLY FUISSE : CHARDONNAY

CARIBBEAN LOBSTER CASSEROLE

Preparation Time: 20 minutes
Cooking Time: 30 minutes
Serves: 6

Kimberly Foote
Oklahoma Crude II

2 lb. lobster meat
1 (15 oz.) can Cream de Coco
¼ cup grated coconut
3 Tblsp. bread crumbs

Small can of Marinara sauce (Progresso is good)
1 tsp. parsley
1 tsp. curry powder

Preheat oven to 400° F. Parboil lobster meat and drain. Layer half in bottom of casserole dish. Pour 1/3 can of each: Cream de Coco and Marinara sauce. Sprinkle coconut, bread crumbs, and spices. Layer lobster, and repeat the process. Top layer should be sauces sprinkled with bread crumbs. Bake at 400° F. for 25 minutes.

MENU:

ARTICHOKE APPETIZER p. 75

. . .

CARIBBEAN LOBSTER CASSEROLE p. 203
FETTUCCINI ALFREDO p. 230
BRUSSEL SPROUTS

. . .

PINEAPPLE CHOCOLATE FONDUE p. 246

. . .

IRISH COFFEE
POUILLY FUISSE : CHARDONNAY

NATIVE SUN LOBSTER BBQ

Preparation Time: 10 minutes
Marinating Time: 30 minutes
Cooking Time: 15 minutes (on BBQ grill)
Serves: 4

Sylvia and Stanley Dabney
Native Sun

2 lobsters (½ lobster per person
   split lengthwise)
MARINADE:
¼ cup lemon or lime juice
½ + cup Seven Seas Italian dressing

1 tsp. paprika
¼ cup minced shallots
3 Tblsp. soy sauce
1 tsp. salt

Mix all except lobster. Leave lobster in shell. Place flesh side down in lasagna type pan and soak in marinade a minimum of 30 minutes, or overnight if you like to do ahead. BBQ over hot coals basting with marinade only until flesh is white and firm. Serve with lots of lemon wedges and melted butter and get ready to smack your lips!

MENU:

TOSSED SALAD

. . .

NATIVE SUN LOBSTER BBQ p. 204
SYLVIA'S RICE p. 235
BASIL TOMATOES p. 220

. . .

ICE CREAM AND PRALINE PARFAIT SAUCE p. 246

. . .

ST. VERAN : CHARDONNAY

TURBOT TURBANS A LA NEWBURG

Preparation Time: 5 minutes   D. Stetson
Cooking Time: 15 - 20 minutes   *Fantasy*
Serves: 6:

2 lbs. white fresh fish fillets (e.g.   2 cups cooked rice
    Turbot or Haddock)   Paprika
1 tsp. salt   Parsley sprigs
¼ tsp. white pepper   Newburg Sauce (Recipe p. 206)
¼ cup butter, melted   Garnish: Watercress, lemon/lime
                or bundle parsley and radish.

Sprinkle serving size portions of fish fillets with salt and pepper. Roll into turbans, and secure with toothpicks. Place on ends in well-greased baking dish (8x8x2). Brush with butter. Bake 15 - 20 minutes at 350° F. until fish flakes easily. To serve, remove toothpicks, and place each turban on a bed of rice. Spoon Newburg Sauce over turbans. Garnish with paprika and parsley sprigs. Watercress should outline the edge of the serving platter with a slice of lemon/lime or a parsley bundle with a radish rose.

MENU:

QUICK SHE CRAB SOUP p. 88

. . .

TURBOT TURBANS A LA NEWBURG p. 205
PAPRIKA-BUTTERED BROCCOLI p. 211

. . .

PEACH AND MARSHMALLOW DESSERT CAKE p. 241

. . .

WHITE BORDEAUX : SAUVIGNON BLANC

NEWBURG SAUCE

Preparation time: 5 minutes
Cooking Time: 10 minutes

1 cup medium white sauce
½ cup heavy cream
4 egg yolks

Salt and pepper
2 Tblsp. white wine

Have the white sauce hot in the upper part of a double boiler. Scald and add the cream, then the egg yolks one at a time, beating well after each addition. Season with salt and pepper and add the wine immediately before serving. Do not allow sauce to boil after eggs have been added.

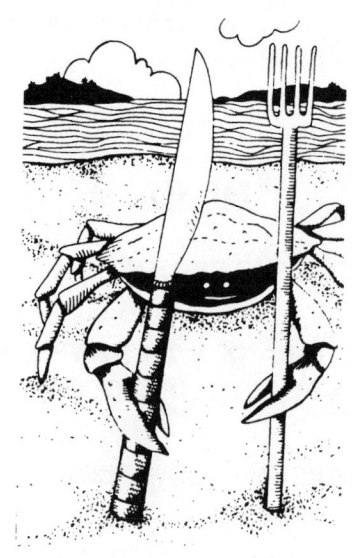

VEGETABLES, PASTA AND RICE

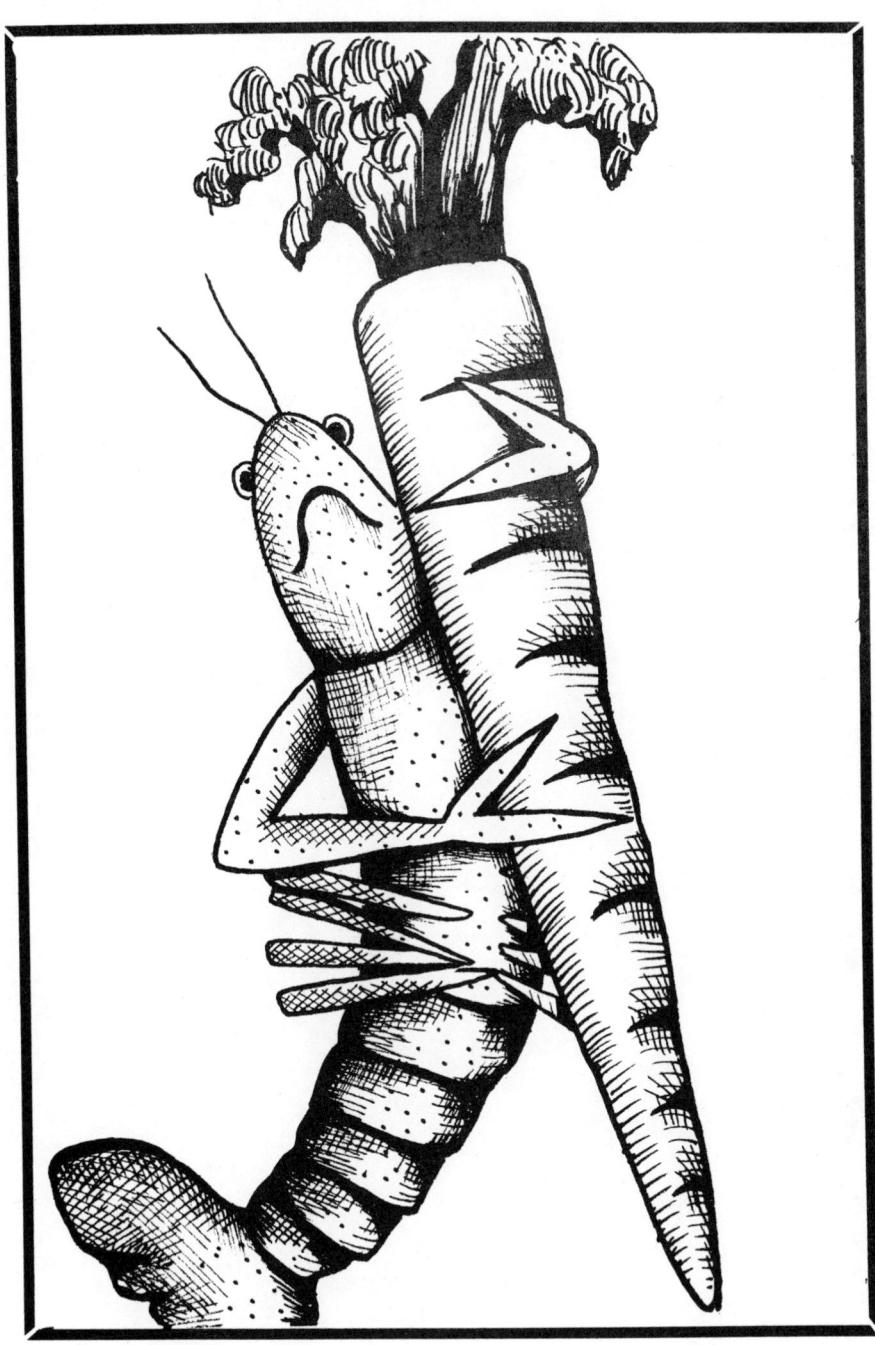

NOTES

ARTICHOKE BOTTOMS
STUFFED WITH MUSHROOMS

Preparation Time: 25 minutes
Cooking Time: 20 minutes
Serves: 4

Jacklyn Johnson Rabinowitz
Almost Heaven

1 lb. finely chopped mushrooms
½ cup finely chopped shallots
¼ cup olive oil
2 Tblsp. chopped fresh parsley
1-1½ tsp. chopped fresh thyme
    or ½ tsp. dried

¼ tsp. salt
1/8 tsp. pepper
2 Tblsp. heavy cream
1 (14 oz.) can artichoke bottoms,
    drained (2 per person)

Saute mushrooms and shallots in oil in large heavy skillet over high heat, stirring for 5 minutes until all moisture has evaporated. Stir in 1 Tblsp. of the parsley, thyme, salt, pepper and heavy cream. Spoon into artichoke bottoms, keeping warm in a slow oven. *Garnish with remaining parsley just before serving.*

ASPARAGUS IN LEMON BUTTER

Preparation Time: 15 minutes
Cooking Time: 5 - 10 minutes
Serves: 8

Lisa Hawkins
Ariguani

2 lbs. asparagus
2 Tblsp. butter
1 tsp. lemon pepper

¼ cup dry Vermouth

Garnish: slice of lemon

Wash asparagus, and cut off tough ends. With a vegetable peeler, peel skins of spears. Saute with remaining ingredients until tender, but still crisp. Do not over cook. *Serve garnished with a slice of lemon.*

HINT: A pinch of baking soda will preserve the color of fresh vegetables.

SESAME BROCCOLI

Preparation Time: 10 minutes
Cooking Time: 15 minutes
Serves: 6

Alison Briscoe
Ovation

1 large bunch broccoli	½ cup water chestnuts, sliced
2½ Tblsp. sesame seeds	3 Tblsp. white wine
2 oz. butter	3 Tblsp. soy sauce
2 cloves garlic	½ tsp. salt (optional)

Saute sesame seeds, remove and set aside. Heat butter in a wok, add pressed garlic and stirfry. Trim broccoli tops. Peel stalks and chop. Add chopped stalks and stirfry 5 minutes. Add water chestnuts, wine, soy sauce and broccoli tops. Mix - cover and cook for 3 - 5 minutes until tender. Serve immediately and sprinkle sesame seeds on top.

BROCCOLI WITH WALNUT BUTTER

Preparation Time: 5 minutes
Cooking Time: 10 minutes
Serves: 4 - 6

Jacklyn Johnson Rabinowitz
Almost Heaven

2 lbs. broccoli	1 Tblsp. lemon juice
½ cup butter	½ tsp. salt
¾ cup chopped walnuts	1/8 tsp. pepper

Steam broccoli florets lightly 'til crisp tender. Drain. While broccoli is cooking, melt butter over medium heat in small skillet. Add walnuts, cook slowly until butter just begins to brown. Add lemon juice, salt and pepper. Pour over hot broccoli. Toss gently to coat.

HINT: To keep green fresh vegetables colorful, cook them with a Tblsp. peanut oil to 2 or 3 quarts of water.

BROCCOLI MOLD

Preparation Time: 20 minutes
Cooking Time: 30 minutes
Serves: 6
Food Processor

Shannon Webster
Chaparral

1 bunch broccoli
    (about 1-1½ lbs.)
3 eggs
¼ cup heavy cream

1½ tsp. salt
¼ tsp. freshly ground pepper
1/8 tsp. freshly ground nutmeg

Preheat oven 350° F. Drain broccoli in colander after cooking it in salted water until tender. Cool, then cut in pieces. Use metal blade, add 1/3 of broccoli. Process until finely chopped. Repeat 2 times adding ½ remaining broccoli each time. Add eggs, one at a time, processing after each addition. Add cream, salt, pepper and nutmeg. Process until smooth. Spoon mixture into a buttered 3-4 cup mold. Place mold in shallow roasting pan on oven shelf. Pour boiling water into pan one-half up sides of mold. Bake at 350° F. for 30 minutes or until knife comes out clean when inserted into center. Invert on serving platter. Lift off mold and serve at once.

PAPRIKA - BUTTERED BROCCOLI

Preparation Time: 5 minutes
Cooking Time: 15 minutes or until fork tender
Serves: 6

D. Stetson
Fantasy

1 cup water
1 tsp. salt
2 (10 oz.) pkgs. frozen whole
    broccoli

PAPRIKA BUTTER:
¼ cup butter
½ tsp. salt
¼ tsp. white pepper
¼ tsp. paprika

Bring water to rapid boil in saucepan. Add salt and broccoli; steam 15 minutes or until broccoli is fork tender, not mushy. Make paprika butter. Melt butter, stir in salt, pepper and paprika. Arrange broccoli on serving platter; pour butter over. Serve immediately.

BREADFRUIT CHIPS

Preparation Time: 5 minutes   *Kimberly Foote*
Cooking Time: 20 minutes   *Oklahoma Crude II*
Serves: 6

2 medium breadfruit	**salt**
oil	**pepper**

Cut breadfruit in half and cut skin off. Slice in french fry sizes. Fry in oil until crisp. Drain on paper towel. Sprinkle with salt and pepper. *Can be reheated in oven to serve warm.*

HARVARD BEETS

Preparation Time: 5 minutes   *Jane Glancy*
Cooking Time: 25 minutes   *Truant*
Serves: 4

1 can beets	**1 Tblsp. cornstarch**
2 Tblsp. vinegar	**1 tsp. sugar**
Pinch of salt	

Drain beets reserving 6 Tblsp. juice. Combine juice with other ingredients except for the beets. Cook over low heat until thickened, stirring frequently. Add beets, and heat through.

SUNSHINE CARROTS

Preparation Time: 5 minutes   *Donna Jaggard*
Cooking Time: 15 minutes   *Thorobred*
Serves: 6

¾ cup orange juice	**2 (16 oz.) cans whole carrots,**
½ cup maple syrup	**drained**
¼ cup orange marmalade	**1 Tblsp. dried mint leaves**

Combine orange juice, syrup, and marmalade in a saucepan. Bring to a boil, stirring constantly. Reduce heat, and add carrots and mint leaves. Heat through.

SWEET AND SOUR CABBAGE

Preparation Time: 10 minutes   *Louise Brendlinger*
Cooking Time: 20 minutes   *Ring-Andersen*
Serves: 6

1 cabbage (red preferably)   1 Tblsp. Worcestershire sauce
½ cup wine vinegar   ½ cup white wine
½ cup brown sugar   1 onion
1 Tblsp. French mustard

Finely slice the cabbage and onion. Bring to a boil with all the other ingredients. Simmer for 20 minutes or until cabbage is tender. Cover while cooking.

MINTY CARROTS

Preparation Time: 15 minutes   *Jean Thayer*
Cooking Time: 15 minutes   *Finesse 60*
Serves: 8

12 large carrots, peeled, thinly   1 tsp. cornstarch
    sliced   Dash of salt
1/3 cup reserved cooking liquid   Juice and grated rind of half of
2 Tblsp. butter   lemon
1 Tblsp. sugar   1 Tblsp. dried mint

Cook carrots till just tender in enough water to cover. Drain, reserving 1/3 of the cooking liquid. Melt butter in medium saucepan. Add sugar, cornstarch and salt. Over low heat, gradually add reserved liquid, stirring continually. When it has thickened slightly, add lemon juice, rind, mint, and carrots. Blend. *May be served immediately or turn off heat and reheat when needed.*

HINT: Run cold water in the sink while you pour hot water from vegetables. It prevents the steam from scalding your hands.

MINTED CARROTS

Preparation Time: 15 minutes   Judith Vegiard
Cooking Time: 15 minutes (approximately)   Ruach
Serves: 8

1 lb. carrots, sliced   1 Tblsp. brown sugar
6 Tblsp. butter   1 Tblsp. dried mint leaves

Boil carrots - not quite until desired doneness. Drain. Add to saucepan
butter, brown sugar and mint leaves. Cover and let simmer over very low
heat for 5 minutes. Stir and serve.

DAVE LOVES CARROTS

Preparation Time: 30 minutes   Kim Turk
Cooking Time: 5 minutes   Antipodes

Carrots, julienned   Honey
Butter   Fresh parsley
Cinnamon or nutmeg

Saute carrots and parsley in butter. Adding to taste, honey and cinnamon or nutmeg. *Dave (a former charter guest) loved these carrots
so much he proposed!*

SWEET AND SOUR CARROTS

Preparation Time: 10 minutes   Denise Wright
Cooking Time: 30 minutes   Parandah
Serves 6 - 8

6 - 8 medium sized carrots   1 tsp. paprika
4 Tblsp. butter   Juice of half a lemon
1/3 cup honey   Garnish: Parsley and lemon slice

Peel carrots and cut into 3" sticks. Cook carrots in lightly salted water
until tender. Drain and set aside until five minutes before serving.
Mix all other ingredients in skillet, add carrots and saute for 10 minutes.
Twisted lemon slice and parsley for garnish.

GLAZED CARROTS

Preparation Time: 20 minutes
Cooking Time: 20 minutes
Serves: 6

Lee Ann LaCesa
Flute

10 medium carrots, sliced ½
    inch thick
½ cube beef bouillon
½ cup water

2 Tblsp. butter
3 Tblsp. sugar
Garnish: chopped parsley

In a 2 quart sauce pan, bring all ingredients to a boil. Simmer until carrots are crisp tender (about 10 minutes). Remove carrots with slotted spoon - keep warm. Simmer liquid until it becomes a glaze consistency stirring occasionally. Add carrots, and mix well. *Garnish with chopped parsley.*

CAULIFLOWER NEOPOLITAN

Preparation Time: 15 - 20 minutes
Cooking Time: 5 minutes
Serves: 4

Didgie Belschner
Tequila

6 pitted/stuffed green olives
½ small onion
1 stalk celery
½ head cauliflower
2 Tblsp. lemon juice

Pepper, freshly ground
1/3 cup olive oil
2 Tblsp. chopped fresh parsley
½ tsp. drained capers

Slice olives, onion and chop celery (reserve). Rinse, core and cut cauliflower into 1" florets. Place in a large saucepan of boiling water. Cook uncovered for 5 minutes. After water boils, drain and rinse with cold water. Pat dry. Whisk lemon juice, salt, pepper in medium bowl. Add oil in slow steady stream whisking continuously. Add reserved olives, celery, onion, parsley and capers. Stir in cauliflower. *Serve at once or refrigerate up to 3 hours.*

GREEN BEANS ALMONDINE

Preparation Time: 5 minutes   Barbie Haworth
Cooking Time: 20 minutes   Ann-Marie II
Serves: 8

2 (10 oz.) packages frozen French   ½ cup blanched, slivered, or sliced
    cut green beans   almonds
½ cup butter   Salt and pepper to taste

Cook frozen green beans per package directions. Saute or brown almonds in butter. Add seasoning and almonds to drained beans. Blend and serve.

MUSHROOMS A LA GREQUE

Preparation Time: 15 minutes   Alison P. Briscoe
Chilling Time: 2 - 3 hours   Ovation
Serves: 8

2 lbs. small mushrooms   12 coriander seeds (optional)
6 tomatoes   12 bay leaves
8 Tblsp. olive oil   2 sprigs thyme
½ pt. dry white wine and water   2 crushed garlic cloves
Salt and freshly ground
    black pepper

Wipe mushrooms and trim stalks level with caps. Nick the skins of the tomatoes; place tomatoes in bowl, cover with boiling water. Let stand for 1 minute, drain and peel off skins. Halve, remove seeds, chop coarsely. Measure oil, wine, water, salt, pepper and coriander seeds, bay leaf, thyme and garlic. Bring to boil and simmer for 3 minutes. Add mushrooms and tomatoes. Cook gently for 5 minutes in covered sauce pan. Remove vegetables into serving dish. Boil wine mixture rapidly for 5 minutes to reduce. Pour over mushrooms and chill for 2 - 3 hours. *(Mushrooms can be replaced by artichoke hearts, zucchini, cauliflower or leeks.)*

SAUTEED LEEKS

Preparation Time: 5 minutes
Cooking Time: 15 minutes
Serves: 8

Chris Balfour
Stowaway

16 small leeks, rinsed and cut
    into ½-inch slices

3 Tblsp. unsalted butter

Steam leeks for 7 - 10 minutes in basket over water. Drain and rinse in cold water. Can be done in advance. When ready to serve, drain leeks. Pat dry. Melt butter in large skillet, and saute until golden for 5 - 8 minutes.

SNOW PEAS AND TOMATOES

Preparation Time: 10 minutes
Cooking Time: 6 minutes
Serves: 4

Margo Ann Muckey
Tuff

2 - 3 Tblsp. butter or margarine
1 clove garlic, minced
¼ cup finely chopped onion
2 (7 oz.) packages frozen
    snow peas, thawed
1 (8 oz.) can water chestnuts,
    drained and sliced

1 Tblsp. soy sauce
1 tsp. salt
1 tsp. dried oregano
3 medium tomatoes, cut into
    ¼ inch dice

Melt butter or margarine with garlic in a large skillet over medium heat. Add onion, and saute until crisp tender about 1 minute. Blend in remaining ingredients except for tomato, and cook for 2 - 3 minutes stirring constantly. Stir in tomatoes, and continue cooking until heated through about 2 - 3 minutes more. Serve.

HINT: Always heat a pan before pouring in oil. In a cold pan, oil burns and foods stick.

ITALIAN PEAS AND ONIONS

Preparation Time: 5 minutes   *Emily Welch*
Cooking Time: 10 minutes   *Wind's End*
Serves: 6

2 (10 oz.) packages frozen peas   ¼ cup butter
1 medium to large onion,   2 tsp. Italian seasoning
    chopped

Melt the butter in a large skillet at medium high heat. Add onions and
peas. Saute for 5 minutes. Add Italian seasoning and cover steaming
for 5 minutes.

GLAZED SNOW PEAS AND CARROTS

Preparation Time: 15 minutes   *Lisa Hawkins*
Cooking Time: 10 minutes   *Ariguani*
Serves: 8

1 lb. snow peas   1 tsp. honey
5 large carrots, peeled   Salt and pepper to taste
Butter

Wash and string snow peas. Slice carrots on a diagonal to reveal an oval
center. Melt butter in large skillet. Add carrots and saute for 5 minutes.
Add snow peas, honey, salt, and pepper. Saute 5 minutes more just
until tender, but still crisp.

MUSHROOM CAPS WITH PETITS POIS

Preparation Time: 10 minutes   *Jacklyn Johnson Rabinowitz*
Cooking Time: 5 minutes   *Almost Heaven*
Serves: 4

3 - 4 large mushrooms per   2 (7¼ oz.) cans Petit Pois
    serving
1 Tblsp. butter

Clean and remove stems of mushrooms. Saute lightly while heating
peas. Spoon peas into mushroom caps.

SPINACH MOUNDS

Preparation Time: 15 minutes
Cooking Time: 20 minutes
Serves: 6

Terrie Thornbjornson
Western Star

2 - 3 tomatoes
2 (10 oz.) packages frozen
    leaf spinach
3 oz. softened cream cheese

2 Tblsp. Lipton's onion soup
2 Tblsp. butter
2 Tblsp. lemon juice
Hollandaise sauce

Preheat oven to 400° F. Slice tomatoes ¼ to ½ inch thick, one per person. Cook spinach, drain, and add cream cheese, onion soup, butter, and lemon juice. Mix until well blended. Scoop a modest amount onto each tomato slice, and bake for 8 - 10 minutes in hot oven or zap in a microwave for 5 minutes. Top with Hollandaise before serving.

HERBED SPINACH

Preparation Time: 5 minutes
Cooking Time: 30 minutes
Serves: 6

Barbie Haworth
Ann-Marie II

1 (10 oz.) package frozen chopped
    spinach, cooked and drained
1 cup cooked rice
1 cup sharp Cheddar cheese,
    shredded
2 eggs, beaten

2 Tblsp. margarine, soft
1/3 cup milk
2 Tblsp. onion, chopped
2 tsp. Worcestershire sauce
½ tsp. salt
1/8 tsp. nutmeg

Preheat oven to 350° F. Combine all ingredients in a bowl. Pour into 1 quart greased casserole dish. Bake at 350° F. for 30 minutes or until set.

BASIL TOMATOES

Preparation Time: 15 minutes
Marinating Time: 30 minutes
Serves: 4

Sylvia Dabney
Native Sun

4 medium/large tomatoes
1 lemon
Salt

Black pepper
Basil
Garnish: Fresh parsley sprigs

Slice tomatoes into thin wheels. Arrange in pretty pattern in large shallow dish. Sprinkle with salt - lots of coarse black pepper - basil (just enough to be visible and tasteable on each slice. Squeeze the juice of 1 lemon all over tomatoes and sprinkle with oil. Let soak at least ½ hour. Decorate with fresh parsley sprigs and serve with lobster or Beef Bourguignonne. *This is delicious particularly on hot evenings when you just do not want to eat everything hot!*

SWEET POTATOES ANNA

Preparation Time: 15 minutes
Cooking Time: 30 minutes
Serves: 4

Cherie Hughes
Skopbank of Finland

¾ cup clarified melted butter
Salt and pepper

3 sweet potatoes

Preheat the oven to 350° F. Peel and thinly slice the 3 potatoes. Melt the clarified butter in ovenproof skillet. Lay potatoes into pan in circles. Do not salt the first layer so as to prevent scorching. Alternate potatoes, butter, salt, and pepper. Heat on the stove for 15 minutes, pressing down with a spatula. Bake for 20 minutes, and invert onto a serving platter.

HINT: Avoid salting food to be deep fried as it draws out moisture from the food causing excess splattering.

POMMES DAUPHINE

Preparation Time: 30 minutes
Cooking Time: 45 minutes
Serves: 8

Chris Balfour
Stowaway

½ cup + 1 Tblsp. melted butter
1 cup cold water
2 tsp. salt
1 cup flour
4 eggs

Freshly grated nutmeg
2 large potatoes, cooked
and mashed
Oil for deep frying

Combine butter, water, and salt in a large saucepan. Place over low heat, and stir until melted. Remove from heat, and stir in flour. Return to heat, and stir constantly to let mixture dry, about 20 seconds. Add 2 eggs at a time, and beat on high speed with mixer. Season with nutmeg. Add 2½ cups potatoes to mixture, and heat well. Can be prepared 1 day ahead and refrigerated). Add oil (3 inches), and heat until hot. Add potato mixture by small tablespoons and fry until golden. Remove with slotted spoon, and drain on paper towel. Keep warm on paper towel-lined platter until ready to serve (pommes can be cooked 45 minutes ahead).

HOT POTATOES VINAIGRETTE

Preparation Time: 20 minutes
Cooking Times: 20 minutes
Serves: 8

Judith Vegiard
Ruach

2 lbs. potatoes
1 Tblsp. wine vinegar
1 Tblsp. Dijon mustard
2/3 cup olive oil

2 shallots, minced
Minced fresh parsley leaves
Salt and pepper to taste

Boil potatoes in a sauce pan until tender. In a bowl, combine the vinegar, mustard, salt and pepper. Add the oil in a stream, whisking and whisk the dressing until it is emulsified. Toss the potatoes while they are still hot with the dressing. Add minced shallots and parsley for garnish.

PARMESAN MASHED POTATOES

Preparation Time: 10 minutes   *Jean Thayer*
Cooking Time: 30 minutes   *Finesse 60*
Serves: 8

4 Tblsp. butter
12 garlic cloves, peeled, chopped
1 cup heavy cream
1 tsp. salt

5 large baking potatoes, peeled
   cut in large slices
1 Tblsp. salt
4 oz. Parmesan, freshly grated
¾ cup minced parsley

In a small saucepan, melt butter. Add garlic, cover, and over low heat cook garlic until tender - 20 minutes. Add cream and 1 tsp. salt. Bring to a boil, reduce heat and simmer for 10 minutes. Remove from heat. Cook potatoes in boiling, salted water until tender. Drain and mash with a ricer. Add garlic-cream mixture, Parmesan and parsley. Top with additional butter, salt and pepper to taste.

BAKED STUFFED POTATOES

Preparation Time: 10 minutes   *Donna Jaggard*
Cooking Time: 1 hour   *Thorobred*
Serves: 6

6 Idaho baking potatoes
1 cup grated Cheddar cheese
4 Tblsp. butter
1/3 cup milk

6 butter pats
Grated Parmesan cheese
Paprika

Preheat oven to 350° F. Wash and bake potatoes until done. Slice off the tops and scoop out the potatoes. Mash potato flesh in bowl with milk, 4 Tblsp. butter, and grated Cheddar. Stuff potato shells with mashed potato mixture. Place a pat of butter on top of each potato. Sprinkle with Parmesan and paprika. Bake 5 - 10 minutes more.

STUFFED POTATO

Preparation Time: 15 minutes
Cooking Time: 25 minutes
Serves: 8

Lisa Hawkins
Ariguani

4 large baking potatoes
3 scant Tblsp. butter
½ cup sour cream
1/3 cup green onions, chopped

½ cup grated Cheddar cheese
Salt and pepper to taste
Milk as needed

Preheat oven to 400° F. Bake potatoes according to your microwave or oven. Allow to cool slightly, and slice in half lengthwise. Scoop out meat of potato in each half, and place in large bowl. Add remaining ingredients, and beat with electric mixer until smooth. Add milk as needed to achieve a very creamy consistency. Spoon potato mixture back into the skins, and place in baking dish. Bake in 400° F. oven for about 20 minutes or until they are golden.

PARSLEY POTATOES

Preparation Time: 10 minutes
Cooking Time: 20 minutes
Serves: 6

Casey Miller
Fancy Free

6 small red potatoes, quartered
    with skin attached
2 Tblsp. butter

1 Tblsp. sour cream
¼ cup chopped parsley
Salt to taste

Boil potatoes until tender, but not soft, about 12 minutes in water to cover. Put butter, sour cream, and parsley in a bowl. Drain potatoes, and add to bowl. Toss, salt, and serve.

SPICY BRAISED POTATOES

Preparation Time: 10 minutes   *Jan Burnes*
Cooking Time: 30 minutes   *Adaro*
Serves: 4

1 cup finely chopped onion	½ tsp. salt
¼ cup olive oil	¼ tsp. pepper
4 medium potatoes, sliced	Water to cover
2 Tblsp. tomato paste	

In a medium sized skillet, saute onion in olive oil until golden, and add potatoes, tomato paste, seasoning, and water to cover. Simmer for 30 minutes. Serve hot. *Delicious with dark meat dishes like broiled steak, roast beef, or lamb.*

CONFETTI SQUASH SAUTE

Preparation Time: 15 minutes   *Donna Jaggard*
Cooking Time: 10 minutes   *Thorobred*
Serves: 6 - 8

1 medium onion	1 Tblsp. olive oil
4 small zucchini	¼ cup butter
4 small yellow squash	1½ tsp. thyme
1 large red pepper	½ tsp. white pepper
1 large green pepper	

Slice all vegetables in julienne sticks. Place squash in colander. Sprinkle with salt, and allow to drain. Pat dry. Heat oil and butter in a large skillet. Saute all the vegetables until crisp-tender. Sprinkle with thyme and pepper. Toss.

SUCCOTASH STUFFED BAKED GREEN PEPPERS

Preparation Time: 10 minutes   *Barbie Haworth*
Cooking Time: 25 minutes   *Ann-Marie II*
Serves: 8

2 packages frozen succotash
   (corn and lima beans)
6 small fresh whole green peppers
3 Tblsp. butter
½ cup pimento - ½ inch squares

2 Tblsp. flour
1¼ tsp. salt
1 cup milk
Parmesan or grated American
   cheese
Paprika

Preheat oven to 400° F. Cut peppers lengthwise, and remove seeds carefully. Cook in boiling water to cover them for 5 minutes. Remove and drain. Cook succotash per package directions. In saucepan, melt butter, add flour, and blend well. Cook for 1 minute. Add milk, a little at a time, stir constantly with whisk. Cook until thick, and add salt. Add vegetables to sauce, and mix gently. Fill peppers, sprinkle with Parmesan or grated American cheese and paprika. Arrange in baking/serving greased pan. Bake at 400°F. for 15 minutes.

STUFFED SUMMER SQUASH

Preparation Time: 10 minutes   *Barbie Haworth*
Cooking Time: 40 minutes   *Ann-Marie II*
Serves: 4

8 small yellow squash
½ cup green pepper, chopped
1 medium tomato, chopped
1 medium onion, chopped

2 slices crisp bacon, crumbled
½ cup Cheddar cheese, shredded
½ tsp. salt
Dash pepper
Butter or margarine

Preheat oven to 350° F. In a large pan, simmer whole squash for 8 minutes or until tender. Slice in half, and remove seeds. Combine other ingredients except butter. Mix well. Fill squash shells, and place in baking pan. Dot each with a pat of butter. Bake at 350°F. for 25 minutes.

PUREED BUTTERNUT SQUASH

Preparation Time: 15 minutes
Cooking Time: 40 minutes
Serves: 4

Carol Lowe
Natasha

1 onion, sliced
2 Tblsp. unsalted butter
½ cup water

2 lbs. butternut squash, peeled, seeded, strings discarded, and sliced thin
½ tsp. ground cardamon

In a large saucepan, cook onion in butter, covered over moderately low heat, until soft. Add squash, cardamon, ½ cup water, and bring to a boil. Cook for 30 minutes until the squash is tender, adding more water if necessary. Blend in food processor in small batches until smooth.

SCRUMPTIOUS SQUASH

Preparation Time: 10 minutes
Cooking Time: 35 minutes
Serves: 8

Alison Briscoe
Ovation

2 cups cooked squash (Crook-neck)
1 (8 oz.) carton sour cream
1 onion, chopped
½ can cream of chicken soup (Campbells)

2 Tblsp. Parmesan cheese
Salt and freshly ground pepper
1 tsp. sugar
2 oz. grated Cheddar cheese (sharp)
2 oz. crushed Ritz crackers

Preheat oven to 350° F. Mix all ingredients apart from the Cheddar cheese and Ritz crackers. Bake for 35 minutes. Remove from oven, cover with Cheddar cheese and crackers and bake until cheese melts.

ZUCCHINI IN GRAND MARNIER

Preparation Time: 15 minutes   *Michelle Mitchell*
Cooking Time: 10 minutes   *Madam*
Serves: 4

2 large or 3 small zucchini   1/3 cup Grand Marnier
2 Tblsp. butter

Cut zucchini up so that it is like toothpicks. Saute in butter. When almost done, add Grand Marnier, and heat through. *Don't let pan get too hot - Grand Marnier will catch alight.*

SHREDDED ZUCCHINI

Preparation Time: 10 minutes   *Jacklyn Johnson Rabinowitz*
Cooking Time: 5 minutes   *Almost Heaven*
Serves: 6

3 zucchini   ½ tsp. garlic salt
   (½ zucchini per serving)   ¼ tsp. freshly ground black pepper
3 or 4 Tblsp. butter

Shred or grate zucchini. Melt butter in large skillet. Add zucchini, garlic salt, pepper. Lightly saute, stirring continuously.

CORGETTES A LA FRITZ

Preparation Time: 30 minutes   *Kim Turk*
Cooking Time: 10 minutes   *Antipodes*

Corgettes (or zucchinis)   Pepper, black and freshly ground
Butter   Parmesan cheese

Prepare corgettes, and saute in butter until bright green. Add Parmesan cheese, and freshly ground black pepper. Do not overcook.

RICE CASSEROLE OVATION

Preparation Time: 5 minutes   Alison P. Briscoe
Cooking Time: 1¼ hours   Ovation
Serves: 8

1 cup brown rice (uncooked)
1 can (10½ oz.) Campbell's onion
   soup
1 soup can of water
4 oz. butter
1 (4 oz.) can mushrooms

1 (8 oz.) can water chestnuts
   (sliced)   or
2 oz. sauteed almonds (sliced)
Salt and freshly ground
   black pepper
Garnish: Fresh parsley

Preheat oven to 325°F. Mix all the ingredients in a casserole dish and bake for 1¼ hours. Sprinkle with parsley.

ZUCCHINI NOODLE CASSEROLE

Preparation Time: ½ hour   Alison P. Briscoe
Cooking Time: 1½ hours   Ovation
Serves: 6

FRESH TOMATO SAUCE:
2 lbs. tomatoes, chopped
1 onion, chopped
1 large carrot, chopped
2 sticks celery, chopped
1 clove garlic, crushed
2 Tblsp. fresh parsley
½ tsp. sugar
2 Tblsp. basil

4 Tblsp. olive oil
2 onions, chopped
8 oz. zucchini, sliced
1 clove garlic, crushed
1 red pepper, sliced
1 lb. fettuccini noodles
8 oz. Muenster cheese
Salt and freshly ground pepper

Preheat oven to 350° F. Sauce: Put first 8 ingredients in a saucepan and simmer until tomatoes have softened and the sauce resembles a puree. Heat oil in a saucepan, fry onions, add zucchini, red pepper, garlic, salt and pepper and sauce. Cover and simmer for ¼ hour. Cook fettucinni in boiling salted water until tender. Drain, stir in the vegetable sauce and grated cheese. Place in a covered casserole dish and bake at 350° F. for 20 minutes

EGGPLANT AND TOMATO CASSEROLE

Preparation Time: 10 minutes
Cooking Time: 45 minutes
Serves: 8

Alison P. Briscoe
Ovation

2 large eggplants, sliced
1 large onion, chopped finely
1 garlic clove, crushed
1 (16 oz.) can tomatoes
2 Tblsp. tomato puree
2 oz. white bread crumbs

1 tsp. oregano
2 oz. olive oil
1 tsp. basil
½ tsp. sugar
Salt and freshly ground pepper
1 (8 oz.) carton plain yogurt
2 oz. Parmesan cheese, grated

Heat olive oil in frying pan, add eggplant slices. Saute until brown on one side. Drain on paper towel. Saute onion and garlic until golden. Stir in tomatoes, tomato puree, oregano, basil, sugar, salt and pepper. Bring to a boil and simmer for 5 minutes to reduce. Divide eggplant into 3 equal parts. Put one part in bottom of shallow casserole dish. Divide tomato sauce into 2 parts and put half on top of eggplant layer. Spoon ½ of yogurt on tomato sauce. Repeat. Finish with eggplant layer, sprinkle top with Parmesan cheese and bread crumbs.

NOODLES WITH CARROTS AND POPPY SEED

Preparation Time: 5 minutes
Cooking Time: 10 minutes
Serves: 4

Jacklyn Johnson Rabinowitz
Almost Heaven

1 carrot, trimmed and scraped
½ lb. medium noodles
   (egg or spinach)

3 Tblsp. butter
1 Tblsp. poppy seeds
Freshly ground black pepper to
   taste

Dice carrot and drop with noodles into boiling water. Cook until noodles are tender. Drain. Return to sauce pan with butter, seeds, pepper. Stir gently.

WALNUT SPAGHETTI

Preparation Time: 10 minutes
Cooking Time: 8 minutes
Serves: 6

Paola Taglia
Stormvogel

½ cup Half & Half (light cream)
1 cup olive oil
2/3 cup walnuts

1 tsp. pepper
½ cup grated Parmesan cheese
Spaghetti (cooked)

Put cream, olive oil, walnuts, and black pepper in the mixer, and mix for 7 minutes. Add to cooked spaghetti, and cover with the grated Parmesan cheese.

FETTUCCINI ALFREDO

Preparation Time: 5 minutes
Cooking Time: 10 minutes
Serves: 6 - 8

Jan Robinson
Vanity

1 pkg. fettuccini or egg noodles
½ - ¾ cup Swiss cheese, grated
2/3 cup Half & Half (light cream)
    or sour cream, room temperature

¼ lb. butter
1 egg yolk, room temperature

Cook noodles as instructed on package. Melt butter and pour over drained noodles. Add grated cheese. Toss. Add cream and egg yolk, which has been lightly beaten. Toss again and remove to hot serving dish. *Serve immediately.*

FETTUCCINI PESTO

Preparation Time: 10 minutes
Cooking Time: 15 minutes
Serves: 6

Sue Griffin
Endless Summer I

1 cup fresh basil
½ cup Parmesan cheese
½ cup nuts
½ cup olive oil

SEASONING:
½ pkg. Fettuccini al verde
½ pkg. white fettuccini

Put all ingredients in blender (except fettuccini) and blend. Cook fettuccini (as per package instructions), strain and mix in desired amount of pesto sauce. *Serve hot.*

GREEN HERBED RICE

Preparation Time: 10 minutes
Cooking Time: 25 minutes
Serves: 4

Jan Robinson
Vanity

2 cups lightly salted water
1 cup long grain white rice
½ cup fresh parsley
3 Tblsp. basil, freshly chopped
    or 1 Tblsp. dried

1½ Tblsp. chopped scallion tops
¼ - ½ cup olive oil
Salt and freshly ground black pepper
1 Tblsp. butter
Parmesan cheese, freshly grated
    (optional)

Bring water to a boil in saucepan. Add rice to boiling water. Stir once so that rice does not stick to bottom of pan. Cover and reduce to lowest heat and cook until done, about 20 minutes. Place parsley, basil, and scallion tops in blender or food processor. Slowly add just enough olive oil to make smooth puree. Just before serving, toss rice with herb puree until well mixed and green in color. Add salt and pepper to taste. *Stir in butter and sprinkle with Parmesan cheese, if desired.*

BULGAR WITH AROMATIC VEGETABLES

Preparation Time: 5 minutes   Jan Robinson
Cooking Time: 25 minutes   Vanity
Serves: 6 - 8

3 Tblsp. butter
¼ cup carrots, chopped
¼ cup celery, chopped
¼ cup onion, chopped
Black pepper, freshly ground

1 cup bulgar
1½ cups chicken broth
¼ tsp. salt
2 Tblsp. fresh parsley, chopped

Melt butter over medium heat and add chopped vegetables and pepper.
Cook, stirring for 1 minute. Add bulgar and toss for 3 to 5 minutes
until vegetables have softened and bulgar is golden brown. Add chicken
broth and salt and bring to a boil. Reduce heat to medium low. Simmer,
uncovered, about 15 minutes, until all liquid has been absorbed. Stir in
chopped parsley.

RISOTTO MILANESE

Preparation Time: 5 minutes   Barbie Haworth
Standing Time: 15 minutes   Ann-Marie II
Cooking Time: 25 minutes
Serves: 6

2 cups rice
3 - 4 cups chicken broth
1/8 tsp. saffron (added to
     the stock)
1 clove garlic, chopped fine

½ cup onion, chopped fine
½ cup fresh mushrooms, chopped
½ cup tomatoes, small pieces
Salt if needed (depends on stock)
½ cup butter

In a saucepan, saute garlic, rice, onions, and mushrooms in butter. Add
hot stock, and cook for 20 minutes covered. Turn off heat, and let
stand for 10 - 15 minutes. Serve hot.   *Note: ¼ cup Parmesan cheese
can be added before cooling.*

SAFFRON RICE PILAF

Preparation Time: 5 minutes
Cooking Time: 20 minutes
Serves: 6

Cherie Hughes
Skopbank of Finland

1 Tblsp. olive oil
3 Tblsp. butter
¼ cup minced shallots
¼ cup chopped onion
1/8 tsp. saffron

1 chicken bouillon cube
Pinch tumeric
Freshly ground pepper
2 cups rice
4 cups water

Saute above ingredients, except rice and water. Add rice, and saute until transparent. Add water. Reduce flame. Cook covered on lowest heat for 20 minutes approximately. Rice kernels will open, and be a mellow yellow color. Fluff, and serve.

RICE BROWNED IN BOUILLON

Preparation Time: 5 minutes
Cooking Time: 30 minutes
Serves: 6

Jane Glancy
Truant

¼ cup butter
1 large onion, minced
1 clove garlic, minced

1 cup raw rice
2 cups bouillon or chicken stock

Heat butter in saucepan. Saute onion and garlic until onion is transparent. Add rice, and saute until golden, adding more butter if necessary. Add bouillon and cover. Bring to a boil, reduce heat, and simmer for 15 - 20 minutes until liquid is absorbed. Remove lid, and allow rice to dry.

HINT: Rice, noodles or spaghetti will not boil over or stick together if you add a lump of butter or a few teaspoons of cooking oil to the water.

RICE PARISIENNE

Preparation Time: 10 minutes
Cooking Time: 30 minutes
Serves: 8

Alison P. Briscoe
Ovation

1 cup uncooked brown rice
8 ozs. fresh sauteed mushrooms
4 Tblsp. butter

2 (10½ oz.) cans onion soup
   (Campbell's)
1 soup can water
Garnish: chopped parley

Saute rice and mushrooms gently in frying pan in butter. Remove and put into sauce pan. Stir in the soup and water. Cover and cook over low flame for 30 minutes or until tender. Sprinkle with fresh parsley.

PARMESAN RICE

Preparation Time: 5 minutes
Cooking Time: 30 minutes
Serves: 4

Jacklyn Johnson Rabinowitz
Almost Heaven

3 Tblsp. butter
¼ cup finely chopped onion
½ tsp. finely minced garlic
1 cup rice - uncooked

1 - 1½ cup chicken broth
Salt and freshly ground black pepper, to taste
2 Tblsp. grated Parmesan cheese

Melt 2 Tblsp. butter in heavy saucepan. Add onion and garlic, stirring until onion wilts. Add rice and stir. Add broth, salt and pepper. Bring to boil and cover. Cook over low heat for 20 minutes. Stir in 1 Tblsp. butter and the 2 Tblsp. cheese.

SYLVIA'S RICE

Preparation Time: 10 minutes
Cooking Time: 25 minutes
Serves: 4

Sylvia Dabney
Native Sun

¾ cup white rice	Salt to taste
¼ cup wild rice	5 chicken bouillon cubes
1 carrot, sliced in thin wheels	2 cups warm water
¼ cup onion, chopped	1 Tblsp. bacon grease or butter

In warm water, dissolve bouillion. Add bacon grease, onions, carrots, and salt. Bring to boil. Add rice, mix, stir with fork to separate. Cover and simmer (lowest heat) for 25 minutes. *Don't look until timer goes off!*

"WILD" RICE

Preparation Time: 1 minute
Cooking Time: 25 minutes
Serves: 8

Lisa Hawkins
Ariguani

2 boxes Uncle Ben's wild rice	2 Tblsp. mango chutney
1/3 cup heavy cream or Half & Half	

Prepare rice as directed on box. When rice has cooked, add cream and chutney.

WILD RICE WITH PLANTAINS

Preparation Time: 10 minutes
Cooking Time: 20 minutes
Serves: 6

Kimberly Foote
Oklahoma Crude II

1 cup Uncle Ben's long grain
    wild rice
4 Tblsp. soy sauce

2 over ripe plantains
¼ cup pecans, chopped

Cook rice as directed on package. Add soy sauce. Slice plantains
in small pieces and add along with pecans about halfway through
cooking time for rice. *An interesting mixture!*

LIME RICE

Preparation Time: 10 minutes
Cooking Time: 20 minutes
Serves: 6

Jennifer Morden
Promises

1 cup regular rice, uncooked
½ cup fresh parsley, minced
¼ cup green onion, minced

Grated rind of 1 small lime
Juice of ½ lime

Cook rice according to package directions, omitting salt. Remove from
heat, and add remaining ingredients. *Great with pork tenderloin.*

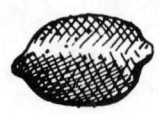

DESSERTS

NOTES

ULTIMATE CHOCOLATE SEX CAKE

Preparation Time: 15 minutes
Cooking Time: 20 minutes
Serves: 8

C.J. Burns
Grace

2 cups flour
2 cups sugar
4 oz. oleo or butter
4 Tblsp. Hershey's cocoa
1 cup water
½ cup crisco
½ cup buttermilk or eggnog
2 slightly beaten eggs
1 tsp. baking soda
1 tsp. cinnamon
1 tsp. vanilla

ICING:
1 box powdered sugar
4 oz. butter, ½ cup
4 Tblsp. Hershey's cocoa
6 Tblsp. milk
1 tsp. vanilla
1 cup chopped walnuts

Preheat oven to 400° F. In a saucepan, bring to a rapid boil (do not mix with mixer!): butter, crisco, cocoa, water. Pour over flour and sugar, and blend well. Then add buttermilk, eggs, soda, cinnamon, and vanilla. Mix well and pour into greased and floured sheet cake pan. Bake for 20 minutes at 400°, 5 minutes before cake is done, melt: 1 stick butter, cocoa, milk. Bring to a boil stirring constantly. Remove from heat and add powdered sugar (a little at a time), vanilla, and nuts. Blend well and spread over warm cake. *Best birthday cake you could ever give a charter guest! Can be made at a moment's notice. Do not overbake. This is the best because it is between chocolate cake, brownies, and fudge.*

MINT CHOCOLATE CHIP CAKE

Preparation Time: 15 minutes
Cooking Time: 1 hour
Serves: 8 - 10

Betsi Dwyer
September Morn

1 pkg. yellow or white cake mix
1 (3 oz.) pkg. instant pistachio
   pudding
1 cup sour cream
4 eggs

1/3 cup vegetable oil
1/3 cup green Creme de Menthe
1 (12 oz.) pkg. chocolate chips
Garnish: whipped cream

Preheat oven to 350° F. Grease and flour a bundt pan or similar pan. Mix all ingredients, except chocolate chips, in a large bowl. Add chips and pour into pan. Bake 1 hour. Sprinkle with powdered sugar when almost cool or serve with whipped cream.

PINEAPPLE UPSIDE DOWN CAKE

Preparation Time: 10 minutes
Cooking Time: 45 minutes
Serves: 8

Rosalind Rice
Endless Summer II

*3 Tblsp. Lyle's Golden Syrup
   for Topping - otherwise,
2 Tblsp. brown sugar creamed
   with equal amount of butter
1 (20 oz.) can pineapple rings,
   reserve juice

8 Tblsp. butter
¾ cup white sugar
2 lightly beaten eggs
1 cup all-purpose flour
Pinch salt
1 tsp. baking powder

Preheat oven to 350° F. Grease 9" cake tin. Pour syrup into bottom or spread creamed butter and sugar mixture evenly over bottom. Arrange pineapple rings over this. Cream together butter and white sugar. Add eggs and beat thoroughly. Fold in sifted flour, salt, and baking powder. Add some pineapple juice to give a dropping consistency. Spread over pineapple rings. Bake in centre of oven until well risen and springy to the touch. Turn out onto a serving plate. Serve with a pineapple sauce made by thickening the remaining juice with a little cornstarch.
Lyle's golden syrup is an English product and I have not come across anything quite the same in the States. It can be bought at Riteways supermarket in Road Town, Tortola.

STRAWBERRY CAKES

Preparation Time: 20 minutes
Cooking Time: 15 minutes
Serves: 4

Gunilla Lundgren
Bambi

3 cups all-purpose flour
2 Tblsp. sugar
½ tsp. salt
1 cup (½ lb.) butter
1 egg yolk

Marzipan cream: ½ lb. marzipan
    paste, grated
1 cup whipped cream
Garnish: Strawberries (½ lb.),
    fresh or frozen

Preheat oven to 425° F. In a bowl, mix flour, sugar, and salt. Mix in butter, and then egg yolk. Work to a dough. Press dough into individual greased tartelettes or a pie pan. Bake for 15 minutes at 425° oven. Let cool. Mix the marzipan with whipped cream. Fill pies with cream mixture and decorate with strawberries.

PEACH AND MARSHMALLOW DESSERT CAKE

Preparation Time: 15 minutes
Cooking Time: 40 minutes
Serves: 6 - 8

D. Stetson
Fantasy

3 Tblsp. butter
¼ cup sugar
½ cup corn syrup
1 egg
2 cups cake flour
2 tsp. baking powder

¼ tsp. salt
½ cup milk
8 peach halves
1 1/3 cup brown sugar
1 tsp. ground cinnamon
8 marshmallows

Preheat oven to 350° F. Grease 8x12 baking pan. Cream 2 Tblsp. butter, sugar, and corn syrup. Add egg and beat well. Sift flour, baking powder, and salt; add to creamed mixture alternately with milk. Pour into prepared pan, arrange peach halves on top. Cream 1 Tblsp. butter; add brown sugar and cinnamon and sprinkle over peaches. Bake 40 minutes. Place marshmallows on top of each peach half; return to oven to brown.

RUM CAKE

Preparation Time: 25 minutes
Cooking Time: 1 hour
Serves: 8 - 10

Jane Glancy
Truant

1 cup chopped pecans or walnuts
1 package yellow cake mix
1 (3 oz.) package instant vanilla
   pudding mix
½ cup cold water
½ cup oil
½ cup dark rum
4 eggs

GLAZE:
¼ lb. butter
¼ cup water
1 cup sugar
½ cup dark rum

Heat the oven to 325° F. Grease and flour 10 inch tube pan or bundt pan. Sprinkle nuts over bottom of pan. Mix all cake ingredients together, and pour over nuts in pan. Bake for 1 hour and cool. Invert on serving plate. Prick the top, and drizzle glaze evenly over the top. Repeat until all the glaze is used. Glaze: Melt the butter in a saucepan, and stir in water and sugar. Boil for 5 minutes, stirring constantly. Remove from the heat, and stir in the rum.

 ## SPECIAL CHRISTMAS RUM CAKE

Preparation Time: depends

Joan Della Dora
Bluewater

Before U start, check the rum to make sure of the quantity. Select large measuring bowl, cup, ect., then check rum again. With an electric mixer beat 1 cup sugar in large fluffy bowl. Check rum again. Add 3 large eggs, 2 cups fried druit, and bat until very high. If fruit sticks to beaters pry out with a drewscriber. Check rum again. Add 3 cups of baking powder, one pint of rum, 1 tsp. of toda, and 1 cup of pepper. Sift in 1 pint lemon juice, and fold in chopped buttermilk and strained nuts. Check rum. Add 1 babblespoon of scrown burger or whatever color U have. Check rum again. Turn pan to 350° , grease oven, and pour whole mess in. What do you mean this ain't a Merry Christmas?!?!?

EBONY AND IVORY CHEESECAKE

Preparation Time: 35 minutes
Cooking time: 2 hours
Chilling Time: 2 hours
Serves: 6 - 8

Sharon Strong
Promises

CRUST:
½ cup butter, melted
1½ cups crushed chocolate snap
    cookies
¾ cup small pecan chunks
1/3 cup whipping cream
10 oz. semi-sweet chocolate chips
1 Tblsp. butter, melted

FILLING:
3 (8 oz.) cream cheese, room
    temperature
1 cup sugar
6 eggs
½ cup whipping cream
1½ tsp. vanilla

Preheat oven to 300° F. Mix together butter and cookie crumbs. Press into a springform pan at least ½ to top. Use pie plate or custard cup to round off edges. Mix together the whipping cream, chocolate chips, and butter. First, sprinkle the crushed pecans over the crumb crust evenly, then drizzle 3 Tblsp. of the chocolate mixture over the nuts. Reserve the rest of mixture for filling. Beat cream cheese and sugar. Next beat in eggs, cream, and vanilla. Separate 1 cup from mixture, and add all but 2 Tblsp. reserved chocolate mixture. Pour chocolate mixture into pan over crust and nuts. Carefully pour ½ cup at a time vanilla mixture over chocolate layer. Use the 2 Tblsp. reserved chocolate mixture to make designs on top of cake. Use evenly spaced dropped tsp. and swirl with knife. Bake for 2 hours, and cool on wire rack. Chill for a few hours.

CHEESECAKE

Preparation Time: 10 minutes   *Carol Lowe*
Cooking Time: 40 minutes   *Natasha*
Serves: 8 - 12

8 - 10 whole graham crackers   2 tsp. vanilla
4 Tblsp. melted butter   1 lb. cream cheese
½ cup + 4 Tblsp. sugar   1 pint sour cream
2 eggs   Garnish: fresh strawberries

Preheat oven to 300° F. Roll out graham crackers. Mix with melted
butter and 1 Tblsp. sugar. Line spring form pan with this. Put cream
cheese in a bowl, and add eggs, ½ cup sugar, and 1 tsp. vanilla. Mix
well with beater. Pour into spring form. Bake 30 minutes at 300°.
Take out and spread pint of sour cream mixed with 3 Tblsp. sugar and
1 tsp. vanilla. Put back in oven for 10 minutes. Cool. *Garnish with fresh
strawberries.*

LEMMON BARS

Preparation Time: 20 minutes   *Denise Wright*
Cooking Time: 40 minutes   *Parandah*
Serves: 8 - 10

1st LAYER: 2nd LAYER:
1 cup butter   4 eggs
2 cups flour   6 - 8 Tblsp. lemon juice
½ cup powdered sugar   2 cups white sugar
                                    4 Tblsp. flour
                                    1 tsp. baking powder

Preheat oven to 350° F. Mix first layer ingredients and pat into 9"x13"
buttered pan. Bake 15 minutes at 350°. Mix second layer ingredients
and pour over crust. Bake 25 minutes at 350°. Sprinkle with powdered
sugar. Cut into bars. (Shirley Dorn Burroughs of Odyssey suggests
using lime juice in place of lemon juice.)

*Note: A 13-year-old guest signed our guest book "Only very good
friends deserve Lemmon Bars" Thus the double "M" spelling!*

CHOCOLATE DIPPED STRAWBERRIES

Preparation Time: 10 minutes
Cooking Time: 5 minutes
Serves: 4

Sylvia Dabney
Native Sun

1 qt. strawberries, washed
    and unstemmed

SAUCE:
2 Tblsp. butter
1 (6 ox.) package semi-sweet
    chocolate morsels

1 tsp. vanilla or orange extract
    (Try it both ways!)
1 (14 oz.) can Eagle Brand Sweet
    Condensed Milk

Arrange strawberries on doilied plate. Place sauce ingredients in top of double boiler, and stir until blended. Serve in bowl over hot water and let guests hand dip the strawberries. If there is any sauce left over, freeze and re-use as fudge sauce for ice cream. *Wonderfully easy - wonderfully delicious!*

GRAND MARNIER CHOCOLATE COVERED PEARS

Preparation Time: 30 minutes
Cooking Time: 10 minutes
Chilling Time: 2 hours
Serves: 6

Emily Welch
Wind's End

2 (29 oz.) cans pear halves
1 (6 oz.) package chocolate chips
½ stick butter

1 cup Grand Marnier
Garnish: Maraschino cherries
    Chocolate sauce

An hour or so, or early in the day, drain juice from pears, reserving juice, and pour Grand Marnier over them in a tightly sealed plastic container to marinate. Chill for an hour. Melt chocolate chips and butter over low heat, or in a double boiler. Let cool to just warm. Drain pears reserving Grand Marnier. Dry well on paper towels. Dip large end half of each pear in chocolate, and place on waxed paper covered cookie sheet. Chill for approximately 1 hour. Mix left over chocolate, Grand Marnier, and pear juice as sauce. *Serve in clear goblets or dessert dishes with maraschino cherries for garnish, and chocolate sauce for that truly rich touch.*

PRALINE PARFAIT

Preparation Time: 10 minutes
Cooking Time: 10 minutes
Serves: 4 - 6

Sylvia Dabney
Native Sun

1½ cups dark corn syrup
½ cup dark bown sugar
4 tsp. flour
¼ tsp. salt

2 Tblsp. butter
1 cup cold water
1½ tsp. vanilla
1 cup chopped pecans

Combine all ingredients except vanilla and pecans and boil for 10 minutes. Remove from heat, add vanilla and pecans. *Serve over ice cream warm or cold.*

PINEAPPLE CHOCOLATE FONDU

Preparation Time: 30 minutes
Cooking Time: 5 minutes
Serves: 8

Kim Turk
Antipodes

1 whole pineapple
1 pint of strawberries
1 bar Cadbury's milk chocolate

Zambuka
½ cup Half & Half (light cream)

Cut off the head and tail of the pineapple. Keep the head. Cut out the inside of pineapple keeping body skin intact. Marinate ¼ of strawberries in Zambuka until cold. When time comes to serve it, arrange pineapples and strawberries around body. Put fondu fork in body, and melt chocolate with cream. *Serve as a casual dessert after big main course. Put a flaming Zambuka on table so you have the choice of either Zambuka or chocolate to dip.*

NUTTY CYN!

Preparation Time: 20 minutes
Chilling Time: 3 hours
Serves: 6 - 8

Nicky Cahi
Once Upon A Time

Graham crackers
2 oz. butter
1 tin condensed milk
½ pint heavy cream

2/3 cup lemon juice
3 egg whites
Garnish: grated chocolate, cherries

Make up biscuit base with graham crackers and butter, and line 9"
pie dish with the base. Beat together condensed milk, cream, and lemon
juice until mixture has fairly thick consistency. Separate eggs and beat
whites until they hold stiff. Fold whites into other mixture, pour all
onto biscuit base and allow to chill for several hours. Garnish with
grated chocolate, cherries, or soft fruit. *Delicious and simple!*

CHOCOLATE TOFFEE DESSERT

Preparation Time: 15 minutes
Cooking Time: 45 minutes
Serves: 6 - 8

Josie Gould
Sevruga

6 oz. butter
3 oz. castor sugar
9 oz. plain flour
4 oz. butter

2 oz. castor sugar
2 Tblsp. honey
7 oz. condensed milk
4 oz. semi-sweet chocolate

Preheat oven to 325° F. Beat the 6 oz. butter and sugar. Fold in the
flour. Knead into a 9 inch dish and bake for 35 minutes at 325°. Melt
4 oz. butter, castor sugar, honey, and condensed milk. Boil for 5
minutes until thick and caramel-like. Pour over cooled cake in dish.
Let cool. Melt chocolate in a double boiler or in a bowl on top of
hot water in a saucepan. Pour over caramel and refrigerate.

'HELIOS' BROWNIES

Preparation Time: 20 minutes
Cooking Time: 40 minutes
Makes: 16

Dawn Drell
Helios

4 oz. unsweetened chocolate
½ cup unsalted butter
1¼ cups and 3 Tblsp. sugar
1 tsp. vanilla extract
3 large eggs, beaten

¾ cup all-purpose flour
½ cup crushed walnuts
4 - 6 chocolate lovers
Garnish: whipped cream
    and Grand Marnier

Preheat oven to 350° F. Grease 8 inch pan. Melt chocolate and butter in a double boiler. Cool 5 minutes. Add sugar and beat 1 or 2 minutes. Add vanilla and eggs, stir only until combined. Add flour and walnuts, mix until batter looks shiny. Bake until toothpick in middle comes out clean, about 40 minutes. *These brownies taste better after a day's "rest" topped with fresh whipped cream. Try adding a dash of Grand Marnier to whipped cream.*

PUFFS OF MOUNTAIN AIR

Preparation Time: 20 minutes
Cooking Time: 12 minutes
Serves: 6

Denise Wright
Parandah

2 eggs, separated
6 Tblsp. sugar
1 Tblsp. flour
1 tsp. vanilla

2 egg whites
Pinch salt
2 Tblsp. butter
Powdered sugar

Preheat oven to 325°F. Beat yolks and 2 Tblsp. sugar until forms a ribbon; add flour, beat again. Add vanilla. Beat 4 whites with salt until stiff peaks; add sugar 1 Tblsp. at a time. Beat stiff. Fold whites into yolks. Spoon into buttered oval dish, making three large mounds. Bake 12 minutes until golden. Dust with powdered sugar. *Serve and listen to the ooh's and ah's. This literally melts in your mouth.*

CHOCOLATE ALMOND FLUFF

Preparation Time: 10 minutes
Chilling Time: 4 hours
Serves: 6

Renie Mousek
Bon Vivant

1 package chocolate almond
    cookies

2 cups whipping cream
½ cup Kahlua or Creme de Menthe

Whip cream. Add Kahlua to whipped cream. In individual attractive dishes layer whipped cream and cookie until glass is full ending with whipped cream. Approximately 5 cookies per serving. Top with crumbled extra cookies and cherry. Chill for 4 hours.

BANANA POUNDS

Preparation Time: 20 minutes
Cooking Time: 15 minutes
Serves: 6 - 8

Kimberly Foote
Oklahoma Crude II

3 ripe bananas
1 (3 oz.) package instant
    yellow pudding mix
2 cups milk

1½ cups rum
Cinnamon
Nutmeg
1 pound cake

Preheat oven to 400° F. Slice bananas, and put in oven proof glass dish. Sprinkle with spices, and dab with butter. Heat in 400° oven. While this is cooking, mix up the pudding and milk according to directions on package. Pour pudding over each slice of pound cake. When bananas are nice and hot, flambe with rum at the table - then dish the bananas over the pound cake and pudding. *A nice mixture!*

BANANAS GOMEZ

Preparation Time: 5 minutes
Cooking Time: 15 minutes
Serves: 6

Annie Scholl
Bon Vivant

¼ cup + 1 Tblsp. butter
½ cup brown sugar
¼ cup honey
¾ cup heavy cream

1/8 tsp. nutmeg
1/8 tsp. cinnamon
2 or 3 bananas, sliced
1 small pound cake, cut into
12 slices

Over medium-high heat, melt butter, and stir in brown sugar until blended. Add honey, and continue stirring and cooking for about 1 minute. Add cream, nutmeg, and cinnamon. Stir until blended. Add bananas, stir, and simmer for about 2 minutes. Place a slice of pound cake on each plate, and spoon over half of banana mixture. Place another slice of pound cake on top, and distribute on top of each serving until gone. *Don't be worried about leftovers with this one — there won't be any!*

MANGOES AU GRATIN

Preparation Time: 15 minutes
Cooking Time: 10 minutes
Serves: 4

Gunilla Lundgren
Bambi

4 mangoes, cut in wedges and
peeled
2 oranges

SABAYONNE SAUCE:
6 Tblsp. sugar
3 egg yolks

Garnish: Sprigs of fresh mint

Preheat oven to 475° F. Place mango wedges in a buttered oven proof dish. Whip egg yolks and sugar until creamy. Mix in juice from 2 oranges, and whip sauce more. Pour sauce over mangoes, and grill in a hot oven until Sabayonne has a golden brown surface.

FLAMING PLANTAINS

Preparation Time: 5 minutes
Cooking Time: 5 minutes
Serves: 6 - 8

Nancy Wilkinson
Hooter

5 Tblsp. butter
6 - 8 plantains, sliced lengthwise
    in half and peeled
¼ cup brown sugar

¼ cup sugar
½ tsp. cinnamon
¼ cup Cruzan rum

In a large frying pan, put butter and plantains over medium heat. Add sugar, brown sugar, and cinnamon. Cook and turn over for about 5 minutes. Pour out excess butter. Add rum, and light up! *Serve with Old Wife.*

PINEAPPLE SURPRISE

Preparation Time: 20 minutes
Cooking Time: 6 minutes
Chilling Time: 8 hours
Serves: 6

Carol Lowe
Natasha

1 large ripe pineapple
2 Tblsp. Kirsch
3 Tblsp. sugar

1½ pints pineapple or orange
    sherbet
6 egg whites
2 Tblsp. sugar

Cut pineapple in half lengthwise including plume. With a curved grapefruit knife, cut out fruit leaving boat shaped shells. Cut fruit into chunks discarding center core. Sprinkle chunks with Kirsch and 3 Tblsp. sugar. Spoon back into pineapple shells. Cover and refrigerate up to 8 hours. Preheat oven to 425° F. Make meringue by whipping whites and adding sugar till stiff. Spoon sherbet over pineapple chunks and cover completely with meringue so heat cannot penetrate to sherbet. Sprinkle with sugar (1 Tblsp.). Bake 6 - 8 minutes until meringue is brown. Serve immediately.

PINEAPPLE PUDDING

Preparation Time: 20 minutes　　　　　　　*Margo Muckey*
Cooking Time: 10 minutes　　　　　　　　　　*Tuff*
Chilling Time: 1 - 2 hours
Serves: 6

2 Tblsp. flour
2 Tblsp. cornstarch
¼ cup lemon juice
1 (20 oz.) can crushed pineapple
　　with juice
1 (8 oz.) can crushed pineapple
　　with juice

3 eggs, separated
½ cup sugar
1½ tsp. lemon peel
½ tsp. baking powder
Garnish: whipped cream

Blend flour, cornstarch, and lemon juice in a 2 quart saucepan until smooth. Add pineapple, egg yolks, sugar, and lemon peel and mix well. Bring to a boil over medium high heat stirring constantly until thickened. Remove from heat, cool slightly. Beat egg whites with baking powder until stiff. Fold into pineapple. Cover and refrigerate until set, about 2 hours. Spoon into bowls and add a dollop of whipped cream to each.

LEMON SYLLABUB

Preparation Time: 5 minutes　　　　　　　*Jan Burnes*
Serves: 4　　　　　　　　　　　　　　　　*Adaro*

1 lemon, grated and squeezed
3 oz. castor sugar
4 - 6 oz. white wine

½ pint whipping or double cream
Garnish: lemon slices

Whisk cream until thick, carefully fold in lemon juice, rind, white wine, and sugar. Whisk until the mixture forms peaks. Pile into wine glasses, and decorate with a slice of lemon. This should be slightly tart. *A light dessert idea for serving after a heavy, spicy dinner.*

DECADENT CHOCOLATE MOUSSE

Preparation Time: 20 minutes   *Lisa Hawkins*
Cooking Time: 5 minutes   *Ariguani*
Serves: 8

12 oz. semi-sweet chocolate	4 egg yolks
¾ cup unsalted butter	5 egg whites
3 Tblsp. unsweetened cocoa	Pinch of salt
powder	Garnish: finely chopped walnuts
1/3 cup sugar	

Combine chocolate, butter, and cocoa in a 1 quart saucepan, and cook over low heat. Remove from heat, and pour into a large bowl. Allow to cool, but not harden. Add sugar, and beat at medium speed until well mixed. Beat in egg yolks one at a time. Set aside. Beat egg whites and salt in another bowl until stiff. Fold gently ¼ whites in chocolate mixture, then the remaining whites ¼ at a time. Pour into ½ cup ramekins, and refrigerate until set. Garnish with nuts. *Serve mousse with a glass of Sauternes wine. Tell your guests to take a bite of mousse and a sip of wine, and let the flavors blend. If you're a chocolate lover you'll think you have died and gone to heaven!*

MIGHTY MOUSSE

Preparation Time: 5 minutes   *Donna Jaggard*
Chilling Time: several hours   *Thorobred*
Serves: 6

2 eggs	1½ cup Half & Half (light cream),
1 Tblsp. Cognac	scalded
Pinch of cinnamon	Garnish: whipped cream and
1½ cup semi-sweet chocolate	shaved chocolate curls
morsels	

Place all ingredients except Half & Half in blender. Blend briefly. Add scalded Half & Half. Blend completely. Pour into bowl or individual dishes. Chill several hours. *Garnish with whipped cream and shaved chocolate curls.*

WHITE CHOCOLATE MOUSSE

Preparation Time: 30 minutes   *Sue Griffin*
Chilling Time: several hours   *Endless Summer I*
Serves: 8

2 sticks white chocolate 8 oz.   ½ cup sugar
   (Toblerone)   1 Tblsp. unflavored gelatin
½ stick butter (4 oz.)   1 cup cream
4 eggs   Garnish: fruit of choice

Soften chocolate and butter and beat until fluffy. Beat in egg yolks, melted gelatin, and sugar. Fold in beaten egg whites. Pour into individual dishes or one large mold. Allow to set. *Decorate with fresh raspberries or fruit of your own choice.*

CHOCOLATE MOUSSE

Preparation Time: 15 minutes   *Marilyn Stenberg*
Chilling Time: 2 hours   *Champagne*
Serves: 6

4 oz. plain chocolate,   2 eggs, separated
   broken up   5 fluid oz. double cream, whipped
5 oz. white marshmallow cream   Garnish: whipped cream, chocolate
4 Tblsp. milk   curls

Gently melt together the chocolate, marshmallow cream, and milk. Cool and then mix in the egg yolks. Leave until cold. Stiffly whip the egg whites, and add to the mousse along with half of the double cream. Leave in refrigerator until thoroughly chilled. Decorate with the rest of the whipped cream and chocolate curls.

STRAWBERRY MOUSSE

Preparation Time: 10 minutes   *Paola Taglia*
Freezing Time: 1 hour   *Stormvogel*
Serves: 6

1 cup frozen strawberries	**1 envelope unflavored gelatin**
½ cup cream, liquid	**½ cup boiling water**
¼ cup alcoholic cassis syrup	**Garnish: cherries and whipped cream**

Put the strawberries, the cream, and the cassis syrup in the mixer. Mix for 5 minutes. Dissolve the gelatin in ½ cup boiling water. Pour in the mixer. Mix for another 5 minutes. Pour into plastic glasses, and put them into the freezer. At the serving moment, garnish with a cherry in the middle of every glass. Optional, some topping cream around the cherry.

SILKY APRICOT MOUSSE

Preparation Time: 15 minutes   *Jacklyn J. Rabinowitz*
Chilling Time: 1 hour   *Almost Heaven*
Serves: 4

1 (30 oz.) can apricots (or peach) halves in syrup	**1½ tsp. vanilla**
¾ cup heavy cream	**Garnish: whipped cream, nutmeg**

Drain apricots. Pat dry. Whirl in blender 'til smooth. Whip cream and vanilla until stiff. Set aside ¼ cup. Fold apricots 1/3 at a time, into whipped cream, blending well each time. Spoon into glasses, and garnish with reserved cream. Sprinkle with nutmeg if you wish. Chill one hour.

SOUFFLE GRAND MARNIER

Preparation Time: 12 - 15 minutes   *Shannon Webster*
Cooking Time: 20 - 25 minutes   *Chaparral*
Serves: 6

2 cups milk   5 egg yolks
¾ cup sugar   7 egg whites
1/3 cup flour   2 oz. Grand Marnier
2 oz. butter - melted

Preheat oven to 400° F. Beat egg whites until stiff. Heat milk, add
sugar, stir and bring to boil. Mix melted butter with the flour and stir
into boiling milk. Blend into a thick creamy consistency. Remove from
stove and add Grand Marnier. Beat egg yolks until lemon in color, and
add to mixture, stirring constantly. Gently fold in the beaten egg
whites. Pour into buttered, sugared souffle dish or mini ramekins.
Bake at 400° F. for 20 - 25 minutes with door closed. Serve at once.
*Cherie Hughes on Skopbank of Finland uses Frangelico instead of
Grand Marnier.*

SOUFFLE DANNON

Preparation Time: 5 minutes   *Sheila Smith*
Serves: 4 - 6   *Victorious*

2 (16 oz.) tubs Dannon raspberry yogurt
1 (16 oz.) tub Cool Whip
Garnish: fresh blueberries or raspberries

*This is an awful cheat, but is instant, good, and it could save your neck
one busy night!. Simply mix and serve topped with raspberries or blueberries. Don't blush.*

PINA COLADA SOUFFLE

Preparation Time: 40 minutes   *Sharon Strong*
Chilling Time: several hours   *Promises*
Serves: 6 - 8

6 egg yolks   2 envelopes unflavored gelatin
½ cup powdered sugar   ¼ cup dark rum
4 egg whites   ½ pint heavy cream
1 cup crushed, drained pineapple   Garnish: toasted coconut
¼ cup cream of coconut   or drained pineapple

Make 1 inch foil tops, and secure with tape to top of 6 tall stemmed
glasses. The entire inside surface should be buttered and sprinkled.
Beat egg yolks and sugar until fluffy. Add pineapple and cream of
coconut. In a small saucepan, sprinkle gelatin over rum. When spongy,
dissolve over hot water. Cool and add to pineapple mixture. Beat egg
whites until stiff. Beat cream until it mounds. Fold cream into pineapple , then egg whites. Spoon carefully into dessert glasses to top
of foil. Chill for several hours. To serve: remove foil top, and sprinkle
with toasted coconut or ½ tsp. of drained crushed pineapple.

ICE CREAM PIE

Preparation Time: 30 minutes   *Sue Griffin*
Cooking Time: 30 minutes   *Endless Summer I*
Serves: 8

MERINGUE: FILLING:
4 egg whites   2 egg whites, beaten
½ cup sugar   1 cup fruit (any over ripe fruit)
                                    2 Tblsp. lemon juice
                                    1 cup cream
                                    ½ cup sugar

Preheat oven to 250° F. Make the meringue, and line a pie dish. Bake
until set in a low oven for 30 minutes. Beat cream, and mix in pureed
fruit, sugar, and lemon juice. Fold in egg whites, and pour into dish.
Freeze. *Decorate with pieces of fruit.*

APPLE CLAFOUTI

Preparation Time: 15 minutes   Carol Love
Cooking Time: 45 minutes   Natasha
Serves: 8

4 Tblsp. butter, 1 Tblsp. softened   3 eggs
4 cups tart apples, peeled, cored,   ¾ cup milk
    thinly sliced about ½ lb.)   ¼ cup Calvados or dark rum
1 Tblsp. strained lemon juice   ¾ cup flour
½ tsp. baking powder   ¼ tsp. salt
¼ tsp. cinnamon   1 - 2 tsp. cinnamon sugar
6 Tblsp. sugar

Preheat oven to 375° F. Spread 1 Tblsp. butter, soft, on bottom and
sides of a 10 inch baking dish. Spread sliced apples evenly in pan.
Sprinkle with lemon juice, cinnamon, 3 Tblsp. sugar, and bake for 15
minutes. Meanwhile, melt 3 Tblsp. butter. Place eggs in blender, cover,
and whirl for 10 seconds. Add milk, rum, and melted butter, and whirl
for 10 seconds (if no blender beat by hand). Combine and sift flour,
baking powder, salt, and remaining 3 Tblsp. sugar. Add dry ingredients,
and blend on high for 30 seconds (or by hand 1 minute) until lumps go.
Pour batter over apples. Return pan to oven for 30 minutes. Sprinkle
with cinnamon sugar, and serve immediately cut into wedges.

CHESS PIE

Preparation Time: 10 minutes   C.J. Burns
Cooking Time: 1 hour   Grace
Serves: 6 - 8

1 unbaked 9" pie shell   ½ cup butter or margarine
4 eggs   ½ cup evaporated milk
2 cups sugar   1 Tblsp. vanilla
1/8 tsp. salt

Preheat oven to 350° F. Mix eggs by hand (wire whisk) until lemony in
color. Add sugar a little at a time. Add salt. Melt the butter. When
cooled add to egg mixture, together with vanilla and evaporated milk.
Pour into unbaked pie shell, and bake at 350° for 1 hour or until knife
comes out clean. *Like a custard pie, makes a wonderful crust on top.*

SOUR CREAM CREPES
WITH CHOCOLATE SAUCE

Preparation Time: 15 minutes — *Judith Vegiard*
Sitting Time: 10 minutes — *Ruach*
Cooking Time: 1 hour
Serves: 8

CREPES:
½ cup flour
Pinch sugar
1 large or 2 med. eggs
¾ cup milk
1 Tblsp. melted butter

1 Tblsp. brandy
CHOCOLATE SAUCE:
1 large Cadbury milk chocolate bar
2 Tblsp. milk
FILLING:
8 ozs. sour cream

Crepes: Sift flour and sugar. Add eggs one at a time, beating thoroughly. Gradually add milk, melted butter, and brandy, beating until smooth. Let batter stand one hour or more at room temperature before cooking crepes.

Chocolate Sauce: Melt chocolate bar in top of double boiler. Add just enough milk to give it a smooth consistency. Keep crepes warm in oven until all are made. Spread sour cream on one half and fold over. Drizzle chocolate sauce on top.

PAPAYA CREAM

Preparation Time: 10 minutes — *Jan Robinson*
Serves: 6 - 8 — *Vanity*

1 papaya (about 1 lb.)
¼ cup honey or ¼ cup sugar
1 Tblsp. lemon or lime juice, or
    2 Tblsp. dark rum

2 Tblsp. sugar
1 cup heavy cream, chilled

Cut papaya in half lengthwise and remove and discard seeds. Scoop out pulp (about 1¼ cups) and place it in blender or food processor. Add honey and juice, or rum, and blend to smooth puree. Beat cream until soft peaks form. Add sugar and beat again until very stiff peaks form. Fold papaya puree into whipped cream, making sure they are well blended. Serve in stemmed glasses.

CREPES A LA PECHE

Kim Turk
Antipodes

Preparation Time: ½ hour
Cooking Time: ½ hour
Chilling Time: ½ hour
Serves: 10 - 12

CREPES:
1½ cup flour
¼ cup powdered sugar
Pinch salt
1 cup milk
¼ cup melted butter
2 Tblsp. Cointreau
1 tsp lemon rind
5 beaten eggs
FILLING:
2 Tblsp. grated orange rind

2 tsp. grated lemon rind
16 oz. cream cheese
1 cup sour cream
¼ cup sugar
SAUCE:
Peaches, 8 large or 1 lb. can
½ - 1 cup butter
Cointreau
Brandy
Sugar

Combine flour, sugar, salt, milk, butter, liqueur, and rind. Beat well.
Add eggs, and beat until smooth. Cover and refrigerate for 30 minutes.
Make and cook crepes. Combine all filling ingredients, and beat until
smooth. Spoon a heaping spoonful on each crepe. Roll and tuck.
Melt butter in chafing dish. Arrange filled crepes around edge of dish.
Add peaches and juice, and heat. Slowly pour Cointreau and warm
brandy into center dish and ignite. Remove to individual serving plates,
and spoon sauce over crepes (very rich).

BAKED ALASKA

Preparation Time: 10 minutes
Cooking Time: 5 minutes
Serves: 6

L. G. Brendlinger
Ring-Anderson

3 egg whites
1 drop vanilla essence
1 Swiss roll

6 oz. fruit, optional
4 oz. sugar
1 8 oz. block ice cream

Preheat oven to 475° F. Place slices of sponge on an oven-proof salva, and cover with fruit if using. Mold the ice cream on top. Put in the freezer until ready to use. Whisk the whites until stiff, add ½ the sugar, and whisk until glossy. Fold in the remaining sugar and vanilla essence. Spread the meringue over the ice cream making sure there are no gaps or holes. Put immediately into a very hot oven 475° for five minutes or until the meringue is golden. Serve at once. Beware of freezing fruit.

BLACK CHERRY & ALMOND CREAM

Preparation Time: 10 minutes
Chilling Time: at least 1 hour
Serves: 4

Fiona Baldrey
Promenade

1 (7½ oz.) can black cherries
½ pint whipping cream
1 Tblsp. confectioners' sugar -
   sieved

3 macaroons
½ tsp. almond extract or 2 Tblsp.
   Kirsch

Drain the cherries, and dry on paper towel. Whisk the whipping cream with the sugar until forming soft peaks. Fold in the almond extract or Kirsch. Break the macaroons into small pieces, and add with the cherries to the cream. Divide between 4 individual dishes (Parfait glasses if you have them) and serve chilled.

CALEDONIAN CREAM

Preparation Time: 20 minutes
Cooking Time: 5 minutes
Chilling Time: one hour
Serves: 8

Jacklyn J. Rabinowitz
Almost Heaven

½ cup thickly cut orange marma-
    lade
¼ cup Scotch whiskey
2 Tblsp. light brown sugar

1 tsp. grated lemon rind
2 Tblsp. lemon juice
2 cups heavy cream
Garnish: 1 orange, sliced

Combine marmalade, whiskey, brown sugar, lemon juice, and rind in
small heavy saucepan. Heat to boiling, stir until sugar melts. Cool
completely. Beat heavy cream and ½ cup of marmalade mixture at
high speed until cream mounds. Spoon into dessert glasses, and chill
1 hour. Just before serving, drizzle remaining marmalade mixture or
garnish with orange slices.

JAN'S KEY LIME PIE

Preparation Time: 25 minutes
Chilling Time: 8 hours
Cooking Time: 10 minutes
Serves: 8

Casey Miller
Fancy Free

4 eggs, separated
1 (14 oz.) can condensed milk
½ cup fresh lime juice

1 9" graham cracker crust
½ cup sugar

Combine egg yolks and milk in a medium bowl. Fold in lime juice.
Pour into crust, and chill for 1 hour. Preheat the oven to 400°. Beat
egg whites until foamy, gradually adding sugar until stiff peaks form.
Spoon over pie, sealing edges. Bake for 10 minutes. Cool slightly,
and refrigerate all day.

STRAWBERRY ICE

Preparation Time: 25 minutes
Freezing Time: 3 hours
Serves: 4

Jacklyn J. Rabinowitz
Almost Heaven

1 pint strawberries, rinsed,
    drained, and hulled
3 Tblsp. honey
1 cup water

2 Tblsp lemon juice
3 Tblsp. orange juice
Garnish: strawberries

Reserve 4 strawberries for garnish. Puree remainig strawberries. Blend in water, honey, and juices. Partially freeze in 8" square metal pan, stir, then freeze 2 hours longer until firm. *Serve garnished with whole berries.*

FROZEN STRAWBERRY MARGARITA PIE

Preparation Time: 20 minutes
Freezing Time: overnight
Refrigeration Time: 30 minutes
Serves: 8

Jacklyn J. Rabinowitz
Almost Heaven

1 9" graham cracker pie shell
1 (14 oz.) can sweetened con-
    densed milk
¼ cup freshly squeezed lime juice
2 - 3 Tblsp. Tequilla
2 - 3 Tblsp. Triple Sec

½ cup frozen strawberries with
    syrup, thawed
2 cups heavy cream, whipped
Garnish: whipped cream, whole
    strawberries and lime slices

Beat milk, lime juice, Tequilla, and Triple Sec in large bowl at medium speed until smooth (3 minutes). At lower speed, beat in strawberries for 1 minute. Fold whipped cream into strawberry mixture until no streaks of white remain. Pour into shell, mounding in center. Freeze overnight. Transfer to refrigerator 30 minutes before serving. *Garnish with additional whipped cream and whole strawberries and lime slices.*

CREAMY COCONUT PIE

Preparation Time: 10 minutes   *Alison Briscoe*
Cooking Time: 30 minutes   *Ovation*
Serves: 8

1 pie shell - pre-cooked   3 beaten egg yolks
¾ cup sugar - if using fresh coconut 1 cup fresh or tinned coconut
1/3 cup sugar - if using tinned   (Baker's)
     coconut   1 tsp. vanilla essence
¼ cup plain flour   2 Tblsp. butter
¼ tsp. salt   3 egg whites
2 cups milk   4 Tblsp. sugar

Preheat oven to 350° F. Mix sugar, flour, and salt in a saucepan. Add
the 2 cups of milk, and cook on a low flame. Stir continuously; bring
to a boil, and cook for 2 minutes. Stir constantly. (Yes, one of those
recipes). Add the beaten egg yolks. Stir, stir, and cook for another 2
minutes. Add the coconut, vanilla, and butter. Stir for the last time,
and pour into the pie shell. Beat egg whites and sugar until it peaks.
Place on top of pie and bake 350° for 12 - 15 minutes.

CHOCOLATE BANANA PIE

Preparation Time: 20 minutes   *Kimberly Foote*
Chilling Time: 4 hours   *Oklahoma Crude II*
Serves: 8

1 pie crust   Whipped cream
1 (3 oz.) package chocolate   Nutmeg
     pudding mix   Ginger
2 bananas   Cinnamon
2 cups milk   Garnish: whipped cream

Preheat oven to 400° F. Brown pie crust in oven. Mix pudding and milk
by directions on package. Let cool, add spices. When crust is browned,
layer bottom with slices of bananas. Pour pudding mix over bananas
until it fills the pie crust. Chill for about 4 hours. *Serve with whipped
cream.*

WALNUT PIE

Preparation Time: 15 minutes
Cooking Time: 40 minutes
Serves: 8

Rosalind Rice
Endless Summer II

1 unbaked 9" pastry shell
4 eggs
1 cup dark brown sugar
½ tsp. salt
¾ cup light Karo syrup

¼ cup melted butter
1 tsp. vanilla
2 cups chopped walnuts
Garnish: Whole walnuts and
  whipped cream

Preheat oven to 400° F. Beat eggs well. Add brown sugar, syrup, salt, melted butter, and vanilla. Mix thoroughly. Sprinkle chopped walnuts over bottom of pastry shell. Pour egg mixture over. Arrange whole walnuts over top of pie. Bake in a hot oven (400°) for 10 minutes. Reduce heat to 325° and bake a further 30 minutes or until pie is set. Remove from oven and allow to cool thoroughly before serving. Top with whipped cream.

NO CRUST CRANBERRY PIE

Preparation Time: 15 minutes
Cooking Time: 50 - 55 minutes
Serves: 8

Donna Jaggard
Thorobred

2 cups cranberries
½ cup sugar
2 eggs
½ cup chopped walnuts

1 cup sugar
1 cup flour
¾ cup melted butter

Preheat oven to 325° F. Grease 10 inch pie plate. Spread cranberries over the bottom. Sprinkle ½ cup sugar and nuts over cranberries. In a separate bowl, beat eggs well. Add 1 cup of sugar, gradually. Beat and add flour and butter. Pour batter over cranberries. Bake 50 - 55 minutes.

E-Z APPLE PIE

Preparation Time: 20 minutes   *Marita M. Tasse*
Cooking Time: 30 minutes   *Flower of the Storm*
Serves: 6

¾ cup sugar
½ cup flour
1 egg
½ tsp. vanilla
¼ tsp. salt

1 tsp. baking powder
½ tsp. cinnamon
½ cup chopped walnuts
1 cup diced apples (2 apples)

Preheat oven to 350° F. Combine sugar, flour, salt, baking powder, and cinnamon. Stir well, Beat in egg and vanilla with whisk or spoon. Stir in nuts and apples. Mixture becomes thick. Spoon into a buttered 8 inch pie plate, and spread evenly. Bake for 30 minutes at 350°. Delicious served warm with ice cream or whipped cream. *A rich apple "cake" consistency.*

PLUM MERINGUE TART

Preparation Time: 20 minutes   *Cherie Hughes*
Cooking Time: 35 minutes   *Skopbank of Finland*
Serves: 6

6 ripe plums
4 egg whites, stiffly beaten
½ cup pecans, chopped
2 tsp. cinnamon

¼ cup sugar
6 leaves filo dough
6 Tblsp. melted butter
¼ cup melted apple jelly

Preheat oven to 350°F. Slice plums in half, and remove the seeds. Slice each half, skin side down, into very thin slices being careful not to cut through skin, then fan them out. Arrange plums into a rectangle. Cut buttered filo dough to fit plums. Make edges for pastry by twisting, and lightly placing long strips of filo to edges. Beat egg whites, add sugar, pecans, and cinnamon. Pile meringue into tart. Lay plums, skin side down, into the meringue. Bake until crust and meringue are golden. Glaze with apple jelly. *Serve with whipped cream.*

PEAR TART

Kim Wharton
Rising Sun

Preparation Time: 15 minutes
Cooking Time: 45 minutes
Serves: 8

CRUST:
1¾ cup flour
12 Tblsp. sweet butter
¼ cup sugar
2 egg yolks
2 Tblsp. water
4 tsp. vanilla

FILLING:
¾ cup melted butter
1 cup + 3 Tblsp. sugar
3 eggs
6 Tblsp. flour
3 Tblsp. Grand Marnier
3 Tblsp. almond extract
6 pears, peeled, cored, and halved
¼ cup sliced almonds

Garnish: Whipped cream

Preheat oven to 350° F. Crust: Mix the flour and sugar together. Cut in butter until crumbly. Add egg yolks, water, and vanilla. Mix until blended. Form in a fluted flan tart pan. Prick the crust and freeze (this prevents the crust from burning). Filling: In a saucepan, melt butter and sugar. Whisk in the eggs, flour, Grand Marnier, and almond extract. Peel core, and halve pears. Slice the pears ¾ way through in a fan design. Lay the flat side down, and fan side up in pan. Pour filling over and sprinkle almonds. Bake at 350° for 40 minutes or until brown. *Serve warmed with whipped cream.*

KIWI-BANANA TARTLETS

Preparation Time: 20 minutes
Cooking Time: 5 - 8 minutes
Chilling Time: 2+ hours
Makes: 8 tarts

Sarah Sheets
Royono

TART SHELLS:
1-2/3 cup graham cracker crumbs
6 Tblsp. butter, melted
¼ cup sugar

FILLING:
¾ cup evaporated milk
5/8 cup sweetened condensed milk
4 oz. cream cheese
¼ cup lemon juice

Garnish: Kiwi slices, banana slices

Preheat oven to 375°F. To make crust, combine above ingredients, and press into 3 inch tart shells. Bake for 5 - 8 minutes at 375° or until browned lightly. Cool. To make filling, blend milks and cheese until smooth. Add lemon juice slowly. Mixture will thicken. Spoon into tart shells. Chill several hours. *Garnish with 3 kiwi slices each, on half of tarts, and 5 banana slices on remaining tarts.*

FRIENDSHIP RECIPE

Preparation Time: none
Cooking Time: a little
Serves: lots

Take some morning sunshine.
Add a smile, some words too . . .
Sprinkle in some happy hours,
It's not very hard to do . . .
Add a little thoughtfulness
Stir just enough to blend . . .
Serve it warm with loving hands
It is the makings of a friend.

POTPOURRI

NOTES

TABLE of MEASUREMENTS and EQUIVALENTS
in U.S. and METRIC

U.S.	EQUIVALENTS	METRIC *volume-milliliters*
Dash	Less than 1/8 teaspoon	
1 teaspoon	60 drops	5 ml.
1 Tablespoon	3 teaspoons	15 ml.
2 Tablespoons	1 fluid ounce	30 ml.
4 Tablespoons	¼ cup	60 ml.
5 1/3 Tablespoons	1/3 cup	80 ml.
6 Tablespoons	3/8 cup	90 ml.
8 Tablespoons	½ cup	120 ml.
10 2/3 Tablespoons	2/3 cup	160 ml.
12 Tablespoons	¾ cup	180 ml.
16 Tablespoons	1 cup or 8 ounces	240 ml.
1 cup	½ pint or 8 fluid ounces	240 ml.
2 cups	1 pint	480 ml.
1 pint	16 ounces	480 ml. or .473 liter
1 quart	2 pints	960 ml. or .95 liter
2.1 pints	1.05 quarts or .26 gallons	1 liter
2 quarts	½ gallon	
4 quarts	1 gallon	3.8 liters

		weight-grams
1 ounce	16 drams	28 grams
1 pound	16 ounces	454 grams
1 pound	2 cups liquid	
1 kilogram	2.20 pounds	

METRIC MEASURE/CONVERSION CHART

Approximate Conversion to Metric Measures

When You Know . . .	Multiply by . . .	To Find . . .	Symbol
	Mass (weight)		
ounces	28	grams	g
pounds	0.45	kilograms	kg
	Volume		
teaspoons	5	milliliters	ml
tablespoons	15	milliliters	ml
fluid ounces	30	milliliters	ml
cups	0.24	liters	l
pints	0.47	liters	l
quarts	0.95	liters	l
gallons	3.8	liters	l

COOKING MEASURE EQUIVALENTS

Metric Cup	Volume (Liquid)	Liquid Solids (Butter)	Fine Powder (Flour)	Granular (Sugar)	Grain (Rice)
1	250 ml	200 g	140 g	190 g	150 g
3/4	188 ml	150 g	105 g	143 g	113 g
2/3	167 ml	133 g	93 g	127 g	100 g
1/2	125 ml	100 g	70 g	95 g	75 g
1/3	83 ml	67 g	47 g	63 g	50 g
1/4	63 ml	50 g	35 g	48 g	38 g
1/8	31 ml	25 g	18 g	24 g	19 g

APPROXIMATE TEMPERATURE CONVERSIONS
FAHRENHEIT TO CELSIUS

	Fahrenheit (°F)	Celsius (°C)
Freezer		
coldest area	- 10°	- 23°
overall	0°	- 17°
Water		
freezes	32°	0°
simmers	115°	46°
scalds	130°	55°
boils (sea level)	212°	100°
Soft Ball	234° to 240°	112° to 115°
Firm Ball	242° to 248°	116° to 120°
Hard Ball	250° to 268°	121° to 131°
Slow Oven	275° to 300°	135° to 148°

Fahrenheit to Celsius: Subtract 32 — Multiply by 5 — Divide by 9
Celsius to Fahrenheit: Multiply by 9 — Divide by 5 — Add 32

TEMPERATURE CONVERSION
FROM FAHRENHEIT TO CELSIUS*

Fahrenheit	200	225	250	275	300	325	350
Celsius	93	106	121	135	149	163	176

Fahrenheit	375	400	425	450	475	500	550
Celsius	191	205	218	231	246	260	288

These are round figures. The important thing to remember in cooking is to use relative amounts in measuring.

VOLUME EQUIVALENTS

		Teaspoons	Tablespoons	Fluidounces	Cups	Pints	Quarts
1 teaspoon	=	1	1/3	1/6	1/48	1/96	1/192
1 tablespoon	=	3	1	1/2	1/16	1/32	1/64
1 fluidounce	=	6	2	1	1/8	1/16	1/32
1 cup	=	48	16	8	1	1/2	1/4
1 pint	=	96	32	16	2	1	1/2
1 quart	=	192	64	32	4	2	1
1 gallon	=	768	256	128	16	8	4

INDEX

PARTICIPATING YACHTS

Adaro: *Captain Bill Burnes, Chef Jan Burnes*

Adaro is a luxurious 53' Sloop offering 3 identical full-sized double cabins, all with en suite bathrooms. Captain Bill has 3 decades of sailing experience and wife Jan, your hostess, is a trained Cordon Bleu cook who also enjoys Asian and Mediterranean cuisine. Join Adaro for a Gourmet's Cruise.

Adela: *Captain Jerry Keller, Chef Donna Keller*

Adella is a 50' sailing yacht comfortably equipped for a cruising vacation you'll never forget. Come sail crystal clear waters, walk on white sandy beaches and enjoy enchanting tropical nights. Donna and Jerry look forward to making you their friends.

Almost Heaven: *Captain Mark Rabinowitz, Chef Jacklyn Johnson Rabinowitz*

A limited edition 51' Morgan Ketch, beautifully appointed with a customized teak interior, she takes four guests in two double staterooms. Equipped with air conditioner, stereo, V.H.S., video camera, windsurfer, and snorkeling gear. Jackie excells in fine meal presentations, and Captain Mark is an entertaining raconteur. Come join us . . . it's Almost Heaven!

Ann-Marie II: *Captain Ken Haworth, Chef Barbie Haworth*

Ann-Marie II, a 37' steel Zealand Yawl was built in Holland 30 years ago. This classic sailboat is unsurpassed in beauty inside and out. Ken and Barbie Haworth take two guests only per charter, offering a sailing vacation you'll always cherish.

Antipodes: *Captains Manfred and Deiter Zerbe, Chef Kim Turk*

Ocean 60' Schooner. Can accommodate up to 8 guests in her 4 identical staterooms. Her captains have both chartered successfully since 1973. They have the valuable expertise necessary for a successful trip. Let Antipodes float your way on a Caribbean vacation unlike any you have ever experienced.

Ariguani: *Captain Billy Hawkins, Chef Lisa Hawkins*

Ariguani, a 72' Cockpit Burger is like a quaint country inn; excellent food and service in a relaxed atmosphere. Chartering together since 1982, Billy and Lisa Hawkins are committed to providing you with a charter vacation that will keep you coming back . . . year after year.

Bambi: *Captain Bjorn Lundgren, Chef Gunilla Lundgren*

Bambi, a Gulfstar 37' is very spacious for her size. Three separate cabins with two heads. She is owned and operated by Bjorn and Gunilla Lundgren, a Swedish couple with extensive traveling experience. Gunilla loves cooking. Try her Swedish recipes here.

Bluewater: *Captain Tim Wenger, Chef Joan Della Dora*

From the workmanship of her fine teak finish to her high performance sailing, Bluewater, a Pearson 53', satisfies even the most discriminating yachtsman, yet possesses every amenity for the comfort of the first time sailor. A continuous feast of fine food flows from the galley capable of pleasing even the gourmet.

Bon Harbor: *Captain Ray McMichael, Chef Pamela McMichael*

Bon Harbor, a 54' Ketch, designed with luxury and comfort in mind. Enjoy sailing, snorkeling, and windsurfing in the crystal clear waters of the sunny Caribbean. Join your captain and learn to sail or watch the dolphins from the bowsprit. Deluxe meals and friendly energetic crew will be your hosts on the Bon Harbor.

Bon Vivant: *Captain Michael Kelly, Chef Renie Mousek*
Captain Jon Reeves, Chef Annie Scholl

Bon Vivant, besides being luxuriously appointed and immaculately maintained, is a unique charter boat. We have two crews that alternate every 3 months! This not only guarantees a fresh, lively crew, it enables our guests to pick the couple that best serves their wide range of interests and needs. Bon Vivant - for the best vacation you'll ever have!

Calypso: *Captain and Chef Pat Rowley*

Enjoy the islands aboard Calypso, a 1982 Morgan 51'. Whether it be swimming and snorkeling in a secluded cove, or sunning on her spacious decks, Calypso offers everything you might want for a memorable vacation. Calypso is available for charter in the Caribbean, November through May, and New England during the summer months.

Caroline: *Captain Ann Avery, Chef Norma Trease*

55' Camper-Nicholson, 2 - 4 guests

Champagne: *Captain Peo Stenberg, Chefs Peo and Marilyn Stenberg*

Peo and Marilyn combine all their years of catering and sailing experience to make your charter vacation truly memorable. Champagne has luxurious accommodations for 4 guests, in 2 double cabins, with all the comforts you need and deserve. Come sail with us and discover the secret spots in Paradise.

Chaparral: *Captains Daniel and Shannon Webster, Chef Shannon Webster*

Chaparral is a Gulfstar 60', boasting excellent accommodations and a wide variety of culinary delights. She is operated and maintained by Captains Dan and Shannon Webster. Their skill of sailing and knowledge of the islands is extensive, but their hospitality is what all guests remember best.

Cinderella: *Captain and Chef Jim Carroza*

Cinderella is a captain only charter. Guests are encouraged to participate in sailing, navigation, and cooking. Family cruises and children are welcome.

Emerald Lady: *Captain Paul Array, Chef Mardy Array*

The world is yours aboard . . . the Emerald Lady! Join Paul and Mardy aboard the newly constructed fiberglas world cruising Ketch, and let them introduce you to their exciting world of ocean cruising adventures. Emerald Lady has the ambience of an old world galleon with every modern convenience. Your wants . . . your desires . . . your fantasies . . . are all aboard the Lady.

Emerald Lady: *Captain and Chef Richard George*

Aboard Emerald Lady, a 65' Irwin, we will take you to secluded coves, beautiful beaches, and interesting and exciting ashore. For the finest in food and sailing, join us on Emerald Lady.

Endless Summer I: *Captain Jim Scott, Chef Sue Griffin*

Endless Summer II: *Captain Barry Rice, Chef Rosalind Rice*

Recipe for the Ultimate Caribbean Experience on Endless Summer I and II:
Ingredients: 3 Friendly British Crew
Up to 8 Congenial Guests
4 Double Bedded Staterooms, Bathroom ensuite
Method: Set temperature at desired sunshine level. Blend ingredients together in a 65' sailing vessel. Add a touch of luxury and wine to taste. Brown slowly for at least one week.

Fancy Free: *Captain Tom Miller, Chef Casey Miller*

Fancy Free is a 51' comfortable Cutter. Two private double cabins for 4 guests with separate crew quarters.. Fully equipped for windsurfing, snorkeling, and enthusiastic sailing. Dine on classic cuisine customized to your taste. Join us for the total vacation experience.

Fantasy: *Captain Fred Stetson, Chef Debbie Stetson*

Fantasy, a Gulfstar 43' Ketch, is a fast, comfortable and beautifully appointed sailing yacht. She offers 2 - 4 guests the maximum of comfort often found on larger vessels. Dine on international cuisine, the very best from around the world. You'll never forget the Virgin Islands after you experience the Fantasy.

Finesse 60: *Captain Doug Thayer, Chef Jean Thayer*

finesse (fi'-nesse) n. Gulfstar 60'. 1. Cruising a. relating to sailors - take wheel, set course. b. For non-sailors - a moveable resort (refer to beaches, dining) 2. Beaches of or pertaining to quiet coves, snorkeling, windsurfing. 3. Dining - fine food and drink. 4. Accommodations for two, four, or six. 5. Families - see Welcome. YACHT FINESSE defines it all!

Firefly: *Captain Rib Collins*

Sailing School, Chesapeake Bay

Flower of the Storm: *Captain George C. Crooks, Chef Marita M. Tasse*

This luxurious Ketch, and Islander Freeport 41', offers many creature comforts found only on much larger yachts. After years of chartering, Flower in New England, Skip now teaches and shares his sailing knowledge in tropical waters while Marita, a biologist, explains Caribbean birdlife, and explores with guests the best snorkeling areas.

Flute: *Captain Rik Van Rensselaer, Chef Lee Ann La Cesa*

Flute is special in every way for a couple, two couples, or a family of six. Happy, fun, relaxing, congenial, and the food is fabulous! Come sail on Flute, and let us take you "away from it all" into paradise on the ultimate sailing holiday.

Freight Train: *Captain George Banker, Chef Candice Carson*

A boat who sails as fast as her name
Operated by owners in the charter game
Escape the cold, the frazzles, and the mundane
Let your body grow healthy, your mind grow sane
If you have gotten this far, you know poets we're not
But good cooks and fun people reside on this yacht.

Grace: *Captain George Yerkes, Chef C. J. Burns*

Grace is a 50' Cutter owned by its captain specializing in romantic cruises in the B.V.I., V.I., or Down Island. With a divemaster, George is sure to fill your platter with fresh fish, lobster, and champagne. 2 guests to maximum of 4.

Helios: *Captain Michael Minett, Chef Dawn Drell*

On Helios, having fun is important to us! Along with great cuisine and warm hospitality, enjoy learning to windsurf (we have 2), swimming, snorkeling, or relaxing in the hammock. Come sailing on this beautiful and graceful swan, and discover what paradise is really all about!

Hooter: *Captain Mason Britton, Chef Nancy Wilkinson*

Impervious Cover: *Captain Paul Soule, Chef Cindy Harhen*

Impervious Cover is a Gulfstar 62' (Hull #1). The first of her kind in the chartering fleet. Captain Paul Soule and Chef/Mate Cindy Harhen are avid sailors and water sports enthusiasts. Both enjoy cooking. Paul comes from the seafood-rich eastern shore of Delaware and specializes in seafood. Cindy enjoys traditional as well as exotic cuisine.

Jolie Brise: *Captain Mike Burrill, Chef Geli Burrill*

Not all the brokers can be wrong!! Jolie Brise, winner of prize for boat which brokers would themselves most like to charter in 1984-85 boat show in the Virgin Islands. This very special and exciting 62' C+C Ketch only takes four guests in comfortable elegant decadence.

Kestrel: *Captain Scott Tucker, Chef Jill Cooper*

Kestrel is a 57' Bowman Ketch. She has successfully been in the charter circuit for 9 years, and continues so, spending summers in New England and winters in the Caribbean and French West Indies.

Lady Columbo: *Captain Meyel Haack, Chef Jan Stoughton*

Madam: *Captain Don Mitchell, Chef Michelle Mitchell*

Madam is a Gulfstar 50' chartering in the Virgin Islands (we also do Down Island charters). We have 6 full sets of scuba gear, and we love to scuba dive. Madam sleeps a maximum of 4 guests. We have T.V., V.C.R., and all the latest equipment.

Madrine: *Chef Kirk Ezell*

Mary Denise: *Captain David E. Wood, Chef Jacqui Hoop*

Mary Denise, a 45' custom Ketch built in 1980 by Ed Masters of Florida, is a spacious world cruiser designed for chartering in comfort. Her menu is top-flight, and her service is dedicated to provide that relaxing or active dream of vacation just for two.

Mischief: *Chef Tom Martin*

Mistral: *Captain Russ Fielden, Chef Laura Greces*

Come sail Mistral, a 50' Sloop that really sails! She was built in 1983 by Morgan, especially for Caribbean chartering. Russ & Laura really love these islands and delight in taking you "off the beaten track." We'll be happy to help you sharpen your sailing skills or let you relax.

My Way: *Captains Warwick and Barbara Lowe, Chef Barbara Lowe*

My Way is a contemporary, spacious new Trimaran. Capable of accommodating up to 10 guests. She will provide total luxury and privacy for 6. With activities that range from scuba diving to windsurfing to fine dining, she is literally a floating resort. Come sail MY WAY with Captains Warwick and Barbara Lowe for an unforgettable holiday.

Natasha: *Captain Peter Morris and Chefs Georgina Morris and Carol Lowe*

Natasha is an 83' Camper and Nicholson Ketch designed by Jon Bannenburg. She sleeps 6 in three air-conditioned cabins, two with double berths. Natasha has a crew of four and provides gourmet dining, water-skiing, windsurfing, diving, and snorkeling. Come join us!

Native Sun: *Captains and Chefs Stanley and Sylvia Dabney*

Valiant 40' (Hull #9). Specializing in day charters, snorkeling, lunch, and entertaining stories of 40,000 miles offshore sailing and ten years of living aboard Native Sun. We welcome every guest as a friend and treat each new friend as family. We consider beautiful Honeymoon Bay on Water Island, our home in the islands, the place where our love affair with sailing began 16 years ago.

New Horizons: *Captain Masm Britton, Chef Nancy Wilkinson*

New Horizons is a 60' shoal draught centerboard Ketch. She is exquisite, one of a kind designed yacht, custom built, and launched in Vancouver, B.C. Since then she has sailed the Pacific and Caribbean waters to the infinite delight of her crew, guests, and everyone who is watching.

Ocean Voyager: *Captain Martin Vanderwood, Chef Marion Vanderwood*

Martin and Marion Vanderwood, your knowledgeable crew, promise you an unforgettable vacation aboard Ocean Voyager, a luxurious Ocean 60', accommodating up to 6 guests.

Odyssey: *Captain Glenn Burroughs, Chef Shirley Dorn Burroughs*

Odyssey, our 40' Endeavour Sloop, is ideal for one couple or family cruising. Featuring private aft stateroom for guests, spacious main salon, two heads with showers, windsurfing, snorkeling, color television, and both 12v and 115v electricity. Gourmet meals by Chef Shirley and sailing instruction by Captain Glenn included. Welcome aboard!

Oklahoma Crude II: *Captain Colin Rees, Chef Kimberly Foote*

This Irwin 52's luxurious accommodations make living aboard a pleasure. The interior of this Ketch is custom designed for charter. The galley is fully stocked with crystal and silver for serving Caribbean delicacies. An experienced crew promises to take you into the most relaxing, enjoyable holiday possible.

Once Upon a Time: *Captain Harry Newton, Chef Nicky Cahi*

Once Upon a Time, there was a beautiful 41' Catamaran built in England for chartering in the Caribbean. News of her luxury, elegance and comfort spread far and wide and soon people arrived to discover the continuing story of this lovely yacht.

Ovation: *Captain Douglas Briscoe, Chef Alison Briscoe*

Charter a true ocean sailing yacht and sample superb meals from this fabulous cookbook.

Parandah: *Captain Gary Wright, Chef Denise Wright*

Parandah, a 47' Ketch built in Greece specially for charter service, is featured in the book, **The Charter Game**, as an example of a yacht's perfect cockpit for chartering. A fast sailing yacht, comfortable for four guests.

Promenade: *Captain David Dugdale, Chef Fiona Baldrey*

Magnificent 60' Trimaran taking up to 10 guests: "Fantastic trip, thoroughly enjoyed all the water activities especially the scuba diving. Great food and wonderful service." From our guest book 3/20/84.

Promises: *Captain Jerry Dudley, Chef Jennifer Morden (Summer Crew)*

Captain Jerry Dudley and First Mate/Chef Jennifer Morden have been sailing, and chartering together in the USVI's since early 1982. They are currently working on the 52' Swan yacht, Promises, as a summer crew.

Promises: *Captain Mike Satterlee, Chef Sharon Strong*

Promises, a luxurious Irwin 52' Ketch, offers 6 guests 3 spacious, private, double staterooms. Sharon and Mike enjoy sharing the treasures of the Caribbean with their guests, and provide them with excellent cuisine and great hospitality. They are an active crew, and sensitive to the needs of their guests.

Raby Vaucluse: *Captain Bill Gibson, Chef Liz Thomas*

Ring-Anderson: *Captain Rick Brendlinger, Chef Louise Brendlinger*

Ring-Anderson combines old world elegance with new world comforts: an experience not to be missed.

Rising Sun: *Captain Brooks Kuhn, Chef Kim Wharton*

Rising Sun offers the best of both worlds cruising the Virgins in the winter and the New England Coast in the summer. She accommodates 4 in 2 private cabins with baths. Fulfill your dreams in the Rolls Royce of high performance yachts. Sail the Rising Sun.

Royono: *Captain Ben Sheets, Chef Sarah Sheets*

Sailing aboard Royono, an 85' Alden/Herreshoff Yawl, is to experience the aura of a time past when life was more leisurely, and yachts were designed by the old masters with an eye towards elegance and beauty. Ben and Sarah Sheets welcome guests aboard for exceptional sailing, excellent food, and gracious service and company.

Ruach: *Captain Michael Vegiard, Chef Judith Myers Vegiard*

September Morn: *Captain Eric Unterborn, Chef Betsi Dwyer*

Sevruga: *Captain Ross Lysinger, Chef Josie Gould*

Sevruga (one of the best caviars) is a 46' Ketch built by Dufowe. With accommodations for 4 guests, diving and snorkeling gear, and a windsurfer, she and her crew will provide you with a great sailing holiday. Join us!

Skopbank of Finland: *Captain Herb Kiendl, Chef Cherie Hughes*

Having completed the Whitebread Round-the-World Race, Skopland of Finland is now refitted for your sailing adventure in comfort and style. Dine on sumptuous food, enjoy refreshing daiquiries, sail under a million stars, (the choice is yours) . . . all with the graceful strength of a fine racing yacht.

Solskin II: *Captain John Long, Chef Irene McClain*

Solskin II is a 37' Albert Yawl where pleasure is the name of the game for our day sailing guests.

Stampede: *Captain Andy Smith, Chef Wendy Smith*

When next winter comes, we know what you'll need, two fun-filled weeks on "LOVELY" Stampede!

Stormvogel: *Captain Ermanno Traverso, Chef Paolo Taglia*

Stormvogel is a very famous 72' Ketch. She has been already three times around the world winning the most important ocean races. She is now successfully chartering the Virgin Islands from where she will start the fourth around the world trip in April 1986.

Stowaway: *Captain Alan Balfour, Chef Chris Balfour*

Tefra: *Captain Robert L. Barker, Chef Lisa Ferry*

Tequila: *Captains and Chefs Bob and Didgie Belschner*

Tequila — The spirit of adventure! Bob and Didgie's sleek 39' Cruiser/Racer is packed with beautiful wood work, maintained with owner pride. As Co-Captains and Cooks, we also like to teach sailing and seamanship, as well as, introduce you to our water sports equipment. For one couple. Come sail with us!

Thorobred: *Captain George B. Brown, Chef Donna Jaggard*

Thorobred, an owner-operated semi-custom Morgan 41', has been chartering in the Caribbean since 1979. George and Donna will make your chartering vacation a most memorable one.

Truant: *Captain Tom Gavin, Chef Jane Glancy*

You are invited to a tropical interlude aboard the yacht Truant. She is a 41' traditionally designed Ketch with generous accommodations. Truant carries only two guests so you are assured of comfort and privacy.

Tuff: *Captain Stephen Beamer, Chef Margo Muckey*

Tuff is a C & C Landfall 48', accommodating 2 - 4 guests.

Valdivia: *Captain Steve Janzan, Chef Kathy Rodrigues*

Valdivia, a classic 92' Ketch, is ideal for a family group being able to accommodate 8 people comfortably. Guests have the option of being able to dine in the spacious 'playpen' on the main deck as well as in the salon. Wide range of Caribbean to French cuisine to delight all palates.

Vanity: *Captains Bob and Jan Robinson, Chef Jan Robinson*

Vanity, a luxurious 60' Motor Sailer. This owner/operated charter yacht is designed for privacy. Taking only four guests, Vanity assures you of individual consideration. Dine comfortably under the stars, enjoy international cuisine. Seven years of chartering give the Robinsons the knowledge of where the action is and where serenity prevails.

Victorious: *Captain John Barry, Chef Sheila Smith*

John has been sailing in the Caribbean for ten years. Sheila has spent the last three years running her own restaurant in Scotland. Victorious is a luxurious new custom built Morgan 62' who sails beautifully. The combination of expert captaining, delicious cooking, and Victorious' spacious accommodation is unbeatable.

Western Star: *Captain Mel Luff, Chef Terrie Thornbjornson*

Sailing, snorkeling, scuba-diving, water skiing, windsurfing, even jet skis are available on Western Star's maxi-fun Virgin Islands charters. Sail with us aboard our 53' Gulfstar and enjoy the ultimate in cruising luxury. Think about the crystal clear waters, warm sun, deluxe meals, and energetic friendly crew.

Wind's End: *Captain Sam Welch, Chef Emily Welch*

Escape in world class comfort with ample space and excellent stability, a truly comfortable boat to live aboard and sail. Wind's End's deluxe accommodations and services belie her size, and welcome you aboard. With two equal cabins, this Endeavour 43' can make your holiday a lovely relaxing vacation.

Winji: *Captain Al Herget, Chef Margo Hall*

Winji, a beautiful 53' Pearson Ketch, is a performance sailing yacht with a luxuriously decorated interior. Experience an unforgettable sailing adventure with your hosts Margo and Al.

RE-ORDER ADDITIONAL COPIES

AUTOGRAPH TO:

Qua.	Description	Price	Total
	SHIP TO SHORE I	$14.95	
	SHIP TO SHORE II	$14.95	
	SWEET TO SHORE	$14.95	
	SEA TO SHORE	$14.95	
	SIP TO SHORE	$10.95	

SHIP TO:

SHIP TO SHORE
10500 Mount Holly Road
Charlotte, NC 28214-9347
(704) 392-4740

6% Tax (NC only)		
Gift Wrap $2.00		
Freight $1.50 Per/Bk		
TOTAL		

AUTOGRAPH TO:

SHIP TO:

Please charge my: MASTERCARD ☐ VISA ☐
AM EX ☐ CHECK ☐ MONEY ORDER ☐
Payable to: SHIP TO SHORE, INC.
MY CREDIT CARD NUMBER IS:

CALL TO ORDER TOLL FREE
1-800-338-6072

Signature:_____ Exp. Date: ☐☐☐☐

- -

RE-ORDER ADDITIONAL COPIES

AUTOGRAPH TO:

Qua.	Description	Price	Total
	SHIP TO SHORE I	$14.95	
	SHIP TO SHORE II	$14.95	
	SWEET TO SHORE	$14.95	
	SEA TO SHORE	$14.95	
	SIP TO SHORE	$10.95	

SHIP TO:

SHIP TO SHORE
10500 Mount Holly Road
Charlotte, NC 28214-9347
(704) 392-4740

6% Tax (NC only)		
Gift Wrap $2.00		
Freight $1.50 Per/Bk		
TOTAL		

AUTOGRAPH TO:

SHIP TO:

Please charge my: MASTERCARD ☐ VISA ☐
AM EX ☐ CHECK ☐ MONEY ORDER ☐
Payable to: SHIP TO SHORE, INC.
MY CREDIT CARD NUMBER IS:

CALL TO ORDER TOLL FREE
1-800-338-6072

Signature:_____ Exp. Date: ☐☐☐☐

FREE !

Share the taste of the Caribbean with your friends.

Simply mail this form or call **1-800-338-6072** and we will send them a **FREE** catalog.

Name _____ Name _____

Address _____ Address _____

City _____ City _____

State _____ Zip _____ State _____ Zip _____

PERFECT GIFTS FOR ANY OCCASION

Ship to Shore Inc.
10500 Mt. Holly Road, Charlotte, NC 28214-9347

FREE !

Share the taste of the Caribbean with your friends.

Simply mail this form or call **1-800-338-6072** and we will send them a **FREE** catalog.

Name _____ Name _____

Address _____ Address _____

City _____ City _____

State _____ Zip _____ State _____ Zip _____

PERFECT GIFTS FOR ANY OCCASION

Ship to Shore Inc.
10500 Mt. Holly Road, Charlotte, NC 28214-9347

RE-ORDER ADDITIONAL COPIES

AUTOGRAPH TO:

Qua.	Description	Price	Total
	SHIP TO SHORE I	$14.95	
	SHIP TO SHORE II	$14.95	
	SWEET TO SHORE	$14.95	
	SEA TO SHORE	$14.95	
	SIP TO SHORE	$10.95	

SHIP TO:

SHIP TO SHORE
10500 Mount Holly Road
Charlotte, NC 28214-9347
(704) 392-4740

6% Tax (NC only)		
Gift Wrap $2.00		
Freight $1.50 Per/Bk		
TOTAL		

AUTOGRAPH TO:

SHIP TO:

Please charge my: MASTERCARD ☐ VISA ☐
AM EX ☐ CHECK ☐ MONEY ORDER ☐
Payable to: SHIP TO SHORE, INC.
MY CREDIT CARD NUMBER IS:

CALL TO ORDER TOLL <u>FREE</u>
1-800-338-6072

Signature:_____Exp. Date: ☐☐☐☐

- -

RE-ORDER ADDITIONAL COPIES

AUTOGRAPH TO:

Qua.	Description	Price	Total
	SHIP TO SHORE I	$14.95	
	SHIP TO SHORE II	$14.95	
	SWEET TO SHORE	$14.95	
	SEA TO SHORE	$14.95	
	SIP TO SHORE	$10.95	

SHIP TO:

SHIP TO SHORE
10500 Mount Holly Road
Charlotte, NC 28214-9347
(704) 392-4740

6% Tax (NC only)		
Gift Wrap $2.00		
Freight $1.50 Per/Bk		
TOTAL		

AUTOGRAPH TO:

SHIP TO:

Please charge my: MASTERCARD ☐ VISA ☐
AM EX ☐ CHECK ☐ MONEY ORDER ☐
Payable to: SHIP TO SHORE, INC.
MY CREDIT CARD NUMBER IS:

CALL TO ORDER TOLL <u>FREE</u>
1-800-338-6072

Signature:_____Exp. Date: ☐☐☐☐

FREE !

Share the taste of the Caribbean with your friends.

Simply mail this form or call **1-800-338-6072** and we will send them a **FREE** catalog.

Name _____   Name _____

Address _____   Address _____

City _____   City _____

State _____ Zip _____   State _____ Zip _____

PERFECT GIFTS FOR ANY OCCASION

Ship to Shore Inc.
10500 Mt. Holly Road, Charlotte, NC 28214-9347

FREE !

Share the taste of the Caribbean with your friends.

Simply mail this form or call **1-800-338-6072** and we will send them a **FREE** catalog.

Name _____   Name _____

Address _____   Address _____

City _____   City _____

State _____ Zip _____   State _____ Zip _____

PERFECT GIFTS FOR ANY OCCASION

Ship to Shore Inc.
10500 Mt. Holly Road, Charlotte, NC 28214-9347